Richard Henry Major

The Discoveries of Prince Henry the Navigator

And their results: being the narrative of the discovery by sea, within one century, of more than half the world

Richard Henry Major

The Discoveries of Prince Henry the Navigator
And their results: being the narrative of the discovery by sea, within one century, of more than half the world

ISBN/EAN: 9783337169503

Printed in Europe, USA, Canada, Australia, Japan

Cover: Foto ©Andreas Hilbeck / pixelio.de

More available books at **www.hansebooks.com**

PRINCE HENRY

THE NAVIGATOR.

LONDON:
GILBERT AND RIVINGTON, PRINTERS,
ST. JOHN'S SQUARE.

THE DISCOVERIES

OF

PRINCE HENRY

THE NAVIGATOR,

AND THEIR RESULTS;

BEING

THE NARRATIVE OF THE DISCOVERY BY SEA,
WITHIN ONE CENTURY,
OF MORE THAN HALF THE WORLD.

BY

RICHARD HENRY MAJOR, F.S.A.

KEEPER OF THE DEPARTMENT OF MAPS AND CHARTS IN THE BRITISH MUSEUM,
HON. SEC. OF THE ROYAL GEOGRAPHICAL SOCIETY.

Illustrated with Portraits, Maps, etc.

London:
SAMPSON LOW, MARSTON, SEARLE, & RIVINGTON,
CROWN BUILDINGS, 188, FLEET STREET.
1877.

[All rights reserved.]

"Conceito digno foi do ramo claro
Do venturoso rei, que arou primeiro
O mar, por ir deitar do ninho caro
O morador de Abyla derradeiro.
Este, por sua indústria e ingenho raro,
N'um madeiro ajuntando outro madeiro,
Descubrir pôde a parte, que faz clara
De Argos, da Hydra a luz, da Lebre e da Ara."
      CAMOENS. *Os Lusiadas*, Canto viii. Stanza 71.

TO HIS

HONOURED AND BELOVED WIFE,

SARAH ELIZABETH MAJOR,

This Work,

FIRST SUGGESTED BY HER

THIRTY YEARS AGO,

IS AFFECTIONATELY DEDICATED BY

THE AUTHOR.

PREFACE.

It may perhaps be fairly regarded as a matter of surprise that no Englishman had until the year 1868 attempted to prepare a monograph of the life of Prince Henry the Navigator. If a phenomenon without example in the world's history, resulting from the thought and perseverance of one man, might be supposed of interest enough to tempt the pen of the biographer, assuredly that inducement was not wanting. When we see the small population of a narrow strip of the Spanish Peninsula, limited both in means and men, become, in an incredibly short space of time, a mighty maritime nation, not only conquering the islands and Western Coasts of Africa and rounding its Southern Cape, but creating empires and founding capital cities at a distance of two thousand leagues from their own homesteads, we are tempted to suppose that such results must have been brought about by some freak of fortune, some happy stroke of luck. Not so: they were the effects of the patience, wisdom, intellectual labour, and example of one man, backed by the pluck of a race of sailors who, when we consider the means at their disposal, have been unsurpassed as adventurers in any country or in any age. Doubtless, the geographical position of Portugal, at the extremity of the European continent, had much to do with the suggestion of its glorious mission; but what else besides danger and death could the formidable waves of the Atlantic have suggested to her mariners, had it not been for the courageous conception and unflinching zeal of one who, during forty long years of even limited success, knew how to blend patience with enthusiasm, and conquer disappointment by devoted persistence in what he had prescribed to himself as a duty. The story of the life of such an one can surely not be deemed an uninteresting or unimportant matter.

The miniature which forms the frontispiece of the present volume is taken from an exact facsimile of that which is in the original manuscript, for procuring which I have to acknowledge my indebtedness to the kind intervention of M. Prosper Merimée. The original miniature in the manuscript is the only authentic portrait of Prince Henry which the Portuguese possess. The prince is represented dressed in mourning, his head covered with the large barret cap without any insignia, and his hair cut short according to the custom of the time on such occasions. As the chronicle was finished in 1448, and as the prince's brother Dom Pedro lost his life at Alfarrobeira on the 20th of May, 1449, it is most probable that the portrait was taken while the prince was in mourning for his illustrious brother, for the fair copy of the chronicle was not completed till 1453.

Preface.

To Prince Henry we are primarily indebted for our knowledge of more than one half of the world; and it is for this reason that this work is entitled, "The Discoveries of Prince Henry the Navigator, and their Results."

The glory of Prince Henry consists in the conception and persistent prosecution of a great idea, and in what followed therefrom. This book, then, is rather a record of the glory than of the mere life of Prince Henry. That glory is not a matter of fancy or bombast, but of mighty and momentous reality, a reality to which the Anglo-Saxon race, at least, have no excuse for indifference.

The coasts of Africa visited;—The Cape of Good Hope rounded;—The New World disclosed;—The Seaway to India, the Moluccas, and China laid open;—The globe circumnavigated, and Australia discovered: within one century of continuous and connected exploration. "Such," as I have stated in my closing chapter, "were the stupendous results of a great thought, and of indomitable perseverance in spite of twelve years of costly failure and disheartening ridicule. Had that failure and that ridicule produced on Prince Henry the effect which they ordinarily produce on other men, it is impossible to say what delays would have occurred before these mighty events would have been realized, for it must be borne in mind that the ardour not only of his own sailors but of surrounding nations owed its impulse to this pertinacity of purpose in him."

When I prepared the "Life of Prince Henry," which

was published in 1868, I had a duty before me from which I am now happily free. Early documents had to be sought out from different countries, their authenticity and accuracy carefully scrutinized, and, as powerful antagonists had to be contended with, every point of evidence had to be faithfully laid before the reader. But while all this was necessary for the satisfaction of the antiquarian student, it was obviously the exact contrary of what is looked for in a work of general interest, and accordingly a very small number of copies were printed. From the present book all controversy has been eliminated, and while the reader who seeks for evidence can find it in the earlier publication, in the present work he has the narrative simply of the adventures which gave glory to the life of Prince Henry, and opened up the two hemispheres to the knowledge of mankind at large.

CONTENTS.

		PAGE
Chapter	I. The Purpose	1
,,	II. The Prince's Parentage	5
,,	III. Ceuta	22
,,	IV. "Talent de bien faire"	43
,,	V. Porto Santo and Madeira	54
,,	VI. Cape Bojador	64
,,	VII. Tangier	73
,,	VIII. The Tawny Moors and the Negroes	89
,,	IX. The Canaries	122
,,	X. The Azores	130
,,	XI. Cadamosto	138
,,	XII. The Death of Prince Henry	178
,,	XIII. The Stormy Cape	194
,,	XIV. Results Westward	222
,,	XV. Results Eastward	242
,,	XVI. Results Southward	269
Appendix		301
Index		311

INSTRUCTIONS TO BINDER.

Portrait of Prince Henry		*Frontispiece*
Monastery of Batalha	*to face page*	17
Queen Philippa	,,	27
View of Ceuta	,,	33
King John	,,	65
Tomb of Prince Henry	,,	183
Plan of Sagres	,,	193
Equatorial Nile Lakes	,,	209
Statue of Prince Henry	,,	245
Jave la Grande (Australia)	,,	297
Large Map of Africa	*End of Volume*	

PRINCE HENRY THE NAVIGATOR.

CHAPTER I.

THE PURPOSE.

THE mystery which since creation had hung over the Atlantic, and hidden from man's knowledge one-half of the surface of the globe, had reserved a field of noble enterprise for Prince Henry the Navigator. Until his day the pathways of the human race had been the mountain, the river, and the plain, the strait, the lake, and inland sea; but he it was who first conceived the thought of opening a road through the unexplored ocean, a road replete with danger but abundant in promise. Although the son of a king, he relinquished the pleasures of the court, and took up his abode on the inhospitable promontory of Sagres at the extreme south-western angle of Europe. It was a small peninsula, the rocky surface of which showed no sign of vegetation, except a few stunted juniper-trees, to relieve the sadness of a waste of shifting sand. Another spot so cold, so barren, or so dreary, it were difficult to find on the warm and genial soil of sunny Portugal. Landwards the north-west winds were almost unceasing, while three-quarters of the horizon were occupied by the mighty and mysterious waters of the as yet unmeasured Atlantic.

In days long past there had stood upon the sister headland of St. Vincent, at about a league's distance, a circular Druidical temple, where, as Strabo tells us, the old Iberians believed that the Gods assembled at night, and from the ancient name of Sacrum Promontorium, hence given to the entire promontory by the Romans, Cape Sagres received its modern appellation. As may be imagined, the motive for the Prince's choice could not have been an ordinary one. If, from the pinnacle of our present knowledge, we mark on the world of waters those bright tracks which, during four centuries and a half, have led to the discovery of mighty continents, we shall find them all lead us back to that same inhospitable point of Sagres, and to the motive which gave to it a royal inhabitant. To find the sea-path to the "Thesauris Arabum et divitis Indiæ," till then known only through faint echoes of almost forgotten tradition, was the object to which Prince Henry devoted his life. The goal which he thus set before himself was at an unknown distance, and had to be attained through dangers supposed to be unsurmountable and by means so inadequate as to demand a proportionate excess of courage, study, and perseverance.

To be duly appreciated, this comprehensive thought must be viewed in relation to the period in which it was conceived. "The last of the dark ages," the fifteenth century has been rightly named, but the light which displaced its obscurity had not yet begun to dawn when Prince Henry, with prophetic instinct, traced mentally a pathway to India by an anticipated Cape of Good Hope. No printing-press as yet gave forth to the world the accumulated wisdom and experience of the past. The compass, though known and in use, had not yet emboldened men to leave the shore and put out with confidence into the open sea; no sea-chart existed to guide the mariner along those perilous African coasts; no lighthouse reared its friendly head to warn or welcome him on his homeward track. The scientific and practical appliances which were to render possible the discovery of half a world had yet to be developed. But, with such objects in view, the Prince collected the information supplied by ancient geographers, unweariedly devoted himself to the study of mathematics, navigation, and cartography, and freely invited, with princely liberality of reward, the co-operation of the boldest and most skilful navigators of every country.

We look back with astonishment and admiration at the stupendous achievement effected a whole life time later by the immortal Columbus, an achievement which formed the connecting link between the old world and the new; yet the explorations instituted by Prince Henry of Portugal, were in truth the anvil upon which that link was forged; and yet how many are there in England, the land of sailors, who even know the name of the illustrious man who was the very initiator of continuous Atlantic exploration? If the final success of a bold and comprehensive idea outstep the life of its author, the world, which always prefers success to merit, will forget the originator of the very result which it applauds. This injustice is specially manifest in the case of Prince Henry, for the vastness of his conception on the one hand, and the imperfection of his appliances on the other, made the probabilities of success during his own lifetime infinitely the more remote. It is in such cases that

Fame needs to be awakened to her task. Thus slept for centuries the fame of Christopher Columbus; thus sleeps the fame of Richard Hakluyt, the pioneer of the prosperity of England.

If it be the glory of Great Britain that by means of her maritime explorations the sun never sets on her dominions, she may recall with satisfaction that he who opened the way to that glory was the son of a royal English lady and of the greatest king that ever sat on the throne of Portugal. The importance of these personages is such as to demand a separate chapter.

CHAPTER II.

THE PRINCE'S PARENTAGE.

PRINCE HENRY the Navigator was the fifth child and fourth son of King João I., " of good memory," (also surnamed " the Great," and " Father of his country,") and of Queen Philippa, daughter of " old John of Gaunt, time-honoured Lancaster." He was thus the nephew of Henry IV. of England, and great-grandson of Edward III. He was also a descendant of the last kings of the line of Capet, and allied to the family of Valois.

Although in reality one of the oldest nations in Europe, it was not till the accession of Prince Henry's father to the throne that Portugal began to assume a prominent position as a kingdom. For six centuries the people had groaned under the yoke of their powerful and implacable enemies, the Moors, and not till the end of that time did their desperate and stubborn patriotism triumph over the almost invincible obstacles which stood in its way. No sooner, however, were the Moors ejected from the Peninsula than the liberties of the Portuguese were again placed in jeopardy by the attacks of Spain, their former ally. It was reserved to King João, the father of Prince Henry, to establish the throne upon a solid basis, to carry into Morocco the sword of the avenger, and to prepare the way for those more expansive movements which were to issue from the genius of his son.

With him commenced the glorious dynasty known as that of Aviz, which lasted two hundred years, and embodied the period of Portugal's greatest dignity, prosperity, and renown.

The accession of this potent monarch to the throne was an event which at first sight seemed most improbable, seeing that he was the youngest, and an illegitimate son of the king, but it was brought about in this wise. His father, Dom Pedro I. had by his first wife two sons, Luiz, who died young, and Fernando, who succeeded him; and by the beautiful, but unfortunate Iñez de Castro, three sons, Affonso, who died young, João, and Diniz. Besides these he had by Theresa Lourenço, a lady of noble birth, a natural son, named João, Prince Henry's father, who at the age of seven received from the king the Grand Mastership of the Order of Aviz. In 1367 Dom Pedro died, and was succeeded by Fernando, who soon after, on the death of Pedro the Cruel without issue, became also heir to the crown of Castile. That kingdom, however, had been immediately seized by Henry of Trastamare, the late king's bastard brother; and, in order to support his own claims, Fernando formed an alliance with the King of Arragon, whose daughter Leonora he engaged to marry. A long struggle ensued between Castile and Portugal, which terminated in a treaty by which Fernando engaged to marry another Leonora, the daughter of Henry of Trastamare; but this difficulty he impartially settled by going through the form of marriage with a third Leonora, surnamed Telles de Meneses, the wife of João Lourenço da Cunha, Lord of Pombeiro, whose marriage he annulled, and publicly took her to wife. The natural result of this proceeding was a new and cruel war between Castile and Portugal, which only terminated in 1373, when Pope Gregory XI. successfully mediated between the two kingdoms.

Leonora, the infamous and adulterous spouse of Fernando, regarded all his brothers with suspicion and hatred, but more especially Don João, the Grand Master of Aviz, whose life she more than once ineffectually attempted. The others she succeeded in banishing from the court, whence they took refuge in Castile. To her other crimes she now added infidelity to her husband, her paramour being Fernando Andeiro, a Castilian subject, but a favourite of the king. The only issue of the marriage of Fernando with Leonora Telles was one daughter, Brites, who in 1383 became the wife of King Juan of Castile, the successor of Henry of Trastamare. King Fernando's failing health prevented him from being present at the brilliant marriage of his daughter. He had at length become aware of the guilt of the infamous queen, but not having the courage to remove her paramour from the court, he called to his aid his illegitimate brother João, the Grand Master of Aviz, with whom he resolved upon Andeiro's death, but before this could be effected the king fell ill and died, on the 22nd of October, 1383. Leonora forthwith assumed the position of Regent, but, on the demand of the King of Castile, was compelled to proclaim her daughter Brites as queen.

The Portuguese chafed at the thought that the Castilian yoke should be imposed upon them through the marriage of their princess with a king of Castile. Leonora and her paramour were universally detested; and not only the nobility, but the whole kingdom, were prepared to hail as their deliverer any one who should take the life of the latter. The Grand Master of Aviz, who was the only son of King Pedro I. now in

Portugal, at once saw in this favourable conjunction of circumstances a chance of obtaining possession of the crown.

Leonora was not blind to the same possibility, and by way of removing him made him governor of the Alemtejo, for the defence of the frontier. This was a crisis in his life. Andeiro's death had been secretly resolved upon by the leading nobles of the kingdom, and the hand of the Grand Master was by all regarded as the one to strike the blow. Accordingly, at the close of an interview with the queen in her palace, he led Andeiro into an antechamber, as if to speak with him, and there slew him. He then gave orders that the gates of the palace should be closed; and in pursuance of a preconcerted plan, his page, Gomez Freire, rode through the streets of Lisbon, crying out that his master was shut up in the palace, and in imminent danger of his life. The people, by whom he was much beloved, rushed in crowds towards the palace gates, threatening to force an entrance unless they were convinced with their own eyes of the Grand Master's safety.

When at length he made his appearance, and rode through the streets, the shouts of joy with which he was received told plainly how near he was to the realization of his most sanguine hopes.

A few of the nobles returned to the queen's party after the death of Andeiro, but the mass of the people were enthusiastic for the Grand Master, especially as Leonora had invoked the aid of the King of Castile, and they looked with dread to the prospect of Castilian dominion. On the 16th of December, 1383, an act was passed constituting the Grand Master defender and regent of the kingdom, with powers little less than royal.

The Prince's Parentage.

In this new and difficult position he displayed talents equal to his responsibilities. To invest that position with befitting dignity, he styled himself in all official letters and ordinances "João, by the grace of God, son of the most noble King Pedro, Master of the Order of Chivalry of Aviz, Regent and Defender of the Kingdoms of Portugal and the Algarves." He placed the royal arms upon the cross of his order, so that only the extremities of the latter were visible, thus skilfully blending the insignia of the Grand Master with those of the Regent of the kingdom.

He was careful, moreover, to represent himself as holding authority only as the *locum tenens* of his half-brother João, who was still a prisoner in Castile, and he caused banners to be painted representing the prince in a dungeon and loaded with chains; by this means he secured to himself the partisans of that prince, and at the same time intensified the national hatred against the King of Castile. Meanwhile the queen had withdrawn for safety to the strong fortress of Santarem, and as the Castilian forces were rapidly approaching, the regent lost no time in securing the alliance of the King of England. As soon as the King and Queen of Castile entered Portugal, Queen Leonora made a formal renunciation of the crown in their favour, a measure which secured to them the majority of her partisans, and placed many strongholds at their disposal. Before long, however, a disagreement arising as to the appointment of the chief Rabbi of Portugal, which ended in Leonora attempting to assassinate the king, and being confined for life in the convent at Tordesillas near Valladolid, her adherents withdrew their support, and the king was left to his own resources.

Lisbon was now the focus both of his hope and his anxiety, and with the view of effectually reducing it he blockaded it from the sea, while his forces ravaged the Alemtejo and endeavoured to hem it in by land. It was absolutely necessary to check at once the advance of the land force, and the Grand Master entrusted this important charge to the gallant but youthful Nuño Alvarez Pereira, his sworn brother in arms.

The undertaking was a critical one, for the Portuguese were far inferior in numbers, but the religious enthusiasm of Pereira surmounted all obstacles. He met the enemy at Atoleiros, and having with his little army first invoked the aid of the God of battles, fell upon the Castilian cavalry with such fury that they fled in the utmost disorder. Meanwhile the king, who had received large reinforcements from Castile, delayed the siege until the arrival of his fleet from Seville, and the Grand Master utilized the interval by refitting his own vessels which lay in the harbour. He also repaired the walls of the city, stocked it with provisions, and stored its seventy-three towers with arms and projectiles. For five long months the devoted city held out bravely; at the end of that time, however, being crowded with refugees, it was threatened by a more formidable foe in the shape of famine.

But amid the ranks of the besiegers stalked a yet more deadly enemy, the plague, which carried off almost two hundred Castilians daily. In this direful position of affairs each party obstinately waited to see which would be the conqueror, the famine or the pestilence; till at length, when symptoms of the malady began to show themselves on Queen Brites, the king struck his camp, and on the 5th of September took his departure for Torres Vedras, uttering bitter imprecations on the city

which had thus successfully resisted him. On the
14th October he crossed the frontier, not in triumph, but
as it were with a funeral procession; for in the van of
his army were carried on biers the bodies of many noble
victims of the plague, whose remains had been preserved
that they might be buried in the tombs of their ancestors.
The gloom inspired by the black trappings of death was
unrelieved either by the gladness of success or by the
consciousness of glory won. Sadness and silence were
the companions of that homeward march. Meanwhile at
Lisbon the joy was that of men restored from death to
life. The people were bent on solemn acts of fervent
thanksgiving to the Almighty, and the bishop and clergy,
the regent, the nobility, and the populace testified their
united and humble thankfulness by walking in reverent
procession barefooted to the convent of the Holy Trinity,
to offer to God the incense of their praise and gratitude.
To none were the glad tidings of this happy event more
welcome than to that truest of friends and patriots,
Nuño Alvarez Pereira. With his usual fearlessness he
sailed down the Tagus from Palmella in a light skiff,
through the enemy's fleet, to offer his congratulations,
and at his instigation a renewal of the act of homage
to the Grand Master by all the nobles, knights, prelates,
and municipal authorities, took place on the 6th of
October, in the royal palace, where the Grand Master
resided. About this time the King of Castile attempted
the assassination of the Grand Master, but the plot was
discovered.

Soon after this the Cortes were convened at Coimbra.
The safety of the kingdom rendered necessary the
appointment of a responsible chief, and it was evidently
the wish of the people to proclaim the Grand Master

king. Some of the nobles, however, thought the only legitimate course was, that the Grand Master should be regent for his half-brother Dom João, or in case of his death, for the infant Dom Diniz, who had been declared legitimate children of King Pedro.

At this juncture the Grand Master had the good fortune to possess in the Chancellor João das Regras an advocate, who served him as well with his tongue as his faithful friend Nuño Alvarez Pereira had already done with his sword. The chancellor's main purpose was to show that the throne was without an heir. He first asserted that Brites, Fernando's daughter, was illegitimate, and further, that she and her husband had, by making a violent entry into Portugal, broken the treaty by which the terms of the succession had been settled. He then dwelt on the doubtful legitimacy of the children of Iñez de Castro, and in conclusion argued that the Portuguese possessed the power of choosing their own king, and that there was no one who by his birth, abilities, and devotion to his country so well deserved to be raised to the throne as the Grand Master of Aviz. The discussions which ensued were set at rest by the chancellor producing the written refusal of Pope Innocent VI. to recognize the legitimacy of the children of Iñez de Castro. His success was complete, and on the 6th of April, 1385, the Grand Master was proclaimed king to the joy of the whole nation.

The new sovereign was only twenty-nine years old at the time of his accession, and his first exercise of power was to show his gratitude towards those to whom he owed his prosperity. Foremost among these was Nuño Alvarez Pereira, on whom, though two years younger than himself, he conferred the highest military honour in the realm, viz. the rank of Constable, a distinction for which he soon had the opportunity of proving his fitness; for before long the King of Castile was again on his way to attack Portugal. Pereira at once set out with all the troops at his command for Santiago, and, collecting men as he proceeded, made himself master of various places which held allegiance to the King of Castile. The king soon after joined him in Entre Douro e Minho, and took possession of the most important places in that province. Meanwhile the Castilians had crossed the frontier by Almeida, and were advancing upon Viseu. King João marched to meet them with an army consisting of three hundred lances, a small band of regular infantry, and a large number of peasants. The Castilians had been pillaging for several days, and were anxious to avoid an encounter, but the Portuguese intercepted them about half a league from Trancoso. The engagement which ensued was long and deadly, for the Castilians being superior in number could not brook the idea of defeat, but the Portuguese were struggling for hearth, and home, and country, and bore down all before them. When the sun set four hundred chosen lances of Castile were laid low, and the Portuguese were masters of the field. The actual loss to the Spaniards was great, but the blow to the *morale* of those who remained was perhaps even more important, while the Portuguese were greatly encouraged for the coming struggle. This determined the King of Castile to bring the whole of his forces into Portugal, and to engage King João in one decisive battle, a plan which was opposed by his more prudent advisers for reasons among which the king's health was by no means the lightest. King João and the constable lost no time in collecting such forces as could be mustered, and happily by this time three large ships arrived at Lisbon from England with about five hundred men-at-arms and archers. The greater part of them were mere adventurers. There were no knights among them, but they were led by three squires named Norbury, Mowbray, and Huguelin de Hartsel, whereas two thousand French knights had joined the Castilian army. On the 14th of August the Portuguese army took up an advantageous position in a plain at a league's distance from Porto de Mos. When the first ranks of the Castilians came in sight they did not offer battle to the Portuguese, but marched in the direction of Aljubarrota, where they halted. The older and more prudent officers of the Castilian army advised that they should remain quietly where they were, as the soldiers were fasting and fatigued with their march. This prudent counsel was overruled by the impatience of the younger soldiers, who clamoured for an instant encounter.

Historians differ as to the respective strength of the two armies in this important battle, but there can be no doubt that the Castilians were very superior in numbers, in experience, and in equipments. They had also the advantage of possessing ten pieces of cannon called "trons," the first ever seen in Spain. The movement of the Spaniards towards Aljubarrota had necessitated a change in the position of the Portuguese army. The ground occupied by King João was a level plain covered with heather, and as his force was small it was divided into only two lines. In the vanguard was the Constable with only 600 lances. In the right wing was a goodly band of gentlemen who, as a point of honour, had resolved to defend to the death the spot on which they might be placed. This division bore the name of the " Enamorados," or "Volunteers," and was distinguished by a green banner. The left wing consisted of Portuguese and foreigners, among whom were some English bowmen and men-at-arms. Behind the men-at-arms in both wings were bowmen and infantry, so placed as to give ready help to the cavalry. The king, with 700 lances and the royal standard with the guard appointed for its defence, were in the rearguard, behind which was a strong barricade formed with the baggage which was begirt by foot soldiers and bowmen. It was evening, and the men had suffered much from the necessity of remaining under arms all day beneath the full blaze of an August sun, especially as, from reverence for the vigil of the Assumption, few of them ate or drank. But the example of the king and the Constable quite sustained the courage of all. On both sides the trumpets sounded for the charge; the war-cries of "Castile and Santiago," and "St. George for Portugal," rang through the air, and the two armies met with a heavy shock. The Portuguese vanguard at first suffered terribly from the arrows of the Castilian bowmen, and the Castilian light horse endeavoured, though in vain, to penetrate the baggage waggons, but the main force of the battle was soon concentrated round the banner of the Constable, the Castilians directing their principal efforts against the division of the "Enamorados," who suffered the most. When the king perceived that the foremost ranks were penetrated, and that the Constable was hard beset, he pressed forward with the rearguard and the royal banner. The contest became fiercer and more deadly every moment, King João himself kindling the courage and valour of his troops by surprising proofs of his own strength and intrepidity. In the height of the combat the royal standard of Castile was thrown down, and at the disappearance of the banner, which had served them as a rallying-point, some of the Castilians began to give way. When the King of Castile saw his standard overthrown, and his soldiers seizing any horses they could find to flee upon, he resolved to look to his own safety before the battle was entirely lost. His keeper of the household, Pedro Gonsalvez de Mendoza, who had foreseen the result of a contest, entered upon against his own advice and that of the most experienced knights of the council, had steadily remained by his master's side to help him in the moment of necessity. That moment had now arrived. Setting the king upon a strong horse in exchange for the mule which, after leaving his litter, he had ridden on account of his illness, he led him from the field, and then, in spite of the king's remonstrances, returned to the fight. "The women of Guadalaxara," said he, "shall not reproach me with having led their husbands and sons to death, while I return home safe and sound." Accordingly he fought his way into the thick of the battle, where he fell like a true-hearted soldier as he was, whilst his master rode for his life, tearing his beard and cursing the day that he had entered Portugal. Meanwhile the Portuguese bowmen and the infantry who protected the baggage, having been taken in flank by the Castilian light horse, King João ordered the constable to hasten to their assistance. The Portuguese were already successfully defending themselves, and on the appearance of the constable the Castilian cavalry ceased from the attack. The wings were now able to bring all their strength upon the Castilian vanguard, and complete its overthrow. The Castilians, finding that their king had fled, lost all hope, and favoured by the darkness took to flight. To this day there is shown, in Aljubarrota, a

VIEW OF THE MONASTERY OF BATALHA, DRAWN BY H. L'ÉVÊQUE, 1810.

baker's shop, which tradition records to have been at that time a bakehouse, in which Brites d'Almeida, the baker's wife, slew with her oven-peel no less than seven Castilian soldiers.

This famous battle of Aljubarrota was fought on the 14th of August, 1385. It was a day the proud memory of which is deathless in the annals of Portugal; for, apart from its incalculable importance to the permanent well-being of that country, the battle then fought was as remarkable for the display of chivalrous courage as any that has been recorded in the history of modern Europe. In accordance with the custom of the period, King João remained three days and three nights upon the field, until the fetid exhalations from the bodies of the slain obliged him to withdraw. The booty taken from the Castilians was very great. The king's tent with all its furniture, the silver triptych belonging to the portable altar of the Castilian army, which is still to be seen in the sacristy at Guimaraens, were taken, as well as the king's sceptre, which was long preserved in the now extinct Convento do Carmo at Lisbon, built by the Constable Nuño Alvarez de Pereira. It was near the site of this famous battle that the king afterwards erected the beautiful convent of Batalha, as a mausoleum for himself and his posterity, and here are still preserved the helmet and sword worn by him on that eventful day.

Meanwhile the King of Castile had fled, accompanied only by a few servants. At midnight he arrived sick and exhausted at Santarem, about twelve leagues from Aljubarrota, where, still alarmed for his safety, he took a boat the same night, and descending the river, reached the port of Lisbon on the 15th of August. Thence he sailed in safety to Seville, where he took the precaution of landing during the night of the 22nd of August. In his despondency at the great calamity which had befallen him, he is said to have worn mourning for seven years.

The disaster which Castile had experienced at Aljubarrota was speedily followed by a scarcely less crushing blow on their own territory, for the Constable attacked them at Valverde and gained another brilliant victory. Most of the Portuguese towns occupied by the Castilians soon surrendered to the king, and, in order to reduce the rest to submission, he was making preparations for levying a considerable army, when news arrived that the Duke of Lancaster was on the point of proceeding to Spain to prefer his claim to the crown of Castile, in right of his marriage with the Princess Constance.

From early times an alliance, cemented by numerous political and commercial treaties, had existed between England and Portugal, and the elevation of the Grand Master of Aviz to the throne, and his victory over the King of Castile, had supplied his ambassadors with reasons for suggesting to the Duke of Lancaster that the opportunity was favourable for carrying out his own designs upon Castile.

Accordingly on the 20th of July, 1386, the duke arrived at Corunna with 2000 lances, 3000 archers, and a fleet of 180 galleys, accompanied by the Duchess Constance, their daughter Catherine, and Philippa, the duke's daughter by a former marriage. Without delay an interview was arranged between him and the king, at which the latter undertook to assist him in the conquest of Castile, and bound himself to supply and maintain 2000 lances, 1000 crossbow-men, and 2000 foot soldiers, for eight months ; while the duke, on his part, pledged himself, in the event of success, to cede to the

King of Portugal several considerable places on the frontier, and to repay the expenses of the campaign.

By way of sealing this new compact, it was agreed that the king should receive one of the duke's daughters in marriage. It was the wish of the Portuguese that the king should choose Catherine, with a view of her thus becoming the heir presumptive to the crown of Castile, but the king himself, both from policy and from real preference, chose the Princess Philippa. Having first obtained from the Pope the necessary dispensation from the vow of chastity which he had taken as Grand Master of the Order of Aviz, he was married to Philippa with great pomp, and to the extreme delight of the people, on the 2nd of February, 1387. The young king had endeared himself to his subjects by his well-proved heroism and wisdom, while Philippa, who was one year his junior, was as remarkable for the modest dignity of her bearing as for her beauty, both qualities well befitting the grand-daughter of Philippa of Hainault. The proposed invasion of Castile, however, which had brought about this marriage, soon proved abortive. The Castilians showed no disposition to acknowledge the Duke of Lancaster as their sovereign, and the forces he had brought with him were insufficient to cope with the King of Castile, although King João assisted him beyond the terms of the treaty. Under these circumstances the duke saw fit to reconsider an offer which the Spanish king had made him on his first arrival in Portugal, and in the September of the same year, the Princess Catherine was affianced to the Prince Royal of Spain, who received from his father on this occasion the title of Prince of Asturias, a title which has ever since been borne by the heir presumptive to that monarchy.

No further hostilities took place between the two countries till the death of Juan I., King of Castile, in 1390; his successor, Don Enrique, made a futile attempt to place the Infant Dom Deniz, son of Iñez de Castro, on the throne of Portugal, but was afterwards persuaded by his wife, Queen Philippa's half-sister, to agree to a cessation of hostilities for ten years. On his death Queen Catherine became Regent for her son, and a definite treaty of peace between the two countries was concluded in 1411.

Meantime the friendship between Portugal and England had become most closely cemented. The riband of the newly established Order of the Garter had been conferred upon King João, who was the first foreign sovereign to receive it, and it had been agreed that in the case of any treaty between either of the countries and Castile, the other should be included. Whilst Portugal was thus gaining importance, King João and Queen Philippa became the parents of a noble family of children, whose names and order of birth are as follows:—

{ 1. Branca, and
{ 2. Affonso, who died in infancy.

3. Duarte (or Edward), so named in memory of his great-grandfather, Edward III. of England, and who succeeded his father on the throne of Portugal. He was born 31st October, 1391.

4. Pedro, born 9th December, 1392.

5. Henrique, the Prince Henry of the present biography, born in Oporto, on Ash-Wednesday, 4th March, 1394.

6. Isabel, born 21st February, 1397, afterwards married to Philippe le Bon, Duke of Burgundy, who established the Order of the Golden Fleece in honour of the occasion.

7. João, born 13th January, 1400, afterwards Grand Master of the Order of Santiago.

8. Fernando, born 29th September, 1402, whose patient endurance of suffering in Morocco won for him the designation of "The Constant Prince."

King João had also two illegitimate children: Affonso, Count of Barcellos, who married the daughter of the Constable Nuño Alvarez Pereira, from which union sprang the royal house of Braganza; and Brites, who married on the 26th November, 1405, Thomas FitzAllan, Earl of Arundel.

CHAPTER III.

CEUTA.

A.D. 1415.

Now that Portugal was at peace with Castile, it began to attain a high degree of prosperity, and King João, though dreaded by his neighbours, was beloved by his people. The glory identified with his name served as a stimulus to the ambition of his sons, the three eldest of whom, Duarte, Pedro, and Henry, were now of age, and had been admirably trained by their father in every chivalrous accomplishment. The princes were anxious to receive the honour of knighthood; but, as this was a distinction only to be gained at the point of the sword, the king proposed to hold a succession of tournaments during an entire year, to which knights of all nations, and of the highest renown in feats of arms, should be invited. His minister of finance, João Affonso de Alemquer, represented to him the useless expenditure inseparable from such a plan, and suggested that an invasion of the Moorish city of Ceuta would offer a far more honourable and fitting opportunity for conferring the rank of knighthood upon the princes, while it would be carrying the sword of the avenger into the country of their former conquerors, and opening a door to the advance of Christianity. The king yielded to the representations of his minister and the wishes of his sons, to whom the idea of winning their spurs at a tournament was most distasteful.

Desiring to obtain as much information as possible respecting the strength and position of Ceuta, he had recourse to the following stratagem. He sent Affonso Furtado de Mendoza and Alvaro Gonsalves de Camelo, Prior of the hospital of St. John of Jerusalem, as envoys to Sicily, to ask the hand of the queen in marriage for Dom Pedro, and as the vessels must necessarily pass near Ceuta, where ships of different nations were in the habit of stopping, he desired the envoys to make the most of the opportunity to examine the place. Accordingly, under pretence of taking in provisions, which, in their character of ambassadors, they were permitted by the governor to do, they remained four days in the city, carefully noting everything about which the king needed information. They then proceeded to Sicily, and delivered their message to the queen, but without success. On their return, the king demanded of Mendoza his information respecting Ceuta. His only answer was an assurance that the king would be successful in his enterprise, but in lieu of any local observations, simply stated that when he was a boy travelling with his father, who had been sent on a mission to Aragon, at a picturesque well near a town called Africa, a long-bearded old Moor, seeing he was a Christian, had with tears in his eyes, uttered to him a prophecy, already partly verified, that a king named John, a natural son of the late king, should be the first of his country to gain dominion in Africa.

The king then turned for information to the Prior of St. John, but it seemed that he was fated to be answered only in enigmas, for this envoy declared his inability to afford any details unless he were supplied with two loads of sand and two bushels of beans. When after some demur these singular materials were produced, the prior formed the sand into a representation of the seven hills from which Ceuta or Septa takes its name, described the double wall on the landward side, with its towers and curtains, and represented with the beans the apparent number and position of the houses, and, what was all important, indicated the most convenient spot for the safe and expeditious landing of the troops.

The king warmly commended his zeal and sagacity, and after consultation with the queen and the constable, at once commenced his preparations for the expedition. The Kings of Aragon and Granada immediately took the alarm. To the former, who sent messengers to him, requesting a frank avowal of his intentions, King João replied that he had no idea of attacking Aragon, but that on the contrary, in case of necessity, he was ready to protect it. The Moorish King of Granada at first sought to allay his fears by asking the intervention of the King of Aragon; but receiving a contemptuous answer, he sent envoys direct to King João himself, begging an assurance of peace under the king's seal, so that commercial intercourse between the two countries might not be interrupted. The king replied that he would take time for consideration. The envoys now had recourse to Queen Philippa, and besought her, in the name of Riccaforna, Queen of Granada, so to use her influence as to induce the king to remain at peace, promising, in requital, to send her choice and costly gifts for the nuptials of her daughter. To this Queen Philippa, who, as the old chronicler says, "being English by birth, held both Jews and Moors in detestation," gave the following dignified reply :—" I know nothing of the methods which your queens may resort to in dealings with their husbands, but with us it would be regarded as an indecent thing for a wife to interfere in her husband's affairs, especially in such as have to be debated in council. As regards the present which your queen has so liberally offered me, I thank her and accept her good wishes, but beg her to dispose of her gifts elsewhere as she may please, for, when the time comes for my daughter to be married, she will have no lack of costly ornaments."

The king at length informed the envoys that he had no intention of invading Granada, and to allay the suspicions of the neighbouring powers gave out that he was about to declare war against the Count of Holland, to whom he sent an envoy with instructions secretly to inform the count of the truth, but openly to threaten war. When the fleet was completed, and while the soldiers were busily engaged in lading the vessels, a pestilence broke out in both Lisbon and Oporto. The king by no means relaxed his efforts on this account, but personally superintended at Lisbon the preparations for the expedition. At Oporto Prince Henry, armed with full authority from his father, equipped seven triremes, six biremes, twenty-six ships of burden, and a great number of pinnaces, with which he set sail for Lisbon, where he joined Dom Pedro, who was awaiting him in the roads with eight galleys. The princes were on the point of setting out when they were recalled by the news that the queen had been stricken with the pestilence. They hastened to Sacavem where she lay, but, though she rallied at the sight of them, it was evident that her end was fast approaching.

The old chronicler, Matteo de Pisano, relates minutely the scenes which followed. The queen had had three swords made, richly set with precious stones, for the purpose of presenting them to her three sons when they were knighted. On the day after their arrival the queen solemnly addressed them in the king's presence, giving each a portion of the true cross with her blessing. In presenting the sword to Dom Duarte, she impressed upon him his duties as a king, especially that of ruling justly. To Dom Pedro she gave, as his knightly duty, the charge of protecting the honour of helpless maidens and widows, and to Prince Henry she commended the care of the soldiery; from which selection and the circumstance that the command of the attack on Ceuta was subsequently entrusted to him by the king, we may infer that Prince Henry had already distinguished himself by his soldierly qualities beyond his two elder brothers. On the thirteenth day of her illness the queen suddenly inquired, "What wind blows so strongly against the side of the chamber?" and when told by her sons that it was the north wind, she said, "It is the wind most favourable for your departure, which will doubtless take place on the feast of St. James." This proved a true prophecy, though it seemed at the time scarcely possible, for the feast of St. James would fall only six days after. The queen died on the 19th of July, 1415, to the sincere grief of the people; for, while sharing for twenty-eight years the throne of the most highly gifted of the kings of Portugal, she had exhibited qualities which would have placed her amongst the most noble of her sex in any country or in any age. To do good was with her a necessity of existence, and her choicest pleasure was in

QUEEN PHILIPPA.

From the Recumbent Statue over her Tomb at Batalha.

Page 27

stilling contentions and reconciling disputants. The virtue of abstinence she carried to an excess, for, from a deeply-seated sense of devotion, she fasted so severely as to seriously undermine her health. In the details of domestic economy she took as much interest as the humblest among her subjects, and encouraged similar habits in the ladies who were about her person. Such an example could not, and did not, fail to produce a notable effect on the bearing, manners, and tone of the nobles of the court. But of all the occupations of the queen, that in which she took the greatest delight, was the training and instruction of her children, in which she communicated to them much of the lofty tone of her own exalted character. She also possessed the faculty of developing their understandings in a manner which was remarkable for the period, and their history shows how eminently qualified she was to be the mother of princes and heroes.

The nature of the queen's disease, together with the heat of the weather, rendered it necessary to hasten the interment of her remains, and on the following day the funeral was celebrated with great pomp in the monastery of Odivellas, but her body was ultimately removed, on the 14th of August, 1434, to the magnificent chapel erected by King João at Batalha, for the joint sepulchre of himself and his beloved queen.

After the funeral Prince Henry joined the king at Restello, a little chapel at the mouth of the Tagus, which the prince had built for sailors on the spot where his nephew, King Manoel, afterwards erected the superb monastery of Belem, and whither the nobles had induced the king to retire for safety from the pestilence. There was much discussion as to the time for the departure of the expedition to Ceuta, but the king overruled the opinion of some who thought that there ought first to be a period of public mourning, by saying that an immediate departure would best carry out the queen's expressed wishes. Accordingly, the expedition started with a favouring wind on the 25th of July, that feast of St. James which had been indicated by the dying queen. Many distinguished adventurers from England, France, and Germany, took part in the enterprise. A baron of the last-named country took with him forty knights, and a wealthy Englishman, or perhaps Scotchman, whose name is difficult to recognize under the transmitted form of Menendus or Mongo, possibly Menzies, brought four vessels laden with provisions. The armament was an unusually large one for the period. It consisted of 33 galleys, 27 triremes, 32 biremes, and 120 smaller vessels, with 50,000 men, of whom 20,000 would seem to have been soldiers, and the remainder oarsmen and mariners.

The armada anchored in the Bay of Lagos at nightfall of Saturday the 27th. On Sunday morning the king disembarked, with all the chiefs of the expedition, and heard mass in the cathedral, after which Father João de Xira, the Preacher-Royal, read the Bull of the Crusade granted by the Pope in favour of those who should be present at the conquest of Ceuta. On the 30th the king departed for Faro, where he was detained by a calm until the 7th of August, and where Prince Henry gave proof of great presence of mind; for the lantern of his vessel having caught fire during the night, and there being imminent danger that the flames would spread to the ship, he, though suddenly aroused from sleep, with much risk to himself seized the burning

lantern and threw it into the sea. On the afternoon of
the 10th the armada anchored at Algeziras, a place
belonging to the King of Granada. Ceuta was to have
been attacked on the 12th, and the fleet was already in
full sail when a strong wind arose, which, combined with
the action of the current in the strait, carried the large
vessels nearly to Malaga, so that only the galleys and
smaller craft reached Ceuta, where many of them
anchored.

This city, in old times called Septa, had been partly
constructed and fortified by the Emperor Justinian. It
was the principal port of Morocco, being the centre of
commerce between Damascus, Alexandria, and other
eastern places, and the nations of Western Europe. Its
position was one of great importance, for in all the
invasions of Spain and Portugal, it had been the point of
muster for the Moorish armies and the rendezvous of the
corsairs. It occupied the western portion of a peninsula
nearly three miles in length, jutting out almost due east
from the mainland. It was divided into two unequal
parts by a wall, the smaller and westernmost part
terminating in the citadel, which covered the neck of
land by which the peninsula was joined to the continent.
The portion of the peninsula eastward of this wall was
called Almina, and contained the outer and larger
division of the city, as well as the seven hills from which
Ceuta derived its name, by far the highest of which was
at the easternmost extremity, and was surmounted by a
fortress called El Hacho. On the north side of the
peninsula, from the citadel to the foot of this last-
mentioned hill, the city was protected by another lofty
wall. Eastward of this hill was a small bay named
Barbazote, in which tolerably large vessels could lie at

anchor sheltered from the west wind and but little exposed to missiles from the northern wall. Here the king determined to await the arrival of the vessels which had been driven out, intending to effect a landing immediately on their return. After much delay Prince Henry succeeded in bringing them up, but a violent tempest frustrated the king's plan by compelling him to seek another anchorage, for while the large vessels turned with difficulty the point of Almina, the current caught the smaller craft which moved more slowly and carried them towards Malaga. This apparent disaster, which in the minds of the superstitious awakened doubts as to the success of the enterprise, actually contributed in no small degree to that success.

The first appearance of the strangers had caused great anxiety to the Moors, who lost no time in preparing for defence, and obtained help from the sovereign of Fez and from other neighbouring chiefs to the extent, it has been said, of one hundred thousand men. When, however, the Moors saw the fleet a second time dispersed, they imagined that it would be impossible again to bring it together, and the Governor of Ceuta, Zalá ben Zalá, accordingly dismissed the auxiliaries, and contented himself with the ordinary garrison.

The Portuguese themselves were discouraged, and, but for the determination of the king, the princes, and the constable, would have abandoned the expedition. Prince Henry having again collected the fleet, preparations were resumed for the attack, which was at length ordered in the following manner. Prince Henry was to anchor off Almina with forty or fifty vessels, and to be ready at daybreak on a signal from the king to land his men with all expedition. The king himself with the main body of the fleet was to anchor opposite the castle. The Moors would naturally flock to the point where the greater part of the fleet lay, and Prince Henry would thus be able to land with comparatively little hindrance; while, if the Moors should turn to oppose him, he would be supported by the king's division.

These movements of the fleet greatly alarmed the Moors. Zalá ben Zalá was so convinced that the issue of the struggle would be disastrous, that, but for the counsel of a few of his confidential advisers, he would have fled. In order to produce an impression that Ceuta was a very populous city, he now gave instructions that the wall on the side where the fleet lay should be crowded with men and that lighted candles should be placed in all the windows of the houses. The effect was brilliant, but, as might have been anticipated, in no way alarmed the Portuguese. The first of these who touched the soil was Ruy Gonsalvez, a man renowned for his daring, who attacked the Moors so desperately that they recoiled sufficiently to allow of others landing. This hastened the movements of the Portuguese, and Prince Henry and Dom Duarte effected a landing with about three hundred men. The Moors poured out in great numbers from the town, and a long and fierce contest ensued, in which the latter were driven back to the Almina Gate which opened on the landing-place, and through which they entered and the Portuguese with them. The first who passed through was Vasco Eannes de Cortereal, closely followed by Dom Duarte, and thus they continued charging the Moors till they reached the gates of the city. Here Prince Henry offered to resign the command to Dom Duarte, but the latter would not accept it. After retreating before the first onset, the Moors made a stand, being protected by the walls, and encouraged by their champion, a gigantic negro who fought naked and used no weapons but stones, which he hurled with terrible force, and with one of which, while the combat was in its height, he struck Vasco Martinez de Albergaria, a nobleman of Prince Henry's household, full on the helmet. The Portuguese staggered under the violence of the blow and stood for a moment half stunned, but recovering himself, he broke his way through the ranks of the enemy, and thrust his spear into the side of the giant. When the Moors saw their champion fall, they fled in confusion into the city, the Portuguese entering with them. Prince Henry's most anxious care now was to secure possession of the city gates, not only for the sake of facilitating the entry of his countrymen, but also in order to prevent those who had already entered being hopelessly shut in by the enemy. The two princes, with the Count de Barcellos, their illegitimate brother, and about five hundred men occupied a mound within the city, and there fixed Prince Henry's standard, the spot being favourable for defence, should the Moors renew the engagement. In consequence of the smallness of their force they were not free from anxiety, lest, before fresh troops arrived, the soldiers might be tempted to begin plundering, which would give the Moors an opportunity to collect in sufficient strength to shut the gates, and so render their position in the highest degree perilous. But reinforcements came in with great rapidity from that part of the fleet which Prince Henry had commanded, and some of the Moors in their alarm announced to Zalá ben Zalá in the citadel, that the city was taken. Some took flight with their wives and children. Zalá ben Zalá, overwhelmed with

dismay, came from the citadel in the hope of checking, if possible, the advance of the enemy through the narrow streets until the citizens could pass the wall to the western or inland side of the city, where, if anywhere, they might receive help from their neighbours.

When Prince Henry perceived that the greater number of his men had arrived he thought it better to waste no more time on the spot where he had waited with Dom Duarte, and gave orders to the captains to occupy various parts of the city, so that no opportunity might be afforded for the panic of the Moors to subside, or for them to reorganize their forces. Dom Duarte took possession of Cesto, the highest of the hills overlooking the city, and Prince Henry of the main street.

Meanwhile the king, who had now inspected the fleet, gave orders for a general landing, and receiving news of the rapid victory of his sons, offered up thanks to God for their success. He then advanced with his retinue towards the town, and, supposing from the quantity of plunder which was being carried on board the ships that nothing more remained to be done, seated himself near the gate.

In the interim the Moors, seeing the Portuguese intent on plunder, and approaching in utter disorder very near to the citadel, had attacked them with such fury that they fled in confusion. The Moors thought this the moment for avenging their injuries, and endeavoured to drive the enemy completely out of the city and close the gates. Prince Henry allowed the flying Portuguese to pass him, knowing that if he checked the foremost those in the rear would be exposed to great danger. He himself was left with but a handful of men; but seeing that the position of affairs was critical, he opposed the Moors with

such vigour that he put them to flight with great
slaughter. Pursuing them, however, too eagerly, he found
himself alone with the enemy, and would certainly have
been cut off had not the narrowness of the road in a great
degree protected him. For a short time he had to sustain
the conflict quite alone, till, his soldiers coming to his
assistance, the Moors were again put to the rout. While
his men pursued them, Prince Henry rested in a house
which the Portuguese had converted into a store for the
goods which they had brought on shore, but the fugitives
having received reinforcements, the Portuguese were again
driven back as far as the house where the prince was.
In vain he endeavoured to rally them, they were worn
out with the heat and thirst, and out of the many whom
he addressed not more than seventeen remained with
him. With these few he boldly met the on-coming enemy,
and forced them to retreat through the gate which led
into the inner part of the city, he himself following with
them. At length after a long and violent struggle he
succeeded in clearing this gate, and thereby secured his
return to his troops.

But evening was now coming on, and the Portuguese
began to seek their respective leaders, from whom they
had been separated in the turmoil of the day, and many
were the anxious inquiries for Prince Henry, whose
gallantry had won all hearts; and it was rumoured that
at the head of a handful of men he had made his way
to the above-mentioned gate, and fighting to the last had
there met his death. The king hearing of this, said with
a calm and unmoved countenance, "Such is the end
which soldiers must expect."

In another part of the town, Dom Duarte was delibe-
rating with Don Pedro and some other nobles as to the

means of storming the citadel, and sent a message to Prince Henry desiring his presence. This Prince Henry at first refused, for he waited to see if the Moors would return to the conflict, but when a second messenger urged on him that it was now evening, and that if the citadel were stormed no further work would remain to be done, he joined the council.

Meantime the Moors, who feared that they would be unable to defend the fortress, after consultation with Zalá ben Zalá, determined on flight. Each man loaded himself with as much as he could carry, and having constructed a testudo at the western gate, which opened landward, they silently retired with their wives and children to the neighbouring towns and villages.

It was now sunset, and the Portuguese, having resolved to attack the citadel at daybreak, sent out a reconnoitering party, who, finding no sentinels on guard, suspected that the Moors had deserted. On hearing this, the king, who now had entered the city, sent a knight, named João Vaz de Almada, to attempt an entrance into the inner part of the city, and if he found the citadel abandoned, to place the standard of St. Vincent, the patron saint of Lisbon, upon the highest tower of the fortress.

When Almada reached the gate in the wall which divided the city into two parts he found it shut, and ordered his men to hew it down. While they were so doing, two Moors, who had waited to see the end, told them in Spanish to spare themselves the trouble, for that they would open the gate. Almada then entered the citadel, and placed the standard on the highest tower.

Meanwhile the king, hearing that Prince Henry was alive and present at the council, sent to summon him to his presence. The king's face grew bright with joy as his son approached and he welcomed him with the proposal that, as he had borne himself so gloriously that day in the midst of so many well-tried veterans, he should receive the honour of knighthood in precedence of his brothers. Prince Henry, however, besought the king, that as his brothers Dom Duarte and Dom Pedro took precedence of him in age, they might likewise do so in honour. The king commended the wisdom of his son's reply, and gave orders that at daybreak all the bishops and priests who were present with the army should assemble in the great mosque, and consecrate it as the site of the cathedral of the city. On the following day this was done, and the three princes presented themselves before the king, in full armour, each bearing unsheathed the sword which the queen had given him, and with all due solemnity they were invested with knighthood, each in the order of his birth.

The night had been passed in the greatest watchfulness. When in the morning the Portuguese entered the city, it lay before them in unbroken stillness. They encountered nothing but the dead bodies of the slain, and some few old men, women, and children, who still lingered near the homes which they loved, even at the risk of becoming slaves to the victorious Christians. The spoil was most abundant in gold and silver, and jewels of great price, with stuffs and drugs in great quantity, but the destruction and waste were immense. The morning was stormy, with rain and hail, and such was the recklessness of the troops that, mingled with the streams of water which flowed down the streets, were oil, honey, spices, preserves, and butter, with fragments of the great jars which had hitherto contained them. This waste was afterwards the subject of much vain regret, when it was found that the provisions in the city were enough to have maintained for a considerable time the garrison necessary to hold it in subjection. The spoil which fell to the share of the nobles was very rich. Dom Affonzo, Count de Barcellos, with princely taste took for his plunder more than six hundred columns of alabaster and marble from the gates and windows of the palace of Zalá ben Zalá and the other chief buildings of the city. From one square was taken an entire vaulted roof of elaborate gilt work, which together with the columns was afterwards used in the construction of the count's palace at Barcellos.

The Moors were now seen ascending the mountains, bearing with them their wives and children, whom after awhile they left in charge of the old men that were unable to bear arms, whilst they themselves returned to the walls of the city, challenging its present occupants to fight, rather with a passionate desire of vengeance than with any hope of recovering what they had lost. Dom Duarte rode forth with a large company and speedily repulsed them, and as, when they again returned, they found the gates shut, they withdrew, uttering such wild, sad wailings of anguish and despair as moved even the hearts of their enemies to pity.

On the Sunday after this important victory, the principal mosque having been purified, the king with his sons and the grandees proceeded thither to the sound of martial music to hear the first mass. They were met at the entrance by a large number of priests in rich vestments, and the sound of the instruments was answered by two bells which were found in the highest tower of the mosque. How came they there? was the natural question of those who knew that the Mahometans

were not in the habit of using bells. The answer was
not without its interest. Some years before the Moors
had attacked and pillaged the city of Lagos, and carried
off these bells, which had been carefully but vainly
concealed, and which now again spread far and wide the
summons to attend a Christian service. Many Moors of
both sexes were witnesses from a distance of this sudden
and for them heart-rending transformation of a structure
which but two days before had been the scene of that
exclusive devotion which regarded the approach of a
Christian foot as a desecration meriting death. When
the hated sound of those bells reached their ears they
stood aghast as if under the influence of a hideous and
unnatural dream.

While the most solemn services of the Church were
being celebrated in the newly consecrated cathedral,
messengers from the king were hastening in different
directions with the news of the victory, the fame of which
rapidly spread throughout Europe, for it was felt to be
one that promised important consequences.

The conquerors were naturally desirous not to prolong
their stay upon the coast of Barbary, and the king,
though by no means inclined to resign into the hands of
the Moors so important a conquest, was anxious to
resume the government of his country. The majority of
the Portuguese doubted the possibility of holding the
place, and one grandee, Martin Affonso de Mello, whom
the king had selected as commander, declined the honour,
though it was a greater than had been offered by the
king to any subject in any of his enterprises. While it
was uncertain who was to accept the charge of the place,
Dom Pedro de Meneses, Count de Viana, of the noble
house of Villareal, happening to have in his hand a stick

of Zamboa wood,[1] uttered the exclamation, "By my faith, with this stick alone, I feel myself man enough to defend these walls against every Morisco of them all." What then appeared an empty boast became afterwards a valuable reality. The king took him at his word, and this stout-hearted knight remained the first commander of Ceuta, and had the honour of being told by the king that he should require of him no other pledge than that which was afforded by his high character and noble birth. Faria y Sousa, who wrote two centuries later, records that this staff was still, in his time, preserved at Ceuta, and placed in the hands of every governor on the occasion of his taking the command of the place. The valiant Dom Pedro held the governorship for nearly two and twenty years. He was engaged in frequent contests with the Moors, but proved himself well able to maintain with honour that dignified but responsible position. From that day to this the Moors have never recovered possession of the city.

The king left Ceuta with the fleet on the second of September, 1415, and a few days afterwards anchored, amidst the exultant welcomes of his people, in the port of Tavira, on the coast of Algarve. At Tavira the king summoned his sons to him, and declared his wish to reward them for the great service which they had rendered him. To Dom Duarte, who was to succeed him on the throne, he had nothing greater to offer, but upon Dom Pedro he conferred the titles of Duke of Coimbra and Lord of Montemoro Velho, Aveiro, and other territories which thence, as forming the appanage of his rank, took the name of the Infantado, a designation which still

---

[1] A variety of the orange tree. Faria uses the words—Azebuche, Azebo, and Azambugeyro.

remains. The title of Duke had not previously existed in Portugal. Prince Henry was made Duke of Viseu and Lord of Covilham.

In Tavira the king discharged with many thanks and ample presents those who had volunteered their assistance, and dismissed with liberal payment the foreign vessels which had been employed in his service. Among these were twenty-seven English ships, which, touching at the port of Lisbon on their way to the Holy Land, had at the king's request joined him in his expedition against the Moors.

This enterprise, which had in the first instance been undertaken mainly with the view of affording a worthy opportunity for the young princes to earn knighthood, proved in many ways of great importance. It was a severe reprisal upon the Moors, who had for so many centuries inflicted their hated dominion on the Peninsula, and it transmuted Ceuta, from being the chief emporium and key of the Mahometan states, into the very bulwark of Christendom against them. But further, and this is especially note-worthy, as a successful naval enterprise it was the parent of those grand achievements which made the close of the fifteenth century memorable in the history of the world.

For three years the Count de Viana was able to hold the Moors in check with the forces which had been left in his command, but in 1418 it appeared necessary for him to seek aid from the mother country. Ceuta was surrounded inland by a large army of Moors, and was attacked from the sea by the forces of the King of Granada, who had sent a fleet of seventy-four sail, and numerous troops, under the command of his nephew Muley Saïd, to attack the city from the sea. Fortunately the munitions in the arsenals of Lisbon were abundant, so that the king was able to despatch a strong force under the command of Prince Henry, who took with him his brother Dom João. At the same time, Dom Duarte and Dom Pedro proceeded to Algarve, in order that they might be ready to reinforce Prince Henry in case of necessity. As the latter was entering the mouth of the strait, he was met by a pinnace, bringing him written information from the Count de Viana that Muley Saïd had already taken possession of the eastern part of the Almina, in combination with the army already *in situ*, while the galleys blockaded the port. The glory of destroying the navy of Granada did not however fall to the lot of Prince Henry, for, before he could reach Ceuta, the Count de Viana had sallied forth at the head of his small but stout-hearted garrison against the position which Muley Saïd had taken up on Mount Hacho. The brave Moor met the count with a desperate resistance, which though it was sufficient to secure his honour, could not win for him success. At the commencement of the engagement, his galleys, which had sailed out of the bay, came in sight of the Portuguese fleet, of the approach of which the Moors had given repeated signals from both sides of the strait. The whole of the fleet of Granada took the alarm and fled, only one galley remaining to aid the escape of Muley Saïd with a small handful of men. By the time the princes landed the action was at an end.

The princes remained two months in Ceuta, expecting that the Moors would make an effort to regain their lost city, but they waited in vain. During this time Prince Henry, who chafed at the thought of returning to the presence of his father without having achieved a single act of distinction, conceived the bold idea of taking Gibraltar by storm. Although he was opposed by the almost unanimous opinion of the council, yet he determined to make the attempt, and set sail accordingly. Fortune, however, did not favour the undertaking. A storm arose which drove the fleet towards Cape de Gat, where it remained fifteen days, and on their return to Ceuta the princes received a letter from their father with positive orders for their return to Lisbon.

CHAPTER IV.

TALENT DE BIEN FAIRE.

"TALENT de bien faire" was Prince Henry's adopted motto, and human wit perhaps could scarcely suggest a better. In his time the word "talent" conveyed not, as now, the idea of "power" or "faculty," but of "desire," and the appropriateness of the motto to Prince Henry himself has in it something remarkable. Its principal characteristic is aspiration, and when the exertions of the prince's life have been depicted they will be found to have been great indeed in effort, but great only in ultimate, not in immediate, result, the most indisputable evidence of a life devoted to the "Talent de bien faire."

The renown of the prince after the taking of Ceuta became so high in Europe that he was invited severally by the Pope, the Emperor of Germany, and the Kings of Castile and of England to undertake the command of their respective armies. In all probability it was in 1420 or 1421 that he received this invitation from the Pope (Martin V.), after the embassy sent to him by the Greek Emperor Manuel Palæologus asking for his assistance against the Turks. The Emperor of Germany was Sigismund, whose close relations with the court of Lisbon and with the ambassadors of Portugal in the Council of Constance would enable him to form a correct opinion of the eminent qualities of the prince. The

Kings of Castile and of England were John II. and Henry V.

When Prince Henry, after the capture of Ceuta, set his mind upon the conquest of Guinea he sent every year two or three vessels to examine the coasts beyond Cape Non, the limit of Spanish exploration, yet none of his ships for many years had the hardihood to round Cape Bojador. It is recorded by Barros, the great historian of the Portuguese, when describing the effect of a storm which assailed one of the earliest of these expeditions, that "the Portuguese mariners of that time were not accustomed thus to venture on the open sea, all their nautical knowledge being limited to coasting in sight of land." Hercules was yet in his cradle. The little nation had but just succeeded in strangling the snakes of Moorish and of Spanish oppression. So far it had done bravely. It had thrown off the yoke and was able to draw breath. What wonder if having achieved such victories it felt its pulse beat strong for greater and yet nobler efforts. True, the ocean was a new and formidable antagonist. Other nations mightier than they had tempted the same danger but had withdrawn disheartened from the contest, and their unavailing efforts, so far from diminishing, enhance the glory due to that persistent bravery which yielded neither to difficulty nor danger. But the inspiration and encouragement to this perseverance emanated from Prince Henry himself.

It was not, however, to the exploration of the West Coast of Africa only that the thoughts of the prince were directed. The hope of reaching India by the south point of Africa was a yet higher object of ambition. The political decay of the Roman Empire had not been accompanied by any decrease in that love of luxury and profusion which necessitated commerce and navigation. The civilization and trade of the world had simply fallen into the hands of new masters. The vast dominion acquired by the followers of Mahomet gave them the control of a gigantic commerce. Not indeed that maritime communication possessed for them any charms; the contrary was the case, and the timidity of their navigation was peculiarly remarkable, but their overland caravans were the means of carrying on a traffic which extended from the Mediterranean to India, and from the heart of Africa to Astrakhan and the countries of the north. One of the most important of these caravan routes was that which traversed the great African desert, and introduced into the Mediterranean the slaves and gold dust, the ivory, and malaguette pepper that were procured from the negroes.

In the middle ages a variety of causes conspired to direct the attention of European nations to the East. The Crusades, mischievous as they were in their primary effects on the nations from which they emanated, not only made them acquainted with distant countries but also with that oriental luxury which supplied a stimulus to the cultivation of mercantile relations with those countries. Another event which had great influence in inciting the western states of Europe to maritime discovery was the war between the Moors and the inhabitants of the Peninsula. The vast mercantile operations of the Arabs had filled Spain with the rich productions of the East, and the luxurious habits of the Moorish courts of Seville and Granada were imitated by the Catholic princes of Aragon and Castile. But as hostilities between the conquerors and the conquered daily became more obstinate and implacable, the lack of these objects of luxury began to be felt by the latter, to whom, at least amongst the wealthy, they had become necessities. So that it may be fairly inferred that the expulsion of the Moors from the Peninsula was one of the great stimulants to the search for a passage to India by the sea. In this expulsion the Portuguese took the lead, and were consequently the first to feel the effect of the incentive. The conquest of Ceuta was the first step towards the desired object, and Prince Henry, with his love of study, his chivalrous courage, and zealous nature, was exactly the man to pursue that object with the perseverance of a fixed determination.

The geographical position of Portugal was eminently suggestive and encouraging. The large revenues of the Order of Christ, of which the Prince was the Grand Master, provided him with resources for which he could imagine no more worthy employment than the conquest and conversion of the heathen, and the general extension of the knowledge of the human race, with its concomitant commercial advantages. During his stay in Africa he gathered important information from the Moors respecting the populous nations of the interior and of the coast of Guinea, and of the passage of large caravans from Tunis to Timbuctoo and to Cantor, on the Gambia, which instigated him to seek those countries by the way of the sea. From Azanegue prisoners he gathered information of the position of certain palms growing at the northern mouth of the Senegal, or so-called Nile, by which he was enabled to give instructions to his navigators for the finding of that river.

As regards the West Coast of Africa, very little indeed had up to this time become known to explorers. Ibn Ihaldoun in the preceding century had placed the limit at Cape Non, but Ibn Saïd had related the chance arrival of some Arabs at the Glittering Cape (Cape Branco) two centuries before, and it is certain that Cape Bojador was known as early as 1375, for it is laid down under the form of Bugeder in the Catalan map of that date. But here was in very truth the limit of known coast. We have not sufficient evidence to show the exact extent of the information which the Prince was enabled to gather respecting the interior of the country, but we are not entirely deprived of the means of forming what may probably be an approximately correct judgment on that point. The seaports on the North Coast of Africa had long been the medium of conveying to Europe the valuable commodities brought from Nigritia, but as these were brought over by land, and not by sea, it is manifest that much had to be learned by inquiry respecting the nations and the countries from which they were supplied. To become acquainted not only with the Moors and their immediate neighbours to the south, but also with the lands both on the Eastern and the Western Coasts beyond the Great Desert, was the object of the prince's desire. And it must be acknowledged that the chances of gaining approximately accurate local knowledge from the Arabs was greater than could be looked for from Europeans, for while the former took diligent notice of individual narratives of travel, and industriously availed themselves of the geographical information which they acquired, the latter made a secret of many of their commercial connexions, and even treated with mistrust the details of explorations which were openly made known, whether by Arabs or by Christians. The one great source and even limit of the knowledge of African geography was commerce, and the kingdoms in the interior with which this commerce took place were Melli, Gana, Tekrúr, Takedda, Burnu, and Kanem. The most important of these was Melli, comprising the cities of Kabra, Timbuctoo, and Kuku on the Joliba. Of Timbuctoo some knowledge was already possessed in the Spanish peninsula, inasmuch as there appear to have been frequent communications between it and the kingdom of Granada. Leo Africanus, himself a native of Granada, who was born at the close of the century which witnessed Prince Henry's explorations, speaks of the Stone Mosque and Royal Palace of Timbuctoo, the only two remarkable buildings in the city, as having been the work of an experienced architect of Granada; and Ibn Batuta, writing in the century in which Prince Henry was born, mentions as one of the curiosities of Timbuctoo the tomb of Abu-Ishac-es-Sahili, a famous poet of Granada, who died at Timbuctoo in 1346. The old accounts leave us in much doubt in respect of the geography of the several kingdoms we have referred to, though many points have been settled in more recent times.

The more entirely to enable himself to carry out his objects without embarrassment, the prince took up his abode, with the king's permission, on the promontory of Sagres in Algarve, of which kingdom he was made governor in perpetuity after his return from the succour of Ceuta in 1419. He originally named his new quarters Terça Nabal, short for Terçena Nabal, or Naval Arsenal, but at a later time when it came to have strong walls, and houses were being continually added to it, it received the name of Villa do Infante, or Town of the Infant.

By the great kindness of his Excellency the Marquis de Sá da Bandeira, late Prime Minister of Portugal, I have been favoured with a drawn copy of an official survey of this interesting promontory, of which the accompanying plate is a reduction.

In this secluded spot, with the vast Atlantic stretching measureless and mysterious before him, Prince Henry devoted himself to the study of astronomy and mathematics, and to the despatch of vessels on adventurous exploration.

Very few details are left to us of the astronomical instruments used in the time of Prince Henry. The altitude of a star was taken by the astrolabe and the quadrant by means of an alidade, or ruled index, having two holes pierced in its extremities, through which the ray passed. The quadrant hung vertically from a ring which was held in the hand. We do not know how these instruments were graduated, but it is to be presumed very roughly. The astrolabe, the compass, timepieces, and charts were employed by sailors in the Mediterranean at the beginning of the fifteenth century. It is quite certain that the needle was used at sea before Prince Henry's time, for he himself speaks of it when urging on one of his navigators to the rounding of Cape Bojador.

It was in the reign of Affonso the Fourth that the sciences of mathematics and astronomy first began to be studied in Portugal, the Moors and Jews being the most eager students, and they principally in judicial astrology. It is not, however, till the time of Prince Henry that we meet with the names of individual cultivators of those sciences. His brother the King Dom Duarte himself gave proof of the interest he took in meteorology by the following observations of the aspects of the moon made by him and preserved amongst his writings in the

Carthusian Convent at Evora. He says that "when the new moon is entirely red, it signifies much wind. If its topmost point be dark, it means rain. If it sparkle like water raised by oars, it shows that there will soon be a storm. If dark in the middle, it shows that there will be fine weather when the moon reaches the full."

It seems highly probable that the chair of mathematics in Lisbon was established by Prince Henry himself, since by a deed dated 12th October, 1431, he conferred on the University of that city, which had no house property, some houses which he purchased of João Annes, the king's armourer, for four hundred coroas velhas, while it is known that in 1435 that chair did exist, and that the subject was one in which he took especial interest.

A most valuable caodjutor of the prince in the prosecution of these studies was his elder brother the Infant Dom Pedro. Excellently educated, as indeed were all the children of Queen Philippa, he was an accomplished student of the ancient languages and mathematics. In 1416,[1] the year after the taking of Ceuta, this prince was seized with the desire to gain enlightenment by travel through the principal countries of Europe and Western Asia. And accordingly on the first Sunday after Easter, with the king's permission, he set forth with that object attended by a small suite of only twelve persons. He first visited his uncle the King of Castile at Valladolid, who not only welcomed him with a present of five thousand gold pieces, but escorted him in person a league forth of the city. The king also

[1] The old chroniclers assign the date of 1424 to the prince's departure on his travels, but his modern biographer, the Abbade de Castro, has found reason to place that event in 1416.

gave him for a companion an interpreter named Garcia
Ramires, who had travelled in many countries and was a
notably able linguist. His first destination was to
Palestine, whence, after visiting the Holy Places, he
proceeded to the Court of the Grand Turk and to that of
the Grand Sultan of Babylonia, where he met with a
magnificent reception. He thence passed to the Court
of Rome, where Pope Martin V. welcomed him with the
highest distinction and at his request conceded to the
Kings of Portugal the important prerogative, afterwards
confirmed by a bull dated June 16th, 1428, of receiving
the rite of coronation by unction in the same manner as
observed in the crowning of the Kings of England and
France. This grace was subsequently confirmed to
King Duarte, King João's successor, by Pope Eugenius
in the year 1436. The prince also visited the Courts of
the Kings of Hungary and Denmark, and Sousa states,
on the authority of the History of Bohemia by Æneas
Sylvius, afterwards Pope Pius II., that in company with
Eric X., King of Denmark, he served the Emperor
Sigismund to such good purpose in the war against the
Turks, and also in the war against the Venetians, that
he granted him in reward the Marca Trevisana.[2] After
peace was established between Sigismund and the
Venetians the prince went to Venice, and there received
from the Republic, in compliment to him as a traveller
and a learned royal prince, the priceless gift of a copy
of the travels of Marco Polo, which had been preserved
by the Venetians in their treasury as a work of great
value,[3] together with a map which had been supposed to

[2] I do not find the passage, but the deed of endowment was seen by Duarte Nuñes in the archives of the Torre do Tombo.

[3] A Portuguese translation of this work was made and edited at Lisbon

have been either an original or the copy of one by the hand of the same illustrious explorer. The prince then proceeded to England, which he much desired to see on account of its being the country of the queen his mother. His reception by Henry the Sixth was marked by every demonstration of honour and regard that could be shown by a powerful monarch to so near a relative. On the 22nd of April, 1427, the prince was elected a Knight of the Garter in place of Thomas Beaufort, Duke of Exeter, who had died on the 27th December, 1426.

At the end of twelve years' travel Dom Pedro returned in 1428 to Portugal, where his safe arrival after so many wanderings caused the liveliest joy not only to the king his father and his brothers, but to the whole population, by whom he was henceforth spoken of as the prince "that had travelled over the seven parts of the world." Unfortunately we possess only a fabulous narrative of this most genuine peregrination drawn up by one of Dom Pedro's own companions, named Gomez de Santo Estevan. This is the more to be regretted as journeys of such length through distant countries were seldom in those days made by royal personages. On his return Dom Pedro devoted himself like his brother Prince Henry to scientific studies, among which the art of cartography took a leading place, and there is little doubt that to the genius and attainments of his elder brother Dom Pedro, Prince Henry owed much of encouragement and enlightenment in his pursuit of geographical investigation. The Marco Polo MS. and the map brought from Venice would doubtless act as a potent stimulus to these investigations.

in 1502 by a learned German printer named Valentim Fernandez, who had established himself in Lisbon at that time.

When in Ceuta in 1415 Prince Henry gathered important information from the Moors of Fez and Morocco respecting the Arabs who lived on the borders of the desert, as well as respecting the kingdom of the Jaloffs near Guinea. He knew that the countries on the North of Africa were enriched by commerce with that country, and derived therefrom a considerable quantity of gold. In this, as a step to yet greater purposes of advancement, he saw a source of prosperity for his own country, which in itself was worthy of new efforts at exploration. The earliest date assigned by any authority of the same century to an expedition fitted out by him is that of this selfsame year of 1415; and he made a practice of sending out an expedition every year as far as was possible along the west coast of Africa.

These various expeditions which resulted in no immediate advantage called down upon the prince much obloquy from the nobles, who complained of an amount of useless expenditure, from which meanwhile they were in no sense the losers. But vituperation fell harmless upon one who was consciously influenced by a noble purpose which could only be effected by perseverance. At length an event took place which silenced clamour for a while, and greatly encouraged the hopes of the prince, but this must form the subject of a separate chapter.

CHAPTER V.

PORTO SANTO AND MADEIRA.

1418—1420.

The discovery of the islands of Porto Santo and Madeira in 1418-20 was the first fruit of Prince Henry's explorations. Two squires of his own household, named João Gonsalvez Zarco and Tristam Vaz Teixeyra, anxious for fame and desirous of serving their master, had set out on an exploring expedition to the coast of Guinea, but were taken by a storm off Cape St. Vincent and driven to the island of Porto Santo. The favourable report of this newly found island induced Prince Henry forthwith to send out to colonize it, and after a while a dark spot was descried on the horizon by the colonists, which on examination proved to be what is now called the island of Madeira. Until the year 1827, the belief had prevailed for nearly three centuries that this group was then discovered for the first time, and that the islands then also received their respective names. But this is not the case. On a map now in Florence, made by a Genoese in 1351, these islands are laid down with the names of " Isola de lo Legname," or Island of Wood, of which Madeira is a translation, " Porto Santo " and " Isole deserte," which last are identical with the more recent names. A vague rumour obtained in the islands themselves that the discovery had been made fortuitously at the close of the same century by an Englishman named Machin, but great discredit was thrown upon this story by many, and none knew for a certainty what to believe. Happily the means have fallen within my power of establishing the truth of this latter story, and I shall therefore narrate it here and describe the process by which Zarco himself was led to his reputed accidental discovery. The story is one of the most romantic that has ever been dignified with the name of history, and has been told a hundred times in as many different shapes; but the following is a digest of it as related by the possessor of the original manuscript account.

In the reign of Edward III., a young man of good family named Robert Machin had the misfortune to become enamoured of a young lady, the wealth and rank of whose parents were so far superior to his own that they treated his pretensions with disdain. To avoid his importunities they obtained from the king an order for his imprisonment, and in the interval united their daughter to a nobleman whose station was more suited to maintain the dignity of their family. As the lady whose name was Anne D'Arfet or Dorset reciprocated Machin's affection, he was no sooner released from prison than he determined on carrying her off. By the aid of a friend who contrived to gain admittance as groom into the lady's family, which was established at Bristol, this plan was finally effected, and from Bristol they set sail together in a vessel which Machin had already provided and manned for the purpose.

The intention was to sail for France, but a north-east wind carried them off that coast and, after thirteen days' driving before a tempest, they caught sight of an island on which they landed. They found it uninhabited, but well wooded and watered and eminently suited for habitation. For three days they enjoyed the peacefulness of security, and while some explored the interior, others in the ship examined the contour of the coast, but on the third night were overtaken by a storm and driven on the coast of Africa. The anxiety and suffering which the unhappy lady had undergone found their culmination in this disaster, and after three days of total mental prostration she expired. She was buried at the foot of the altar which had been erected in gratitude on their arrival, and, on the fifth day after her death, Machin also was found dead on the grave of his mistress. The survivors buried him, and then embarked in the ship's boat and, on reaching the coast of Africa, were carried before the King of Morocco, by whom they were thrown into captivity. In the same unfortunate circumstances they encountered their missing companions who had previously been carried away in the ship.

Among their fellow-captives was one Juan de Morales, a native of Seville, a good seaman and originally a pilot, to whom they gave a description of the land they had discovered. Now on the 5th March, 1416, died Don Sancho, the youngest son of King Ferdinand of Aragon, and by his will he left a large sum for the ransom of Christian captives from Morocco. Amongst those who were redeemed was this Juan de Morales, but the vessel which brought him over was captured by the Portuguese navigator João Gonsalvez Zarco. From pity, however, the latter liberated the unfortunate captives, reserving only Morales, whose experience in nautical matters he thought might be of service to his master, Prince Henry. Now, as we have already had occasion to say, this Zarco had gone out in company with Tristam Vaz Teixeyra, to explore the west coast of Africa, and had been driven by a storm on the island of Porto Santo. This appears to have occurred at the close of 1418 or at the beginning of 1419. From Morales he heard the account of Machin's discovery, and, with the permission of the prince and under the guidance of Morales, he set sail and made the important re-discovery of the island of Madeira, to one half of which he gave the name of Funchal and to the other that of Machico. Now it so happened that the narrative of this discovery written by Alcaforado, one of the adventurers, was preserved for two centuries and a half in the Zarco family, when by marriage it fell into the possession of a distinguished writer, Francisco Manuel de Mello, who published it in Lisbon in 1660, and from it we derive very satisfactory proof of the genuineness of the romantic story of Machin's adventure, which had been so much doubted.

None of Machin's crew had been left behind, and as the importance attached to Zarco's re-discovery in 1419-20 proves that the island had not previously been colonized by the Portuguese, it follows that the names of Machico and Funchal were newly given by Zarco and Vaz at the time of the partition of the island between them. The etymology of the word Funchal is exclusively Portuguese. It signifies a place where fennel (in Portuguese, funcho) grows, and the name is distinctly declared to have been given from that plant having been found there in great quantities. The entirely different Spanish form of the word "hinojo," and the Italian form "finocchio," prove that the name could not have survived from any previous Spanish or Italian discovery. And since no Englishman remained on the island to preserve the name of Machin, the conclusion is inevitable that, at the time of the partition, the Portuguese showed their recognition of Machin's previous discovery, communicated to them by the Spaniard Juan de Morales, by themselves giving the name of Machico to the place where they found the grave and cross, and other indications of Machin's tragic adventure. Further, it is past belief, that Manoel de Mello, himself a Portuguese, should gratuitously detract from the glory not only of his own country but of his own family, by setting forth that his ancestor had been preceded in a grand discovery by an Englishman, and, even more, had been guided thereto by a Spaniard, if it had not been true.

But to return to Zarco, who, although his discovery was not original, had accomplished a feat of very great importance and added honour to a name which he had already greatly distinguished. He had won his spurs at Ceuta, and had continued to serve bravely in the other African expeditions. He is also supposed to have been the first who introduced artillery on board the Portuguese vessels. In the June of 1420 he set sail for Porto Santo with two vessels, accompanied by João Lourenço, Ruy Paes, Alvaro Affonso, Gonzalo Ayres Ferreira,[1] and Francisco Alcaforado, the author of the narrative. On arriving he had his attention called to a dark line which was visible on the horizon towards the south-west,

---

[1] We learn from Cordeiro's Historia Insulana, liv. 3, cap. 15, that in a charter of Prince Henry's dated 1430, this Ferreira is mentioned as a companion of Zarco. He was the first who had children born in Madeira. The eldest he called Adam and the second Eve. From him descended the noble family of Casta Grande of Madeira and the Ferreiras of San Miguel, who also derive from the Drummonds and the Royal Stuarts. It may here be observed that Prince Henry, as I am informed by the Count de Rilvas, was careful to institute family registers at that early period in the island of Madeira.

an appearance which had astonished those whom he had left in the island. The pilot Juan de Morales conjectured that this would be the island they were in search of, and suggested that the thick fog was occasioned by the action of the sun on a soil covered with forests. After a stay of eight days, Zarco sailed in the direction of the fog, and as he approached it found that it diminished in extent and intensity towards the east; and, steering in this direction, he reached a point of low land to which he gave the name of Ponta de San Lourenço. Doubling this he coasted along the southern shore, and came to high land covered with thick wood from the shore to the top of the mountains, where the fog still rested.

The next day Ruy Paes was sent with a sloop to explore the coast. He found it answer to the description given of it from memory by Morales, and at length discovered the tomb with the epitaph and wooden cross which had been left by Machin's party, but no human being did he encounter. Zarco took formal possession of the island in the name of the King of Portugal, Prince Henry, and the Order of Christ.

He then went on board his sloop, and accompanied by Alvaro Affonso in command of the other vessel, made an exploration of the coast. He soon fell in with four fine rivers of very pure water, to one of which he gave the name of Rio do Seyxo or river of the flint, which name still remains. From a valley further on, which was full of trees, he collected several samples of the different woods, and at the point of the river which flowed through it he set up a great wooden cross, which gave the name of Santa Cruz to the town afterwards built on the spot. Further on there arose from a point of land a great number of jackdaws, which caused him to name it

"Ponta dos Gralhos" (Jackdaw point). The name survives in the form of Cabo do Garajão. Two leagues further was another point, which with the first formed a spacious and commodious gulf, into which several valleys opened; the first was clothed with majestic cedars, and down the second flowed a broad river, which offered a convenient place for landing. Gonçalo Ayres was sent with some soldiers to explore the interior. He brought back word that from the top of the mountains he could see the outline of the whole island. The river has borne the name of that explorer ever since. On the west of the valley, the beach, which was broad and unsheltered, was one vast field of fennel, whence they called it "Funchal," the name which it has ever since retained. It is observable that the Portuguese instead of seeking grand names for their colonies contented themselves with preserving those which existed already, or adopting those which nature supplied. Some islets, opposite this "Funchal," offered an excellent roadstead where Zarco anchored to take in wood and water, and summoned the crews on board for the night.

Next day the sloops set sail with the view of doubling the westward point of the bay of Funchal. On that point they planted a cross and gave it its present name of Ponta da Cruz, or Point of the Cross. Beyond it extended a beautiful beach, to which they accordingly gave the name of "Praya Formosa." This ended in a considerable torrent, the beauty of which tempted the curiosity of two soldiers from Lagos; they went to reconnoitre it, and imprudently attempted to swim across it, but would certainly have been drowned, had they not received prompt assistance. This circumstance caused the torrent to be named, as at present, the "Ribeira dos Socorridos" (River of the Succoured).

Continuing still to advance, Zarco came to a little creek sheltered by a rock, and entered it with the sloops; his arrival disturbed the repose of a troop of sea wolves or phocas, which fled into a cavern at the foot of the rock, which was their dwelling-place. This "Camara dos Lobos" (Chamber of the Wolves) was the terminus of Zarco's exploration of the coast. After taking in a good supply of water, wood, plants, and birds at Funchal, he returned to Portugal, where he arrived at the end of August.

The king received him with great distinction, bestowed on him the title of Count of Camara dos Lobos, and gave him the hereditary command of his new discovery. He returned in the May following with his wife, his son, and all his family, and landed at the port of Machico, the name of which, given in remembrance of Machin, still survives. On the spot where the unfortunate Englishman was buried, he founded a chapel dedicated to the Saviour. He then went to Funchal, where the bay offered a better anchorage, and there founded a city, which rapidly increased in size, and in which his wife founded the Church of St. Catherine.

The entire island was divided between Zarco and Tristam Vaz, so as to form two Captaincies of about equal extent. The northern half, with Machico for its capital, was given to Tristam, and the southern, with Funchal for its capital, and the three Desertas, to Zarco.

Soon after Zarco had established himself at Funchal he erected a church, which from the great quantity of flint found on the coast he named Nossa Senhora do Calhão, or our Lady of the Flints, but as, inland from

thence, the forests were so thick that they could not
open a road, he had it set fire to, and it is stated by
Gaspar Fructuoso that for the incredible period of seven
years the fire was unextinguished. However this may
have been, it seems clear from a formal act signed by
Prince Henry on the 18th of September, 1460, a few
months before his death, by which he endowed the Order
of Christ with the spiritualities of these islands, that it
was not till he was thirty-five years of age that he began
to colonize the island of Madeira and Porto Santo, which
would be in the year 1425.

The province of Machico was richly wooded, and we
learn from Azurara how, twenty years later, this wood
was imported into Portugal by Prince Henry in such
quantity that a great change took place in the architecture
of the country, lofty houses being substituted for those
which had previously been built in the Roman or Arabic
style. The north of the island produced large quantities
of corn and honey. The sugar cane was introduced from
Sicily, and the first sugar grown in the whole island was
in Machico. It is to Prince Henry that we are indebted
for the royal wine, the temporary loss of which in our
own days through the ravages of the *aphis* is so regretable.
He imported from Candia the Malvasia or Malvoisie
grape, which came originally from Napoli di Malvasia in
the Morea, and hence under the corrupted form of the
name we have our Malmsey Madeira. The best wine
was produced in Machico. Thirty years later when the
island was visited by Cadamosto, a Venetian navigator
in the service of Prince Henry, the Italian described them
as bearing as many grapes as leaves, in bunches two or
three or even four palms in length, and said it was the
most beautiful sight in the world.

On the return of Zarco and Vaz from their first discovery of Porto Santo, they suggested to the prince the desirableness of colonizing the island. The prince greatly approved of the idea, and provided them with the requisites for the colonization, and among those who offered to accompany them was a gentleman of the household of Prince João, named Bartollomeu Perestrello. He had in a cage a pregnant rabbit, which had been given him by a friend. She littered during the passage, and with her young ones was taken to the island. Unfortunately the race increased so rapidly that they consumed everything that was planted by the colonists. On returning the following year after a short absence from the island, the colonists found the rabbits increased to such an extent that in spite of all their efforts to destroy them, they produced no sensible diminution of their numbers. Perestrello then returned greatly discouraged to Portugal, Zarco and Vaz having by this time discovered Madeira, and received from Prince Henry that island in partition between them. The prince however subsequently caused Perestrello to return to Porto Santo, of which he gave him the governorship, and although the multitude of rabbits entirely prevented all vegetable cultivation, yet the island nourished a considerable number of goats, and the dragon-tree grew in abundance, so that they were able to export dragon's blood to Portugal and many other places. The daughter of this same Perestrello afterwards became the wife of the illustrious Christopher Columbus.

CHAPTER VI.

CAPE BOJADOR.

1434—1436.

The last years of the reign of King João, after the taking of Ceuta, were employed in the peaceful pursuit of the internal prosperity of his kingdom, and the dynasty of Aviz was now firmly established. Even the warlike constable, Nuño Alvarez Pereira, who had never known defeat, had retired in 1423 to his magnificent Convent do Carmo, and, adopting the habit of a monk, laid aside all his titles, and, by his own desire, was addressed by the simple name of Nuño. Had he followed his own inclinations, he would have existed on the alms of the charitable and have made a pilgrimage as a mendicant to Jerusalem.

For ten years more the kingdom enjoyed profound peace, when in 1433 the king's health began to fail, and he went by direction of his physicians to Alcochete, a village on the banks of the Tagus, the air of which was considered more suitable for him than that of Lisbon. But as his weakness increased and he became convinced that his end was approaching, he desired his sons to take him to Lisbon, for he did not think it befitting that he should remain to die in an obscure place, and in the house of a private individual, as he was so near to the capital of his dominions. He was therefore removed to

KING JOÃO I., OF GOOD MEMORY.

From the Recumbent Statue over his Tomb at Batalha.

the palace of Alcaçova, where he breathed his last on the
14th of August, 1433,—being the eve of the assumption of
the Blessed Virgin, and the anniversary of the battle of
Aljubarrota,—in the 77th year of his age and the 49th of
his reign. His subjects mourned for him as for a father.
Nor is this difficult to understand. For him they had
suffered much, and willingly sacrificed life and substance,
while on his part the wisdom, skill, and courage which
had made these sacrifices only the offerings of a willing
loyalty, had procured for them a condition of prosperity
and dignity which they had never before enjoyed.

The king had directed by his will that he should be
buried in the convent of Batalha, in the noble tomb
which had been already constructed for himself and
Queen Philippa.[1]

King João was a man of a firm and resolute countenance, of large and well-proportioned frame, and of great
strength, as shown by some pieces of his armour still
existing, such as his helmet and battle-axe, which latter
only a man of great power could have wielded. He was
a man of remarkable self-control, and never allowed his
features to betray emotion even in the extremes of joy or
sorrow. His magnanimity was remarkably shown in the
readiness with which he pardoned and restored to his
favour those who offended him or who had conspired
against his life. In his gifts he was always open-handed,
and those who served him well either in peace or in war
he rewarded almost always beyond their expectation. He
was the founder of a great number of the buildings in

---

[1] The portraits of King John and Queen Philippa given in this volume
are drawn from casts from the statues on their tomb, expressly made for
the author by order of his valued friend His Excellency the Marquis de
Souza Holstein.

Portugal, most remarkable for beauty and magnificence; as for example, the splendid palaces of Cintra, of Lisbon, of Santarem, and of Almeirim; the sumptuous church of our Lady of Batalha, so named in memory of the battle of Aljubarrota; the church of Peralonga of the Order of St. Jerome, the first of that order founded in the kingdom, and the monastery of Carnota, of the Order of St. Francis, near Alemquer.

He was a man of great piety, and was the first sovereign who ordered the Hours of the Blessed Virgin to be translated into the Portuguese language, that all might make use of them in prayer. He also had the Gospels and the life of Christ and other spiritual books translated into the mother tongue. As Grand Master of the Order of Aviz, he had the royal escutcheon placed upon the green cross of the order, as a memorial of the care which as Grand Master he maintained over the kingdom. This is seen in the coins of his reign and those of his successors, until altered by King João II. Being also Knight of the Garter, from devotion to St. George, its patron saint, whose name was at all times his battle-cry, he bore for his crest the dragon, the saint's well-known symbol. He was a man intellectually in advance of his age. One of the latest acts of his life, was a requirement that all public ordinances should be dated from the Christian era, instead of from the era of Cæsar, as had until that time been the practice; the alteration involved a difference of thirty eight years, the era of 1460 corresponding with the year of our Lord 1422.

During the later years of his life the military ardour of his earlier days was allowed to give place to purposes of usefulness, and while he cultivated the chivalry that he loved, in the character and habits of the youthful nobility, he devoted himself to the internal improvement of his kingdom. With so many claims upon their reverence and their love, well might the Portuguese in after years speak of him as the "Father of his country" and "The King of happy memory."

The court of King João adopted for the most part English habits and usages, and the intercommunication between the two countries was much more extensive than it had previously been. The adoption of the French language as it was used at the English court and the devices and mottoes adopted by the king's sons attest this influence. The king himself was an exceedingly accomplished Latin scholar, and wrote in that language with remarkable skill and good taste. And so in that age of discoveries the reading of the "Wonders of the World" and the "Voyages of Marco Polo" brought from Venice by Dom Pedro would doubtless give the greatest delight to the distinguished men who were trained in the households of Prince Henry and his illustrious father and brothers. It has been generally believed that the king on his death-bed exhorted Prince Henry to persevere in his laudable purpose of prosecuting the extension of the Christian faith amongst their hereditary enemies in the as yet unexplored regions of Africa. Such an injunction would fall with redoubled force upon a mind whose views, religious, patriotic, and scientific, were already so strongly directed to that object. For a long series of years the prince had with untiring perseverance continued to send out annually two or three caravels along the West Coast of Africa. Cape Non was passed, but the increasing violence of the waves that broke upon the dangerous northern bank of Cape Bojador had till now prevented his sailors from rounding its formidable point. As yet they feared to venture out of sight of land and risk their lives upon the unknown waters of the Sea of Darkness.

One of the earliest acts of King Duarte after ascending the throne was to testify his satisfaction with Prince Henry's efforts in the progress of discovery by making him a donation of the islands of Madeira, Porto Santo, and the Desertas by a charter given from Cintra on the 26th of September, 1433; and in the following year, by a charter dated from Santarem on the 26th of October, he granted the spirituality of these to the Order of Christ, of which the prince was the Grand Master.

Each time that the prince sent out a fresh expedition he stimulated his explorers with promises of increased reward, to aim at excelling their predecessors in throwing light on this dark subject. Accordingly, in 1433, the year of his father's death, undismayed by so many years of disappointment, he again sent out a squire of his, Gil Eannes, a native of Lagos, but with the usual bad success, for he reached no further than the Canary Islands, where he took some captives and returned home. In the following year the prince strongly urged him to make another effort, at any rate to pass Cape Bojador, which if he could do, it would suffice for that voyage.

It is manifest that fanciful alarms suggested by sailors from other countries were superadded to the real dangers of the ocean to deter the prince's mariners, for in his injunctions to Gil Eannes we find him thus remonstrating with him for giving heed to such fables:—

"If," he says, "there were the slightest authority for these stories that they tell, I would not blame you, but you come to me with the statements of four seamen who have been accustomed to the voyage to Flanders, or some other well-known route, and beyond that have no knowledge of the needle or the sailing-chart. Go out then again and give no heed to their opinions, for, by the Grace of God, you cannot fail to derive from your voyage both honour and profit."

The prince was a man of commanding presence, and his injunctions had great weight with Gil Eannes, who now firmly resolved that he would not appear again before his master without bringing a good account of his errand. Accordingly, disregarding all danger, he put well out to sea, and succeeded in doubling the Cape. Although the exploit was in truth but a small one in the eyes of those who afterwards had gained greater experience, yet the hardihood of it was thought much of at the time, for if the first who reached that Cape had done as much, he would neither have been praised nor thanked, but the greater the sense of danger that others had attached to it, the greater was the honour that accrued to him who overcame it.

The prince was as good as his word, and Gil Eannes on his return was handsomely rewarded. He informed the prince that he had landed, but had found no human beings or signs of habitation, but as he thought he ought to bring back some evidence of his having been on shore, he presented to the prince some plants that he had gathered, which were such as were called in Portugal St. Mary's Roses.

The prince in consequence fitted out in the following year, 1435, a larger vessel than he had yet despatched, called a varinel, or vessel with oars, in which he sent out Affonso Gonsalves Baldaya, his cup-bearer, together with Gil Eannes in his barque, and they passed fifty leagues beyond the Cape. They found no habitations, but only

some traces of men and camels. Either in obedience to
their orders or from necessity they returned with this
report, but did nothing further. They named the place
which they had reached Angra dos Ruivos, *Anglice*
Gurnard Bay, on account of the great number of those
fish which they caught there.

These traces of men and camels satisfied the prince
either that there was a population at no great distance,
or that there were travellers who came to the coast.
Accordingly, he again sent out Baldaya in the same
varinel, and recommended him to proceed as far as he
could, and to do his best to capture one of the people,
so as to gather some information respecting the natives.
Baldaya passed seventy leagues beyond the point
previously reached, making a hundred and twenty from
the Cape, and here found what might be the mouth of a
large river with many good anchorages, and the entrance
of which extended eight leagues along the shore. This
was what has ever since been known as the Rio d'Ouro,
but it is only an estuary.

Here they cast anchor, and as Affonso Gonsalves had
brought with him two horses, given him by the prince
for the purpose, he sent out two young men to
reconnoitre and see whether they could discover any
signs of villages or travellers. To make this task the
easier they wore no armour, but simply took their lances
and swords by way of defence, for in the event of their
meeting any people in numbers, their best chance of
safety would be in their horses' heels. The lads were
but about seventeen years of age, but although they had
no notion what sort of people or wild beasts they
might encounter, they boldly set out and followed the
course of the river for seven leagues.

They came at last upon a group of nineteen men, neither wearing armour nor carrying any weapons but azagays. When the lads saw them they rode up to them, but the men, although so many, had not the courage to meet them in the open field, but for safety collected near a heap of stones, and there withstood the onset of the youths. They fought till evening warned the latter to make their retreat and return to the vessel.

It is difficult to imagine what those men must have thought of this sudden appearance of two boys, of complexion and features so different from their own, mounted on horseback, and armed with weapons which they had never seen before, and withal so courageously attacking a great number of men.

The two Portuguese lads wounded several of their antagonists, and one of them was himself injured in the foot. "I afterwards knew one of these boys," says the old chronicler, "when he was a noble gentleman of good renown in arms. His name was Hector Homem, and you will find him in the chronicles of the kingdom well proved in great deeds. The other was named Diego Lopez Dalmeida, a nobleman of good presence, as I have heard from those who know him." They reached the ship towards morning, and took some rest.

At daybreak Affonso Gonsalves took some of his people with him in his boat, and ascended the river accompanied by the boys on horseback. They came to the place where the natives had been on the day before, hoping to fight with them and capture one of them, but after the boys had left them, they had decamped, leaving the greater portion of their poor property behind them. This Affonso Gonsalves took and put on board his boat, as an evidence of what had been done, and, judging that it would be of no use to continue the pursuit, returned to his ship. They named the bay Angra dos Cavallos, or Bay of the Horses. Near the mouth of the river they found an immense number of phocas, amounting, as some reckoned, to five thousand. They killed as many as they could, and loaded the ship with their skins.

Nevertheless Gonsalves was not contented, because he had not taken one of the natives. He therefore proceeded fifty leagues further, to see if he could not capture some man or woman or child in order to gratify the prince's wish, and at length reached a headland where was a rock which looked like a galley, for which reason they called that port ever after the port of Gallée. Here they landed and found some nets, which they took on board. These nets were a novelty, for they were made of the bark of a tree of such a texture that without any tanning or admixture of flax it could be woven excellently well, and made into nets, or any other cordage.

Hence Affonso Gonsalves returned to Portugal, but without having been able to gain any certain knowledge whether those people were Moors or heathen, nor what was their manner of life.

The result may at first sight appear but insignificant. Such was, however, far from being the case, for it must be borne in mind that now for the first time within the Christian era Cape Bojador, which had hitherto presented an impassable barrier to Europeans into the Sea of Darkness, had at length been rounded. Unfortunately political troubles necessitated a pause in the progress of these explorations during the next five years.

CHAPTER VII.

TANGIER.

1437.

The personal qualities of King João's successor, Dom Duarte, promised most favourably for the maintenance of that prosperity which had been bequeathed to the kingdom by the energy and wisdom of his father, yet was his reign destined to misfortune from its beginning to its close. On the morrow of his father's death, as he was about to be proclaimed king at Lisbon, his physician Mestre Guadalha, who was held in high consideration as an astrologer, counselled him to postpone the ceremony, on the ground that the stars at that time forboded him misfortune. The king gave no heed to the superstitious words of the soothsayer, who forthwith, in the presence of a great concourse of people, prognosticated that the years of the king's reign would be few and full of troubles. The prediction and its accurate fulfilment have been consolidated in the records of history. The ceremony nevertheless took place in conformity with the usual custom.

From Lisbon the king went to Cintra, where his wife and children were, and here a noticeable novelty was introduced, for when the princes of the royal household did homage and took the oath of allegiance, the eldest son of the king, afterwards Affonso V., but then little more than a year and a half old, received the style and title of "Prince of Portugal," instead of that of "Infant." This change was adopted in imitation of the title of "Prince of Wales," given to the eldest son of the Kings of England.

The trouble with which the king had been threatened began to show itself betimes. The king's youngest brother Dom Fernando was especially desirous of emulating the prowess of his brothers in Africa. In this desire he was greatly encouraged by Prince Henry, the aim and object of whose life was to make discoveries and conquests in that direction, and together they decided on attempting an attack upon Tangier. Accordingly they besought the king their brother to fit out an expedition for them against the Moors. The king at first affectionately but firmly refused, for the exchequer had been seriously reduced by many causes, but at last their arguments and the influence of the queen prevailed, and against his judgment he reluctantly gave his consent.

Prince Henry has not been held entirely free from blame in this matter. True it is that the advancement of Christianity and civilization, the good of his country, the dictates of chivalry, the furtherance of his brother's wishes, and his own love of glory, all conspired to set before him in the light of duty, the enterprise which he thus warmly advocated. True it is, also, that the original invasion of Ceuta had been attended with an unlooked for success in the highest degree encouraging to the aspirations of a courageous and ardent mind, and that in that invasion his judgment, no less than his valour, had given him so high a standing in the estimation of his illustrious father, as to gain him the chief command in preference to his elder brothers, yet there can be no doubt that in this instance, as on the occasion of his proposed attack on Gibraltar, his zeal was allowed to outrun his discretion. The dictum of the Papal consistory respecting the indiscreet sacrifice of Christian life in waging war against the infidels might, had it arrived in time, have been accepted by him as a wholesome warning, but it did not arrive in time; and it may be further urged in his extenuation, that if a hesitating cautiousness had always been allowed to repress enthusiasm, history would now be wanting in the records of full many an heroic achievement.

At length the preparations were completed, and on the 26th of August, 1437, the princes landed at Ceuta, of which Count Pedro de Menezes was still the commander. The prince then reviewed the force which he had brought with him and found that of fourteen thousand men which had been promised him, eight thousand were missing. This shortcoming was caused by the reluctance of the people to risk their lives and property in what they considered a rash adventure, and also by the lack of ships to convey a greater number of men to the African shore. On the 13th of September Prince Henry arrived with his army before Tangier and made arrangements to encamp along the sea-coast, but while the troops were thus engaged, a report was spread that the inhabitants of Tangier had opened the gates with the intention of abandoning the place. This news proved to be so far from the truth that the Portuguese were engaged till nightfall in endeavouring but in vain to force the gates. There were in the city about seven thousand fighting men, including many crossbow-men from Granada. They were commanded by Zalá ben

Zalá, the same who had twenty-two years before lost Ceuta.

On Saturday, the 14th September, Prince Henry had completed his encampments, and from that time till the following Thursday was occupied in landing the artillery and munitions. On the morning of Friday, the 20th of September, Prince Henry ordered the trumpets to sound to battle. Dom Fernando, the Count Arrayolos, and the Bishop of Evora were to scale the walls at different points, and Prince Henry took upon himself the attack on the gate of the fortress, where the greatest resistance would be made. For this purpose he took with him only two mantas or mantelets,[6] without any scaling-ladder.

The engagement commenced in the morning and lasted till six o'clock, when the Portuguese were obliged to retire with loss. All attempts to force the gates had been utterly useless, for they had been very strongly walled up by the Moors, with stone and mortar. The contemplated attack with the scaling-ladders proved abortive, for the ladders were too short to reach the top of the wall. Prince Henry was therefore compelled to withdraw, and on mustering his people found that he had five hundred wounded and twenty killed. He now sent to Ceuta for longer scaling-ladders and also for two large pieces of cannon, together with powder and shot, for the guns which he had were too small and ineffective. During ten days there were repeated skirmishes, in which several Portuguese noblemen were slain.

At length, on the 30th of September, a body of ten thousand Moorish horsemen and ninety thousand foot

---

[6] Mantelets were temporary and moveable defences formed of planks, under cover of which the assailants advanced to the attack of fortified places.

came to the assistance of the city, and took their stand on a hill within sight of the camp. But when Prince Henry went out to meet them with fifteen thousand cavalry, eight hundred crossbow-men, and two thousand infantry, they were seized with a panic and took to flight. The next day the same manœuvre was repeated, and on Thursday, the 3rd of October, the Moors advanced in yet greater numbers and drew near to the camp. The prince again went out to meet them, and drove them from their position with considerable loss. Meanwhile another attack was made upon the camp by the Moors, but they also were repulsed by Diogo Lopez de Souza, who had been left to defend it. This engagement was of the highest importance, for had either of the attacks proved successful, the Portuguese army must inevitably have been destroyed.

On the 5th of October the scaling-ladders were replaced, and a wooden tower moving on wheels, and containing men supplied with missiles, was provided for the purpose of being brought up to the level of the walls, to facilitate the escalade by driving from the parapets those who were stationed there. The prince then ordered a second assault to be made upon the town, at a spot where the batteries had made a breach in the wall. This attack was led by himself in person, the remainder of the troops under arms being entrusted to Dom Fernando, the Count de Arrayolos and the Bishop of Evora, to make a stand against the Moorish army, in the event of their attacking the lines during the action.

This assault was as unsuccessful as the former, for only one scaling-ladder was brought to rest against the wall, and that was burnt by the Moors, and those who were upon it were killed. Not one of the others, nor even the wooden tower could be brought up to the wall, for as no other attack, either feigned or real, was made elsewhere, the whole garrison was able to repair to the point assailed, and with fire-arms and other missiles compelled the Portuguese to withdraw with great loss.

On the 9th the Moors appeared in great multitudes, accompanied by the Kings of Fez and Marocco and the other neighbouring princes. They forthwith attacked the advanced posts of the Portuguese army, and opened communication with the fortress, at the same time taking possession of the Portuguese batteries with all the artillery and munitions for the siege. Prince Henry had his horse killed under him, and found himself fighting on foot in the midst of the enemy, from which peril he escaped at the sacrifice of the life of his chief engineer, Fernando Alvarez Cabral, who with devoted gallantry came to his rescue. An additional act of devotion on the part of a page of Dom Fernando provided him with another horse, mounted on which he cleft his way in safety through the enemy.

When the prince reached the camp he found the Portuguese overwhelmed with the great odds against which they had to contend, and to add to his dismay he found that about a thousand of his men had fled to the ships. Happily Dom Pedro de Castro, who was in command of the fleet, came to his aid with reinforcements. Oppressed as he was with toil and anxiety, the prince showed no sign of shrinking from the high requirements of his responsible position. Though surrounded by danger the most imminent, he encouraged his men by an appearance of confidence and cheerfulness, which he was far from feeling in his heart.

On the following day the Moors again attacked the

trenches, but they were now more strongly fortified, and after four hours of hard fighting the Moors were repulsed with immense loss.

At length when the provisions of the Portuguese were well-nigh all consumed, Prince Henry came to the resolution to force a passage in the night-time to the shore and withdraw with the fleet. In this plan however he was frustrated by the treachery of his chaplain, Martin Vieyra, who deserted to the Moors and informed them of the prince's resolution. The Moors now suspended their attacks and deliberated as to the best course to pursue in the probable event of the Portuguese falling into their hands. Some were for exterminating them without mercy, others with greater wisdom suggested that such a massacre would only provoke the Christians to revenge, and that therefore the most prudent course would be to let them freely depart, upon condition that they surrendered Ceuta, and delivered up their artillery and arms and baggage, with all the Moors that had been taken prisoners. This proposal was made, and accepted by the Portuguese, who in fact had no alternative.

Meanwhile a great number of Moors, who either were ignorant of the importance of Ceuta or were very doubtful of its being surrendered, were determined to make another vigorous onset upon the Portuguese camp. They principally directed their attack upon the side which was defended by Dom Fernando, and their numbers and the ferocity of the onslaught placed the prince in considerable danger. But the Portuguese fought with desperation, and the neighbourhood of the intrenchments was soon covered with the bodies of the dead and wounded Moors. The Moors then endeavoured to set fire to the palisades, but the indefatigable energy of Prince Henry averted this danger also. At his side fought the Bishop of Ceuta, whose intrepidity encouraged the soldiers with a fervour of pious zeal which worked wonders in the unequal contest. The struggle having lasted for seven hours without any decisive result on either side, the prince determined on reducing the area of the camp and bringing it nearer to the sea, a task which, in spite of the fatigues of the preceding day, was effected in one night. The Moors offered no opposition, but contented themselves with occupying the ground between the camp and the shore, and guarding the neighbouring passes.

Meanwhile the Portuguese were obliged to kill their horses for food, and to use their saddles for fuel to cook them. In addition they were tormented with thirst, for within the lines there was but one well, which was not sufficient to supply a hundred men with water, so that if some rain had not fallen, they must all have perished. Many of these disasters would have been averted, had Prince Henry in the first instance kept his camp near to the sea-shore, in accordance with the wise instructions which had been given him by the king. Before leaving Lisbon he had received an autograph despatch from the king, containing a special injunction so to fix his camp before Tangier that he should touch the shore at two points, and if, from a deficiency of numbers, that could not be effected, he was by no means to neglect retaining a communication with the sea at least at one point. This recommendation was accompanied with an urgent request that it might often be read and never infringed, and Prince Henry had promised to observe it to the fullest possible extent. Nor does there appear to have been any reason for deviating from these precautionary monitions, and men of calm judgment attributed much of the disastrous result of the expedition to this want of implicit attention to the king's instructions. To establish a communication with the fleet had now become a matter of great difficulty and danger, if not of impossibility.

Fortunately for the Portuguese the enormous losses suffered by the Moors gave them an inclination to subscribe to terms of peace. Hence happily it followed that on the 15th of October a treaty was concluded, by virtue of which the Portuguese were at liberty to embark, but simply in their clothes as they stood, delivering up their arms, their horses, and their baggage. Ceuta, with all the prisoners therein, was to be surrendered, and a pledge given by the King of Portugal, on behalf of his country, that peace should be maintained with all Barbary for a hundred years, both by sea and land, Dom Fernando, with twelve other nobles, being given over as a hostage until the surrender of Ceuta and the prisoners.

When the delegates returned to the prince, they informed him that the Moors had conceived the treacherous plan of taking all the Portuguese prisoners, if they availed themselves of the conditions of the capitulation to enter the town with the view of embarking. Prince Henry consequently gave orders for every preparation to be made for embarking as quickly as possible. In the attempt, however, to reach the boats, about sixty men of the rear-guard were slain.

On Sunday, the 20th of October, the fleet set sail. Out of thirty-seven days that they had been under the walls of Tangier, twenty-five had been occupied in besieging the Moors, but during the remaining twelve they had been themselves besieged. Their losses, however, they reckoned at only five hundred men, while the Moors must have counted at least four thousand slain and many thousands wounded. To the latter this loss was insignificant when compared with the extent of their population, whereas Portugal, with its limited range of territory, had no superfluity of men to spare; but, worst of all, the Portuguese had failed in their object.

Such was the disastrous termination of this imprudent enterprise, and however much we may admire the distinguished heroism of Prince Henry, or honour the nobility of the motives which overruled his judgment, it must be confessed that to him the blame of the disaster must be mainly attributed. The foresight and wisdom which he had so often exhibited in matters of detail were wanting in his consideration of the requisites for an enterprise which was dictated to his feelings and his fancy by the prevailing instinct of his nature, viz., a chivalrous devotion to what he conceived to be religious duty to God and to his country. It was, in the first place, unjustifiable to imperil on a foreign shore the lives of a courageous little army so inadequate in their numbers to the work set before them, and, in the second place, it was an imperative duty to secure, as far as possible, the safety of such courageous followers by every prudent precaution; and proportionately culpable was the dereliction from that duty when enforced by the most emphatic injunctions, even in the handwriting of the sovereign. Of the indomitable energy and valour of the prince we have already witnessed proofs of an extraordinary kind, yet even these, supported by efforts to which they proved a most encouraging example, were insufficient to avert the melancholy result which we have had to describe. But this was not the end of the tragedy. We have now to recount the sad story of the sufferings and death of the devoted but hapless Dom Fernando, who was left behind as a hostage in Barbary.

After the departure of the army, the prince and his companions were conducted by Zalá ben Zalá, on the 22nd of October, 1437, to Arzilla. On their road they were treated with every insult by the Moors, who were still smarting from the losses they had suffered from the Portuguese. Meanwhile Prince Henry, having despatched the Bishop of Evora and the Count of Arrayolos to Portugal, retired to Ceuta to await his brother's release, but on his arrival there his fatigues and grief induced an illness which entirely prostrated him. About this time he was joined by his brother, D. João, who agreed to negotiate with Zalá ben Zalá the exchange of the Moorish prince, his son, for Dom Fernando, and if the terms were rejected to release his brother by force of arms. He set sail on the 20th October, but his project was frustrated by a violent tempest, which forced him, after many perils, to take refuge in the Algarves.

The king, in great grief at the sad fate of his brother, and desiring to save him, even at the cost of Ceuta, convoked the Cortes in the beginning of 1438, that he might have their consent and council on the subject. It was finally resolved that Ceuta should not be abandoned, but that every other possible step should be taken for the release of the prince. King Duarte, in despair at this decision, applied to the Pope, the King of France, and other friendly powers, for active assistance, and received from them nothing but condolence and words of consolation. His attempt to ransom his brother was also fruitless.

After seven months of suffering and illness Dom

Fernando and his followers were transferred by Zalá ben Zalá to the King of Fez, May 25th, 1438, and were consigned to the power of the ferocious Lazurac, an unscrupulous monster, who, in the name of Abdallah the young King of Fez, exercised unlimited authority over the State.

After three months' captivity, they were set to work loaded with chains in the royal gardens. The only food allowed them was two loaves daily without meat or wine. Their bed was composed of two sheepskins, their pillow a bundle of hay, and they had no covering but an old cloak. The prince slept with eleven persons in a room only large enough for eight, and they suffered much from filth, vermin, and hunger.

In the May of 1439, Ceuta was offered in exchange for the Infant, but Lazurac, hoping for a large ransom, contrived to protract the negotiations. On one occasion letters directed to the prince from Portugal were intercepted, and in consequence he was thrown into solitary confinement in a wretched dungeon where he languished out the remaining fifteen months of his existence.

At length he was attacked with dysentery, and his enfeebled frame being unable to struggle against the malady, the Constant Prince, for such was the title which his pious resignation has won for him, breathed his last on the evening of the 5th of June, 1443.

Even the ferocious Lazurac was forced to offer tardy homage to his virtues, and to declare that, had he been a Mahometan, he would have been a saint, and that the Christians were much to blame in leaving him thus to die.

Lazurac had the body embalmed, that it might be

preserved till he saw what the Portuguese would do to regain the body of their prince. But his companions managed to secure and to carefully preserve the heart, and kept it in a secret place till an opportunity should occur of conveying it in safety to Portugal. The corpse was hung up at the gate of the city head downwards, and exposed to the brutal insults and mockeries of the people for four days. It was then placed in a wooden coffin fixed in the same place on two stakes fastened into the wall, where it remained for a long time.

The Prince's servants, with the exception of five who died soon after him, returned to Portugal on the death of Lazurac, and brought with them the heart of their dead master, on the 1st of June, 1451. By order of the king it was conveyed with great solemnity to Batalha, and placed in the tomb destined for the prince by his father. The melancholy procession was met at Thomar by Prince Henry, who was about to undertake a journey. When he saw them he dismissed his equipages and joined with them in rendering the last tribute of love and respect to his devoted brother. Two-and-twenty years afterwards, the corpse of the prince was recovered from the Moors, and brought with much pomp to Batalha, and laid in the tomb which already contained his heart.

The thought of the hapless condition of his unfortunate brother had weighed so heavily on the mind of Dom Duarte that it shortened his life. The recollection that, in spite of his own convictions and the counsels of Dom Pedro and the wisest of his grandees, he had sanctioned the attempt on Tangier, was an unceasing torment to him. Nor was his brotherly affection, wounded as it was by the pitiable sufferings to which Dom Fernando was exposed, the only cause of his distress, for he was contravened in his desires to rescue his brother from captivity by the expressed wish of the Pope, the clergy, and his ministers of state. A weak and sickly prince was by them regarded as of little worth in comparison with the retention of Ceuta, the key to the extension of Portuguese conquest on the continent of Africa, the portal, already in their possession, to the introduction of Christianity amongst the infidels, and the brightest jewel in the crown of Portugal. To him these considerations, while not without their weight, were ineffectual in removing remorse for what he regarded as an unpardonable weakness in himself, and he would thankfully have resigned his crown if he could thereby have secured the restitution of his unfortunate brother. Prince Henry, when appealed to for advice, brought no relief to the mind of the embarrassed king, for with that firm adherence to the course of duty which marked his character, great as was his love for his brother, he set aside every personal consideration when weighed in the balance with the advancement of Christianity and the welfare of his country. The surrender of Ceuta therefore was not to be thought of as the means of delivering Dom Fernando.

Two courses alone remained open for accomplishing that object; ransom, or a crusade against the Moors. The former was impracticable, and the latter by no means promised success. The deep chagrin experienced by the king at length completely undermined his health. It has been generally believed that he was struck with the plague by means of an infected letter, and that his frame, enfeebled by mental trouble, was unable to contend against the attacks of so serious a malady. In his last will, however, he left injunctions to his successor that the freedom of Dom Fernando should be secured at all costs, and, if every other means failed, even by the surrender of Ceuta.

This good but unfortunate king died on the 9th of September, 1438, after a reign of five years, a reign remarkable for well intentioned effort, and as remarkable for unvarying misfortune and disappointment. Active and powerful of frame, he was unsurpassed by any of his day in feats of arms and horsemanship, yet kindliness and grace were far more noticeable in his appearance than the power and energy which he really possessed. This effect may have been in some degree increased by his habit of wearing his hair long and floating, and by his round and almost beardless face. His love of justice and of truthfulness was so great that "the king's word" became a proverbial expression for that which could be implicitly relied upon. The love of study had been inculcated and cultivated in him betimes by his excellent mother. With a mind well stored with information and manners graceful in the extreme, the keenness of his intelligence and correctness of his judgment gave to him a power of expression which won all hearts, and thus he obtained the cognomen of "the Eloquent." Nor did he content himself with communicating pleasure and instruction to his contemporaries; as an author he has left a valuable legacy to posterity in a variety of treatises on ethics and philosophy, not so much distinguished by any profoundly scientific investigation into the principles and bases of these sciences as the expression of a warm and noble nature whose instincts were directed by integrity and clearness of judgment. One of these, entitled the "Leal Conselheiro," or "Faithful Adviser," was published in Paris in 1842, by the Rev. J. I. Roquete. So simple, dignified, and loveable a picture of the homo affections as existing among the members of a regal family, is perhaps not to be found elsewhere. It is the unaffected, nay almost unconscious, exposition of every manly and gentle virtue that could dignify the character of a prince as a Christian, a patriot, and a soldier. But more conspicuous than all the other qualities which are therein exhibited as characteristic of the members of this family, is the strong and loving affection existing between all of them, tempered by a lofty tone of mutual honour and respect which finds its culmination in the profound reverence of all of them for the sacred persons of the king and queen. No higher eulogium could be unconsciously paid to the training bestowed upon their children by King John and Queen Philippa than the *tone* as well as the words of this noble production.

After the disastrous affair of Tangier, Prince Henry retired to Sagres, and continued there until September of 1438, when the King Dom Duarte fell ill at Thomar, and from that time till 1440 the troubles which existed in the kingdom obliged the prince to occupy himself with public affairs and the reconciliation of parties, in order to avert a civil war. So that these events interrupted the course of expedition and discovery from 1437 to 1440.

CHAPTER VIII.

THE TAWNY MOORS AND THE NEGROES.

1441—1448.

In 1441 the affairs of the kingdom becoming somewhat tranquilized, Antam Gonsalves, the prince's master of the wardrobe, was sent out in command of a small ship, but solely with the order to bring home skins and oil of *seacalves*, for as he was but young, the prince put less charge upon him than upon his predecessors. When he had taken in his cargo, Gonsalves proposed to continue the voyage, in the hope of being the first to take captives to present to the prince. He took nine sailors inland and succeeded in capturing two natives, but as he was about to set sail on the following day, there arrived an armed caravel, commanded by Nuño Tristam, a young knight who had come out with a special command from the prince to pass as far as he could beyond the port of Gallée, and to endeavour by all means to make some captures.

He had brought with him a Moor, to act as interpreter, but it turned out that the language of the captives was entirely different. The small capture made by Gonsalves by no means contented Nuño Tristam, and the two agreed to set out together in search, with men selected from their respective crews, and after a sharp contest, they took ten natives, one of whom was a chief.

When the conflict was over, at the unanimous request of his companions, Gonsalves was knighted by Tristam, in spite of his modestly disclaiming his right to such honour. Hence the place was named the "Porto do Cavalleiro," or Port of the Knight.

The chief alone among the captives understood the Moorish language, and was able to converse with the interpreter. The rest spoke the language of the Azanegues, or Tawny Moors. Hoping to treat for the ransom of some of the prisoners, the interpreter went on shore with one of the female captives, but he was detained prisoner, after having in vain tried to negotiate with the natives.

Gonsalves now returned to Portugal, but, as Tristam had orders to proceed farther, and found that his caravel needed repairs, he put into land and careened her, keeping his tides as if he were in Lisbon roads, a bold feat which astonished many of his crew. He then pursued his voyage, and passing the port of Gallée, came to a cape to which from its whiteness he gave the name of Cabo Branco. Here were found tracks of men and some nets, but they gained speech of no one. And as Tristam observed that the coast took the form of a bay, in which the currents seemed likely to impede their progress beyond the time that their provisions would last, he resolved to return to Portugal.

Prince Henry was in the highest degree gratified by the prospect thus opened of bringing these barbarous natives under the influence of Christianity, and extending the honour and prosperity of his country, and rewarded the two captains commensurately with the value which he set upon this successful issue of their labours.

Although the language of the other captives was

unintelligible, the prince was nevertheless able to gather from the chief whom Gonsalves had captured considerable information respecting the country where he dwelt. Foreseeing that he would have to send out many expeditions to contend with the infidel natives of that coast, he sent to the Pope the news of this discovery as the first-fruits of his long-continued exertions, and prayed for a concession in perpetuity to the crown of Portugal of whatever lands might be discovered beyond Cape Bojador to the Indies inclusive, especially submitting to His Holiness that the salvation of these people was the principal object of his labours in that conquest. The news of this discovery was considered so valuable by the Pope and the College of Cardinals that a Bull was forthwith issued in conformity with the request, which was subsequently confirmed by the Pope Nicholas V. and Sixtus IV. The Regent Dom Pedro also granted to his brother Prince Henry a charter, authorizing him to receive the entire fifth of the produce of the expeditions appertaining to the king, and in consideration of the great labour and expense which the prince undertook at his own sole charge, issued a mandate that none should go on these expeditions without Prince Henry's licence and especial command.

The captive chief, although treated with all gentleness, chafed under his servitude much more than those of lower condition, and repeatedly begged Gonsalves to take him back to his country, where he engaged to give as ransom five or six negroes. He also said that there were two boys among the captives, for whom a liberal ransom would be given. This and the hope of gaining further information induced Gonsalves to ask permission to return to Africa.

He was accompanied in his voyage by a nobleman named Balthazar, of the household of Frederick III., Emperor of Germany, the husband of the Infanta Leonora of Portugal. This Balthazar had joined the household of Prince Henry with the intention of winning his spurs at Ceuta, and gallantly he won them. He had often expressed a desire to witness a storm off the coast of Africa, for he had been told that storms on that coast were very different from those on the coasts of Europe. In this wish he was gratified to his heart's content, for they encountered so severe a tempest that Gonsalves and his crew narrowly escaped with their lives, and were compelled to put back to Lisbon. Once more, however, they set forth on their expedition, and when they reached the point where the ransom was to be effected, they landed the chief, and Gonsalves agreed with him where they should meet after he had made his arrangements. The chief was handsomely dressed in clothes which the prince had given him, for Prince Henry hoped thereby to induce the natives to enter into commercial relations with him. Gonsalves was blamed for the trust he placed in the chief's faith, and a detention of seven days at the appointed place, four leagues up the Rio d'Ouro, seemed to justify the blame. At the end of the week, however, a Moor on a white camel appeared with full a hundred slaves, out of which number ten negroes of both sexes were given up in exchange for the two boys. Besides the negroes, Gonsalves received in that ransom a small quantity of gold dust, a leathern buckler, and a great number of ostrich eggs, three dishes of which rarity were one day served at the prince's table perfectly fresh and good.

The natives stated that there were merchants in those

parts who trafficked in gold, and it was supposed that they meant that the gold was found in their own country. This, however, was a mistake, for the gold was brought thither from the interior by the caravans which for many years had carried on that trade across the desert, and principally since the invasion of the Arabs. During the sovereignty of the Caliphs this commerce with the interior of Africa extended not only to the western boundaries of that continent, but even as far as Spain. The caravans crossed the valleys and plains of Sus, of Darah, and of Tafilet to the South of Morocco. Thibr, the Arabic name for gold, was brought from Wangara. The Rio d'Ouro, or River of Gold, received its name from the fact that gold was there first received in barter, by the Portuguese. It has retained that name ever since, although it is in fact no river at all, but simply an estuary occupying an indentation in the coast of about six leagues in depth.

Gonsalves now returned to the prince, and met with a grateful reception, as did also the German knight, who afterwards returned to his country with much honour to himself and large reward from the prince's bounty.

In the year 1443, the prince sent out Nuño Tristam, in another caravel, which reached to twenty-five miles beyond Cape Branco, and found a small island, to which they gave the name of Gete, in the Bay of Arguim.

Here twenty-five canoes put out from shore, containing a host of natives entirely naked. This was not on account of their being on the water, but it was their habitual custom. Each canoe held three or four, who hung their legs over in the water and paddled with them as with oars. The Portuguese at first took them for birds of monstrous size, but when they found their mistake they pursued them to the island and captured fifteen of them. They would have taken more but for the smallness of their boat. The discovery of this point was of great importance to the Portuguese. It facilitated their obtaining information and establishing intercourse with the negro states on the Senegal and Gambia. The prince subsequently had a fort built there, the foundations of which were laid in 1448.[1]

Near the island of Gete they found another, on which was an infinite number of herons which came there to breed, and many other birds which afforded them a good supply of provisions. They gave this island the name of Ilha das Garças, or Heron Island. Nuño Tristam returned the same year with his booty, which was a greater source of satisfaction to him than on his former adventure, for not only had he taken more, but he had reached to a greater distance, and moreover had not to divide his gains with any one.

When the prince began to colonize the islands which he had discovered, and to open a road to the people to turn the discoveries to profit, those who had been loudest in their censure were the first to turn their blame into praise. After the return from Tangier the prince was almost always at his own town, which he then had built in the kingdom of Algarve near to Lagos, where vessels discharged the prizes which they brought; and the first to beg permission to make a voyage at his own cost to the newly-discovered country was Lançarote, an esquire

[1] In 1638, this fort was taken from the Portuguese by the Dutch. In 1665 the English took it, but again lost it. In 1678 the French gained possession of it, and destroyed the old fortress built by the Portuguese. The Dutch recovered the place in 1685, and retained it till 1721, when the French took it by surprise, but were once again driven out by the Dutch in the following year.

who had been educated from his childhood in the prince's household, but who was now married and held the post of king's almoxarife, or receiver of customs, in that city of Lagos.

Having fitted out six caravels, he sailed from thence in 1444, taking with him as commanders Gil Eannes, the same who had first passed Cape Bojador, Stevam Affonso, Rodrigo Alvares, João Dias, and João Bernaldes. After a successful expedition he returned with about two hundred captives, chiefly taken from the islands of Naar and Tider in the Bay of Arguin. The prince received him with great honour, and knighted him at the instance of the companions of his exploit. The captives, who presented every variety of colour, from nearly white to the deepest black, very soon became Christians, and were treated with great kindness by their Portuguese masters. Some of the young girls were adopted by noble ladies, and brought up as their own children.

In the year 1445, some time after the return of Lançarote, the prince gave the command of a caravel to Gonsalo de Cintra, an esquire of his household, with strict orders to go straight to Guinea without putting in anywhere on the road. He, however, allowed himself to be deceived by the natives and his own ambition into disobedience of these orders, and landing on the island of Naar for the purpose of taking captives, was slain in a fight on the shore, not being able to swim back to his boat. The unwieldy name of Angra de Gonsalo de Cintra has been given to a bay some forty miles south of the Rio d'Ouro as commemorative of the death of this unfortunate commander, but the island of Naar is in the Bay of Arguin.

In the same year Prince Henry again sent out Antam Gonsalves in a caravel to the Rio d'Ouro, with one of his own servants, Diogo Affonso, in another. They were accompanied by Gomes Pires, who was sent out by the Regent, Dom Pedro, in a third caravel. The express purpose of the voyage was to treat with the natives and endeavour to make converts to Christianity, but they returned without effecting anything worth notice. João Fernandes went out with this expedition, and remained seven months alone in the wilds of the interior, in order to gain information for the prince respecting the language and manners of the people.

An old Moor returned voluntarily with Gonsalves, wishing to see Prince Henry, who received him with great kindness, and afterwards sent him back to his own country.

No fresh progress, however, was made in discovery on the west coast of Africa, until in this year Diniz Dias, a bold adventurer, who had already distinguished himself in the service of King João, begged permission to make explorations in the service of Prince Henry, who fitted out a caravel for him. Diniz had made up his mind to sail further than any of his predecessors, and this resolution he carried into effect, for he never struck sail till he reached the land of the Negroes. It was not till now that the mouth of the Senegal was passed, which separates the Azanegues or Tawny Moors from the Jaloffs, the first real Blacks.

The Portuguese gave the name of Guinea to the eastern country of the Senegal or Senegambia, whereas it is now confined to the southern coast. In fact, originally Guinea was supposed to commence at Cape Non. Even so late as the beginning of the sixteenth century, in a treaty between Spain and Portugal about the boundaries of their respective conquests in Africa, the opinion was held that the borders of Guinea began between Capes Non and Bojador.

The Guinea Coast, as now understood, began to be known by that name after the construction of the Fort el Mina by the Portuguese in 1481, when the King of Portugal assumed the title of Lord of Guinea. But we must return from our digression.

As Diniz Dias coasted along this newly-visited shore, the caravel caused great astonishment among the natives, till at length four of the latter, being unable to decide whether it was a fish, a bird, or a phantom, took courage and approached it in a canoe, but when they found it contained men they fled with such speed that the Portuguese could not overtake them. As, however, it was far more Dias's purpose to discover land for the service of the prince than to take slaves for his own profit, he proceeded still south till he reached a remarkable headland, to which he gave the name of Cabo Verde. Little more is known respecting this voyage, but as the prince set very great value on this new discovery of the negro country, he largely rewarded Diniz Dias and his companions.

Seven months had now passed since João Fernandes had been left by his own desire among the Moors at the Rio d'Ouro. Antam Gonsalves therefore reminded the prince of the circumstance, and volunteered to do his best not only to bring Fernandes back, but to make the voyage repay its expenses. Three ships were promptly provided, and the principal command given to Antam Gonsalves.

A remarkable accident brought them to the object of their search. Missing the island of Arguin, from ignorance of its position, they passed beyond it to the south, and within an hour of their anchoring they saw a man on the opposite shore who proved to be Fernandes, and who had been watching with anxiety on the coast to see if any vessel were coming to fetch him away.

It appeared that he had engaged the affections of the natives during his sojourn amongst them, and he told Gonsalves of a chief named Ahude Maymom, who wished to barter with him some negroes whom he had taken captive. Gonsalves received the offer gladly, and exchanged articles of trifling value for negroes and gold. The place received the name of Cabo do Resgate, or Cape of the Ransom. In his homeward passage Gonsalves put in at Cape Branco, and made a capture of about sixty natives.

However pleased the prince may have been with the general success of this voyage, his principal satisfaction was in seeing João Fernandes back safe and sound, and able to give him information respecting the country and the people. Fernandes related that the first thing the natives did was to strip him of his clothes, and give him a mantle such as the rest of them wore. The people among whom he lived were shepherds, who wandered with their cattle wherever they could find pasture. The fodder was scanty, the land desert and sandy, with no trees except small ones, such as *figuieras do inferno* (*Palma Christi*), thorn-trees, and a few palms. There were very few flowers. All the water was from wells, except a very few running streams.

The people were called Alarves, Azanegues, and Berbers. They were Mohammedans. Their language, written and spoken, differed from those of other Moors.[2] They waged

---

[2] This would seem to indicate that the Berbers had not at this time adopted the Arabic character.

war with the negroes, and took a great number prisoners. Some of these they would sell to the Moors, who came to their country for that purpose; others they would take to Barca, beyond Tunis, to sell them to the Christian merchants who resorted thither, receiving in exchange bread and other commodities, just as they did at the Rio d'Ouro. The people had negro prisoners in their possession when Fernandes was among them, and some gold which was obtained from the land of the negroes. Their camels were very numerous, and could travel fifty leagues in a day, and they had plenty of cattle in spite of the thinness of the pasture. There were a great number of emus, antas, and gazelles, partridges, and hares. The swallows left in the spring and returned to winter on the sands; the storks went to the land of the negroes to winter.

Fernandes further related that one day two horsemen came up to him, who were going to join the beforementioned chief, Ahude Maymom, and asked him to accompany them. He accepted their invitation with pleasure, and they mounted him on a camel and they went their way. On the road their water failed them, and for three days they had nothing to drink. There was no certain road except by the sea-shore, and they guided themselves by the signs of the sky and the flight of birds. At length, after bearing their thirst as best they could, they came up with Ahude Maymom and his family, which, with their retinue, were about one hundred and fifty in number. Fernandes made his obeisance, and was welcomed by the Moor, who ordered milk to be given him, and treated him so well that when he was received by the caravels he had recovered his good looks and was in his usual health, though he had suffered much from the heat of the country and the sand of the desert.

Their principal food was milk and sometimes a little meat with seeds of wild herbs gathered on the mountains. Wheat was considered a luxury. For many months they and their horses and dogs lived entirely on milk. Those on the sea-shore ate nothing but fish, mostly raw or dried. Their garments were vests and breeches of leather, the better classes wore mantles. They had a few good horses, with saddles and stirrups, and some few of the chiefs kept brood mares. The women wore mantles over their faces, but the rest of their body they left uncovered. The women of the chiefs wore rings of gold on their ancles, and other jewels. Their merchandise, besides the slaves and gold which they got from the negro country, consisted of wool, butter, cheese, dates, which they imported, amber, civet, gum anime, oil and skins of sea-wolves, which were abundant at the Rio d'Ouro.

The success of Antam Gonsalves' expedition induced a gentleman of Lisbon named Gonsalo pacheco, who belonged to the household of the prince, to request permission to make the voyage. He obtained leave to equip a caravel which he had built for himself, and two others which he wished to accompany him. Sailing well to the south they came to a cape which they named "Cabo de Santa Anna," beyond which they sailed eighty leagues yet further south, and would have landed, in spite of the hostile appearance of the people, but were prevented by the roughness of the sea. From the distance they could see that the land was very verdant, with a large population, and abundance of domestic cattle. They would have proceeded further south, but a storm which lasted three days drove them back.

Between Cabo Branco and Cabo Tira they saw a small sandy island, where they found traces of men, fishing nets, and abundance of turtles.

The next day they returned and found the nets had been removed, but there were some turtles with ropes round them just as they had been caught. Observing another island near, they went to it, little suspecting an ambush. They were attacked by a large body of natives, and compelled to retreat with the loss of seven men killed, and one of the boats, which was taken to Tider and broken up for the sake of the nails. The ships then proceeded to Arguin to take in water. In this voyage they took eighty two captives.

Meanwhile the recollection of the death of Gonsalo da Cintra caused the inhabitants of Lagos to appeal to the prince to send out an expedition of sufficient strength to intimidate the natives, who were in such great numbers at the island of Tider and the neighbourhood, so that Portuguese vessels might henceforth pass along any part of that coast without jeopardy. To this Prince Henry gave his approval, and fourteen vessels were forthwith equipped for that object.

At this time (1445), Prince Henry was summoned to Coimbra by his brother, the Regent Dom Pedro, to invest with knighthood his eldest son Pedro, who was Constable of the Kingdom and under orders for Castile; for in such profound esteem did the Regent hold Prince Henry, that he regarded it as the greatest honour that could be conferred upon his son to receive knighthood from such hands.

Before Prince Henry started from Lagos, he entrusted

the chief command of the fourteen caravels to Lançarote, who had already proved himself so able and successful a navigator on the African coast. This was a great distinction, for the other commanders were men of great eminence—Sociro da Costa, Alcaide of Lagos, Lançarote's father-in-law, a fine old soldier; Alvaro de Freitas; Gomes Pires, captain of the king's caravel; Rodrigueannes de Travaços, of the regent's household; Pallenço, who had distinguished himself in the wars against the Moors; Gil Eannes, who first passed Cape Bojador; Stevam Affonso, and other distinguished natives of Lagos. Besides these fourteen ships, there were sent out from Madeira three others, the captains of which were Tristam Vaz, commander of Machico, and Alvaro Dornellas, each in his own caravel, but these were driven back by the weather before they reached Cape Branco. Alvaro Fernandes also came out in a caravel, belonging to his uncle João Gonsalves Zarco, commander of Funchal. From Lisbon Diniz Dias (who first reached the land of the negroes) went out in a caravel of D. Alvaro de Castro, chief chamberlain of King Affonso, and João de Castilha in another belonging to Alvaro Gonsalves d'Ataide, the king's tutor. Altogether there were six-and-twenty caravels, besides the pinnace in which Pallenço went out. The expedition set sail on the 10th of August, 1445.

When some of the vessels had arrived, and among them those of Lançarote, Sociro da Costa, Alvaro de Freitas, Gil Eannes, and Gomes Pires, two hundred and seventy-eight men were selected for the attack and sent on shore in three boats, steered by pilots who had been there before and knew the locality. They had intended to take the natives by surprise, but everything went against them. The pilots proved unequal to their work, the night was dark, the water was low. The boats stranded and were obliged to wait for the tide, and the sun was well up before they reached the island. They proceeded for three leagues along the shore till they reached Tider, near which they perceived a host of natives showing every readiness to fight. A conflict ensued, in which eight natives were killed, and four taken. They then took to flight, leaped into the water and swam to the mainland, having already sent away their wives and children. Before returning to the ships the Portuguese went to the village which the natives had deserted, and to their great delight discovered water, for they were nearly perishing of thirst. They also found a few cotton-trees. On the following day the natives returned to about a stone's throw from the caravels, and danced on the shore as if in defiance. A number of Portuguese, headed by a brave youth of the prince's household, named Diogo Gonsalves, and Pero Alleman, of Lagos, swam ashore and soon put them to flight and fifty-seven were captured.

The object of the expedition was thus effectively accomplished; and now that Tider had been conquered, and its inhabitants dispersed, Lançarote announced to the commander of the fleet that his duty as captain-general ceased; for the prince's orders were, that after that island was taken, each of the captains should be free to take his course in any direction that might seem to promise best. After a fair distribution had been made of the captives they had taken, several of the captains decided on returning to Portugal, as their caravels were small, and the winter was coming on.

Gomes Pires, who was captain of the king's caravel,

declared his intention to proceed to the land of the
negroes, in which purpose he was joined by Lançarote,
Alvaro de Freitas, and others. Two of the other caravels
now parted company with them, one from Tavila, and
another called the *Picanço*, or the *Wren*, belonging to a
man of Lagos, but as they did not go to the land of the
negroes, they will be spoken of hereafter.

Six caravels accordingly sailed southward till they
came to two palm-trees which Diniz Dias had specially
noticed and by which they knew that they were very
near the country of the blacks. They would have landed,
but the surf on the coast prevented them. The smell
from the shore was so fragrant that it was as if some
delightful fruit garden had been placed there for their
especial delectation. The prince had told them from
information he had received from the Azanegue prisoners,
that twenty leagues beyond the palms they would find
the western outlet of the river Nile, called by the natives
Çanaga. This expression shows how full of purpose
these explorations were, and that the prince did not seek
simply to add to his knowledge of the West African coast,
but to compare the information which could be gathered
from the natives themselves with the scientific, historical,
and geographical notions of ancient and mediæval times,
so as ultimately to reach the east. The river here
spoken of is the Nile of the Negroes, or the Senegal,
to which river the name of Niger adhered even so late as
to the close of last century. As they proceeded along
the coast, keeping a look-out for the river, they observed
before them at about two leagues distance from the land
a colour in the water different from the rest, which was
mud coloured. This proved to be the fresh water from
the river, and they soon came to the river's mouth, where

they anchored. Eight of the sailors of Vicente Dias' caravel pulled ashore, and among them Stevam Affonso, who had partly fitted out the caravel. One of them pointed out a cabin near the mouth of the river, and proposed that they should try to take the inhabitants by surprise. Stevam Affonso and five others landed, and hiding near the cabin, saw issue from it a negro boy quite naked, who was immediately taken; and when they went up to the cabin, they found his sister, a girl of about eight years old.

The prince afterwards had this boy educated, and it was supposed that he intended him for the priesthood, that he might go and preach Christianity to his people; but the youth died before he came of age.

When the Portuguese went into the cabin, they found a shield made of leather from the ear of the elephant, quite round, somewhat larger than the ordinary size, with a boss in the middle made of the same leather. They afterwards learned from the natives that all their shields were made from the hide of this animal. When the skin was thicker than they required, they stretched it more than half its original size by means of contrivances which they had for that purpose. They made no use of the ivory, but exported it. "I learned," says Azurara, "that in the Levant one of these tusks was worth on an average a thousand dobras"—a remark which shows that his knowledge of the ivory trade extended only to the ports of the Mediterranean, and not to any exportation of that commodity from the coasts of Guinea. They presently came upon the father of the children, who was busy carpentering, and did not perceive them. Stevam Affonso approached him stealthily, and springing on him clutched him by the hair, and as he himself was a little man and the African very tall, when the latter stood upright he lifted his assailant off his feet. Powerful as the negro was, he could not rid himself of his antagonist, but tossed himself about like a bull that some fierce dog had seized by the ear. The Portuguese then came up and held his arms, intending to bind him, and Stevam Affonso, imagining that he was secured by the others, loosed his hold, but no sooner did the African find his head free than he shook off the others from his arms, and fled. He was much swifter of foot than the Portuguese, and soon plunged into a forest of underwood, and while the rest were trying to find him, he made his way to his hut in search of his children and of his weapon which he had left with them. The bereaved father was furious when he could not find them, and as he looked along the shore in search of them, he saw Vicente Dias walking towards him with nothing but a gaff in his hand. The enraged African fell upon him with his azagay and inflicted a severe wound on his face; after which they closed in a deadly struggle. A negro youth came to the assistance of his friend, and obliged Dias to loose his hold; but at the approach of the other Portuguese, the two negroes made their escape.

The caravels now made their way to Cape Verde, and lighted on the Magdalen Islands, in one of which they found a great number of long-eared goats, and on another fresh goat-skins lying about, which showed that other caravels were in advance of them, a fact which was confirmed by their seeing carved on the trees the arms of Prince Henry and the words of his motto, "Talent de bien faire." The natives on the mainland had mustered in such numbers that the Portuguese had no chance of landing either by day or night; but

Gomes Pires, by way of trying to bring about some intercourse, placed on shore a ball, a mirror, and a sheet of paper on which was drawn a crucifix. These the negroes broke and destroyed as soon as they found them. The Portuguese now drew their bows on them, but they returned the compliment both with arrows and azagays. The arrows were not feathered and had no notch for the string. They were short and made of reeds or canes with long iron heads, and some of the shafts were of charred wood. All their arrows, without exception, were tipped with vegetable poison. Each azagay had seven or eight barbed points. The poison used was very deadly.

In that island in which Prince Henry's arms were found cut on the trees, they found many large baobab-trees, and among them one which measured a hundred and eight palms round in the stem.

From this point they made sail for Lagos, but Gomes Pires became separated from the other caravels, and on his way homewards, put in at the Rio d'Ouro, where some of the natives came to him and sold him a negro for five doubloons. They also gave him water from the camels, and meat, and in other respects gave him a good reception. Indeed, they were so confiding, that they came without hesitation on board his caravel, which he had rather they had not done. At length he managed to have them put on shore without the occurrence of any unpleasantness, and promised them that in July of the following year, he would return and treat further with them. He also laid in a good cargo of seal-skins, and then made his way home.

The other captains also, having had good reason to be contented with the success of their voyage, returned together to Portugal.

Hitherto it has been seen how almost all these explorers had been intent on their own gains in addition to the prince's service; but João Gonsalves Zarco, whose acquaintance the reader has already made in Madeira, was an exception to this rule. He fitted out a splendid caravel, and gave the command of it to his nephew Alvaro Fernandes, with injunctions not to land in the country of the Tawny Moors, but to proceed straight to the negro country, and make his way as far as he could, so as to bring back some new information that should give pleasure to the prince. The caravel was well victualled, had a crew well disposed for work, and Alvaro Fernandes was young and zealous. They proceeded as far as the Senegal, where they filled two pipes with water, one of which they afterwards took to Lisbon. They then passed Cape Verde and came to an island where they landed and found some tame goats, without any one tending them, of which they took some for food. It was they who left those indications of the arms of the prince, and his device and motto cut on the trees which were seen by Lançarote and his companions, for this Alvaro Fernandes was the first who came there.

They anchored about a third of a league from the Cape, hoping to communicate with the natives, though only by signs, for they had no interpreter. Two boats containing ten negroes put off from the shore and made straight for the ship, as if with peaceful intentions. As they approached they made signs asking for assurance of safety, which was given, and immediately five of them entered the caravel. Alvaro Fernandes received them with all possible kindness, gave them plenty to eat and drink, and showed them every attention in his power. They left with every sign of being greatly pleased. When, however, they reached the shore they encouraged other natives to make an attack, and six boats put out with thirty-five or forty men in them prepared for fighting ; but they did not venture to come close to the caravel, but remained at a little distance. When Alvaro Fernandes saw this, he launched his boat on the opposite side of the caravel so as not to be seen by the negroes, ordered eight men into it, and waited for the negroes to come nearer. At length, one of the boats containing five powerful negroes, took courage to approach. When Fernandes observed that it was in such a position that his own boat could reach it before the others could bring help, he ordered his men to sally forth suddenly and row down upon them. From the great advantage they possessed in their mode of rowing, the Portuguese were speedily on the enemy, who being thus taken by surprise and having no hope of defending themselves, threw themselves into the water, and the other boats pulled for the land. The Portuguese had great difficulty in catching them as they were swimming, for they dived like cormorants, so that they could not easily get hold of them. However they took two and brought them on board.

Alvaro Fernandes saw clearly that, after this, no advantage was to be gained by staying there. He therefore proceeded further south, and reached a cape where there were many dry palm-trees without any branches, and to which he gave the name of Cabo dos Mastos (the Cape of the Masts). As they proceeded, Alvaro Fernandes sent out a boat with seven men to go along the shore, and presently they lighted on four negroes sitting on the beach, who were out on a hunting expedition, and armed with bows. When these saw the Portuguese, they rose quickly and fled, not giving themselves time to adjust their bows, and as they were naked, and had their hair short, the Portuguese could not catch them, but they took the bows and arrows, together with some wild boars which they had taken. Among the larger animals found there was an antelope, which was so tame that they would not kill it. They now returned to the ship and sailed back to Madeira, and thence to Lisbon. There they found the prince, who received them with very great favour, and showed especial honour to Zarco, who had thus at his own expense sent out a vessel which went further than any of the others of Lançarote's expeditions that made the voyage to Guinea that year.

Hitherto both the gains and the losses of the Portuguese in these various expeditions had been but small. Dangers had been surmounted and captures had been made, but it may be questioned whether the greed of gain alone would have kept alive the spirit of exploration, in the face of dangers which greatly outbalanced the profit secured to individual adventurers. To the far-sighted vision of Prince Henry, the results, though small and slowly conquered, were far more promising than to those whose object was immediate profit, and hence his resolution never wavered, his zeal in the prosecution of his purpose never flagged. It needed all that zeal, supported by his princely position, and the great weight of his personal authority, to induce men to prosecute yet further search through unknown seas for lands which, with no certainty of advantage, might so easily offer dangers entirely unanticipated. Such dangers were now to be encountered, and with disastrous result.

In the year 1446, Nuño Tristam set sail in a caravel,

by the prince's command, to make explorations beyond
the Cabo dos Mastos, which had been discovered by
Alvaro Fernandes, and, being a resolute man, he passed
a long distance beyond Cape Verde, and reached a very
large river, at whose mouth he anchored and took two
small boats with two-and-twenty men, intending to pull
up the river in search of a village. The tide soon
carried him up a considerable way beyond the bar, when
he encountered twelve canoes containing some seventy
or eighty negroes with bows in their hands, who, having
seen the boat when it first entered the river, had
assembled to meet him. As the tide rose, one of the
native boats passed him, and landed its crew, who began
discharging their arrows at the Portuguese. The others
who remained in the boats came near, and also discharged their poisoned arrows at the new comers. The
Portuguese hastened back to reach the caravel, but
before they got on board, four men were dead from the
effect of the poison. They then made all haste to get
out to sea, and were obliged to cut their cables and leave
their anchors and boats behind, so fierce was the shower
of arrows with which they were assailed. Of the two-
and-twenty that had set out, two only escaped, the
poison being so subtle that the slightest wound touching
the blood caused death.

So perished the brave knight, Nuño Tristam, who
would have coveted a more glorious death, and with him
another knight named João Correa, and three other
gentlemen of the prince's household, named Duarte
d'Olanda, Estevam d'Almeida, and Diogo Machado. In
all one-and-twenty were killed, for one was struck in
endeavouring to raise the anchors. Five only now
remained in the ship: a common sailor who knew little

enough of the art of navigation; a lad named Aires Tinoco, one of Prince Henry's grooms of the chamber, and who went out as scribe to the expedition; an African boy, one of the earliest captures in that country; and two little fellows who had been attached to the persons of some of the deceased adventurers. The pitiable position of this feeble crew on that inhospitable shore may be imagined. They naturally turned their hopes to the sailor, as the best navigator amongst them, but he freely confessed his want of skill. Aires Tinoco, however, had the good judgment to direct him to steer to the north with a little bearing to the east. For two months they knocked about without seeing land, at the end of which time they caught sight of an armed vessel, which terrified them considerably, for they feared it was a Moorish ship. It proved, however, to belong to a Gallician corsair, named Pero Falcom, who, to their great delight, told them that they were off a place called Sines, on the coast of Portugal. They then lost no time in making for Lagos. The grief of the prince at the melancholy story related by the boys was enhanced by the fact that nearly all that had perished had been brought up from childhood in his own household. He therefore made it a duty to take the wives and children of all of them under his especial care and protection.

From the survivors' report of the above tragical occurrence the large river where it happened was at the time named Rio Grande, but ten years later, as will by-and-by be seen, it was ascertained to be the River Gambia.

In proportion as Nuño Tristam had been unfortunate, good fortune seemed to await on Alvaro Fernandes, the nephew of João Gonsalves Zarco, commander of Madeira, for in that same year he returned to the coast of Guinea, and passed a hundred leagues beyond Cape Verde. At some distance beyond the Cabo dos Mastos they landed and came to a village, the inhabitants of which showed a great inclination to fight, and one of them came forward armed with an azagay. Seeing this, Fernandes hurled his lance at him and struck him dead, upon which the rest took to flight.

On the next day they came to a river, probably the River Lagos, which they entered in a boat, and meeting four or five canoes full of negroes, had an encounter with them, in which Alvaro Fernandes received a wound from an arrow in his leg. As he was aware of the poison, he drew the arrow out instantly and bathed the wound with acid and oil, and afterwards anointed it well with theriack[3] as an antidote, and by dint of great care he recovered, but for some days was in great peril of his life.

In spite of their captain being thus wounded, the caravel pushed on to the south and reached a point of sand in front of a great bay, where a boat was sent out to explore. As it approached the shore, some hundred and twenty negroes made their appearance, some armed with shields and azagays and others with bows, and when they reached the water-side began to play and dance in the merriest fashion, but the boat's crew not feeling any particular wish, under the circumstances, to share in their jollity, thought best to return to the ship. This was a hundred and ten leagues south of Cape

---

[3] This now disused antidote, the name of which means treacle (Græce), was a compound of a great number of drugs with a basis of viper's flesh. It was held to be sovereign against the bites of venomous beasts. The name, which was given by Andromachus, Nero's physician, doubtless arose from the preservative nature of treacle against putrid air and other deleterious agents.

Verde. But for the wound of Alvaro Fernandes they would have gone further.

On their return they put in at Arguim, and afterwards at the Cabo do Resgate, where they fell in with that same Ahude Meimom who had kindly treated João Fernandes. Unfortunately they had no interpreter, but by signs they negotiated with him the exchange of a negress for some cloths, and if they had had a greater quantity, the Moors would gladly have made a larger traffic with them of the same kind. This caravel made more way to the south than any of its predecessors, and received as a reward for so doing two hundred doubloons, one hundred from the Regent Dom Pedro and another hundred from Prince Henry.

These rewards encouraged many who would otherwise have been deterred from these explorations by the sad fate of Nuño Tristam, and accordingly in this same year nine caravels were fitted out, the captains of which were Gil Eannes, who first passed Cape Bojador; Fernando Valarinho, who had distinguished himself at Ceuta; Stevam Affonso, Lourenço Dias, Lourenço d'Elvas, and João Bernaldes, an esquire of the Bishop of Algarve, commanding a ship belonging to the bishop; and three others, residents of Lagos. They first proceeded to Madeira to victual, and thence made their way to the Guinea coast, and passed sixty leagues beyond Cape Verde.

Here they came to a river of great size (Rio Grande), which they entered with their caravels; but the bishop's vessel stranded on a sand-bank and was lost, although the crew and contents were saved. While some of them were engaged on the salvage, Stevam Affonso and his brother followed some tracks that they lighted on, and found some plantations of cotton-trees and rice, and other trees of various kinds They presently entered a thick wood, from which issued some natives armed with azagays and bows. Seven of the foremost of those who went to meet them were wounded, and of these five fell dead, two Portuguese and three foreigners. When Stevam Affonso and the others saw the peril of their position, they retreated and escaped with great difficulty, for the natives were there in numbers. On reaching their ships, they determined to return. At the Cabo do Resgate, they succeeded in taking eight-and-forty natives, with whom they made their way to Portugal.

In this year (1446) Gomes Pires did not forget his promise to the Moors in the year before, that he would return to the Rio d'Ouro, and on his petition the prince gave him two caravels, with twenty men, among whom was a youth of the prince's household named João Gorizo, who had charge of the accounts of the receipts and expenditure which occurred in the Moorish traffic. It was now the custom for all the vessels bound to the west coast of Africa to go first to Madeira to victual, and on their arrival Gomes Pires desired Gorizo to remain and take in the stores, while he proceeded straight in the smaller vessel to the Rio d'Ouro. Although he burned fires night and day on a hill near the harbour, it was three days before any Moors made their appearance. When they came, he proposed to them by his interpreters to barter cloth with them for Guinea slaves. They answered that they were not merchants nor were there any thereabouts, though inland there were traffickers in merchandise who had abundance of gold and Guinea slaves, but to reach the spot where they were would involve a very laborious journey. Gomes Pires requested the Moors to fetch these merchants, and gave them in advance a remuneration for their trouble. They pretended to go, but although he waited for them one-and-twenty days they never returned. Meanwhile Gorizo arrived with the other vessel, and they then set sail, and landing at different points within a range of only eleven leagues of coast with considerable toil and fatigue, contrived to capture seventy-nine Moors. As they had brought out a large quantity of salt for the purpose of salting the seal skins in the event of their failing to make a better capture, they were compelled to discharge the salt in order to make stowage room for their captives, and so they returned to Lagos.

"Up to that period, 1446," says the contemporary chronicler Azurara, "there had been fifty-one caravels to these parts. These caravels went four hundred and fifty leagues beyond the Cape. It was found that that coast ran southward with many points, which the prince caused to be added to the sailing chart."

In the following year, 1447, in consequence of the failure in establishing friendly relations with the Moors at the Rio d'Ouro, Prince Henry resolved to try if better success might be met with at Messa, a town on the Atlantic coast of Morocco, midway between Mogadore and Cape Non. Accordingly he placed a caravel under the command of Diogo Gil, a man who had already done good service against the Moors, both by sea and land; for he had heard that a Spanish merchant named Marcos Cisfontes had in his possession twenty-six Moors from that place, the bargain for whose ransom had been already stipulated for in exchange for some negroes of Guinea, and proposed to the merchant to convey those Moors to Messa in this vessel, with the understanding that he should receive in return a certain number of the negroes that were to be given in ransom. The proposal was readily accepted, and João Fernandes, the same who had lived seven months among the Moors at Arguin, accompanied the party, and on arriving volunteered to negotiate the ransom. He was so successful that he procured fifty-one negroes in exchange for eighteen of the Moors. It so happened that while he was yet on shore there came on so strong a wind from the south that they were compelled to trip their anchor and sail for Portugal. They brought back with them for the prince a lion, which he afterwards sent to Galway by way of a present as a curiosity to an Englishman who lived there, and who had been formerly in his service. João Fernandes remained till another ship returned for him.

In this same year also Antam Gonsalves returned to the Rio d'Ouro, to try if it were possible to bring the Moors of that part to terms. He anchored at some distance within the estuary, and a number of Moors came to the shore, among whom was one who was evidently a chief. This man spoke assuringly to Gonsalves, but warned him not to trust the rest unless he were present. It happened once that while he was at a distance, the other Moors made a show of friendliness to the Portuguese, and Gonsalves, thinking the chief was among them, was about to land, but the boats no sooner neared the shore than the Moors attacked the Portuguese with their azagays, and, but for the promptitude of Gonsalves, they would all have been slain. They managed, however, to effect their escape, but with one of their men so seriously wounded that he died in a few days. Another expedition to the Rio d'Ouro under the command of Jorge Gonsalves, in which he brought back a large quantity of oil and skins of sea-wolves, completed the list of voyages in the year 1447.

In January, 1448, the fame of these expeditions brought out to Portugal a nobleman of the household of the King of Denmark, named Vallarte, who begged the prince to grant him a caravel to go to the land of the negroes. It was the kind of request that Prince Henry was always ready to listen to, and accordingly he had a caravel quickly fitted out to go to Cape Verde. To Vallarte he gave the principal command, but as he was a foreigner he sent with him one Fernando d'Affonso, both to aid in the command of the vessel, and as a sort of ambassador to the king of the country. With them also went two natives of that country as interpreters, by whose means the prince hoped that something might be done towards the conversion of the people. The weather was so exceedingly adverse that it took them six months from the time they left Lisbon to reach the Cape Verde. Proceeding further, they anchored at a place called by the natives Abram, where Vallarte went on shore with some others and found a considerable number of negroes assembled. To these Vallarte proposed that as a guarantee for friendly intercourse they should give him one of their people in exchange for one of his. This was agreed to by the permission of Guitanye, the governor of the country. As soon as they had one of the negroes on board the caravel, Fernando d'Affonso told him that their object was to instruct him to inform his master that the Portuguese were servants of a great and mighty prince of western Spain, and were come by his command to treat for him with the king of that country. The negro told them in reply, that the residence of their King Boor was six or seven days' journey off, and that the king was then at a great distance fighting against a rebel.

Fernando still desiring to treat with the king himself,

the governor Guitanye, who seems to have been very friendly with the Portuguese, promised, after some delay, to send the message. During the absence of the governor, Vallarte ventured on shore with a boat's crew, and fell into an ambush of the natives, who attacked them with their azagays to such effect that, of the whole number, only one saved himself by swimming and returned to the ship. Of the end of the rest no news survived, except that the man who swam away declared that he only saw one killed, and the three or four times that he looked round as he was swimming, he always saw Vallarte sitting at the stern of the boat. But at the time that Azurara was writing his chronicle in 1448, some natives of that part came into Prince Henry's possession, who stated that in a fortress far in the interior, there had been four Christian prisoners, one of whom had died, but three were still alive, and these were supposed to be the remnants of the boat's crew. After this miserable adventure Fernando d'Affonso, not having even a boat remaining, returned to Portugal.

The people of Lagos had gained too much experience of the west coast of Africa to be insensible of the value of its fisheries, and they obtained permission from the prince, on payment of a royalty, to turn their knowledge to account in that respect. Off the Cabo dos Ruyvos they found a large abundance. After they had been there some days, and had taken a great quantity of fish, some of which they had dried, and the rest were drying, the Moors came down upon them, and they only narrowly escaped with two men wounded.

In the course of the above explorations, to the period of Azurara's completing his chronicle, nine hundred and twenty-seven souls had been taken to Portugal.

We gladly turn from these scenes of capture of unoffending negroes; for while there can be no doubt that the prince's first motive was to gain information respecting the mode of traffic in that country, to rescue these negroes from heathenism and confer on them the blessings of Christianity, and his second to add to the wealth of his own country by an accession of valuable labour cheaply paid for by the real advantages bestowed on these captured negroes, it is no less sure that his captains were influenced by the love of gain. Of the genuineness of the advantages conferred, however, we have the following most explicit declaration of an eye-witness, the chronicler Azurara:—" They were treated with kindness, and no difference was made between them and the free-born servants of Portugal. Still more: those of tender age were taught trades, and such as showed aptitude for managing their property were set free and married to women of the country, receiving a good dower just as if their masters had been their parents, or at least felt themselves bound to show this liberality in recognition of the good services they had received. Widow-ladies would treat the young captives that they had bought like their own daughters, and leave them legacies in their wills, so that they might afterwards marry well and be regarded absolutely as free women. Suffice it to say that I have never known one of these captives put in irons like other slaves, nor have I ever known one who did not become a Christian, or who was not treated with great kindness. I have often been invited by masters to the baptism or marriage of these strangers, and quite as much ceremony has been observed as if it were on behalf of a child or relation."

The comprehensive purposes which the prince had in view,

in the matter of exploration alone, made the capture of natives of the west coast necessary, in the first instance, for the sake of acquiring local information. The mere process of capture is in itself in the highest degree offensive to us, as we sit in our easy chairs, free from the necessity of making any exertion in subduing the evils of barbarism beyond a little loosening of the strings either of the heart or of the purse. But no sooner do we take a survey of the active processes which, through all history, even up to the present time, have been brought to bear in the extension of civilization by encroachment on barbarian soil, than we find that violence, the details of which, if presented to us equally closely, would be equally offensive, has invariably had to be resorted to. It will, however, be observed that this violence was highly repugnant to the prince's nature. In Azurara, we find that, so soon as he found himself in a position to do so with a fair hope of safety to his mariners, he charged them to resort to peaceful means with the natives, and to refrain from doing them injury. We have the same testimony from Diogo Gomez de Cintra, and the same from Cadamosto. It must be acknowledged that three independent cotemporary witnesses are sufficient to clear the prince from the imputation of cruelty as to the *mode* of deportation of these negroes.

That the importation of negroes into the West Indies and America is not due either directly or indirectly to Prince Henry is indisputable. The very time when that importation commenced is not known, but the earliest date that any one has ever ventured to suggest was half a century after the death of the prince. The country was Spanish, and jealously exclusive of Portuguese encroachment of any kind.

CHAPTER IX.

THE CANARIES.

THERE has been a belief prevailing in every religion from the oldest times that the souls of the departed cannot enter into bliss without first crossing a river. The doctrine originated apparently in India, whence it passed into Assyria and Chaldea, and so into Persia. From Asia it extended into Greece and Egypt, thence through Ethiopia to the country of the Gallas, and at length we find it, as Bowdich tells us, among the natives neighbouring on the country of the Ashantees. Even to the mythic Jordan of the Christian the idea has still obtained. In the poems of Homer the ocean is treated as a river beyond which, at the earth's confines, were the Elysian fields, which Hesiod and Pindar made to be surrounded by water, so that the habitations of the blest were transformed into islands, and hence, as it has been supposed, originated the name of the Insulæ Fortunatæ or Fortunate Islands. These remained, however, no better than islands of fable, lying remote wherever fancy suggested, till solidity was given them by the discovery of the Canaries in the outlying ocean, and at length the land of spirits had assigned to it in men's mind a somewhat more definite geographical position. It is in the highest degree probable that the Phœnicians had been the original discoverers of the Canaries. It may therefore be reasonably presumed that the Canary Islands were known to the Carthaginians established at Gadir or Cadiz, but that the monopolizing policy of that nation induced them to conceal from other countries the extent of their commercial relations.

It was not till the beginning of the fifteenth century, when the Norman Jean de Béthencourt established himself in these islands, that something like substantial information respecting them was made accessible to Europeans. Much earlier expeditions, it is true, had been attempted, but of the navigators who visited them before the fifteenth century, some only landed accidentally, and others went for the purpose of taking slaves, or goat's flesh, or else to gather orchil for dyeing, and dragon's blood or other products that might be useful in commerce.

In 1402, Messire Jean de Béthencourt, Lord of Grainville la Teinturière, in the lovely valley of the Durdent, some twenty miles from Dieppe, having conceived the project of conquering the Canaries, assembled a body of adventurers, among whom was a knight named Gadifer de la Salle, who joined him at Rochelle. He first made a descent on the island of Lançarote, established himself there, and undertook the conquest of the other islands; but not having enough people to effect this enterprise, he went to ask help of the King of Castile, to whom he made homage of the islands. The king conceded to him the sovereignty of the Canaries, with the right of coining money. He also gave him twenty thousand maravedos for present expenses, and a well-found ship with eighty men. By means of these reinforcements Béthencourt subjugated the island of Forteventura. He then revisited France, and there collected a new troop of people of all classes, with their wives and children, whom he brought to his new states, and succeeded in conquering the island of Ferro. Resolving now to finish his days in France, he distributed his lands to those who had helped in his conquest, and named his nephew Maciot de Béthencourt governor-general, as his representative; enjoining him to do justice according to the customs of France and Normandy. He set out on the 15th December, 1405, first for Spain, where he renewed his homage and obtained a bishop for the Canaries. Thence he went to Rome, where he received from the Pope the bull of installation for the Spanish bishop. He returned in 1406 to his lands in Normandy, and died in 1425. It was not till twenty years after this, that we find the sailors of Prince Henry appear upon the scene.

It has already been stated that after the six caravels of Lançarote's expedition had sailed for Guinea, two separated from them and turned northward, viz., that from Tavila, and the Picanço. On their way they met with a caravel commanded by one João de Castilha, going to Guinea, whom they induced to join them in an expedition to the island of Palma. On reaching Gomera they were well received, and two chieftains of the island, named Bruco and Piste, after announcing themselves as grateful servants of Prince Henry, from whom they had received the most generous hospitality, declared their readiness to do anything to serve him. The Portuguese told them they were bound to the island of Palma, for the purpose of capturing some of the natives, and a few of the chieftain's subjects would be of great use as guides and assistants, where both the country and the people's mode of fighting were alike unknown. Piste immediately offered to accompany them, and to take as many

Canarians as they pleased, and with this help they set sail for Palma, which they reached a little before daybreak. Unsuitable as the hour might seem, they immediately landed, and presently saw some of the natives fleeing, but, as they were starting in pursuit, one of the men suggested that they would have a better chance of taking some shepherds, chiefly boys and women, whom they saw keeping their sheep and goats among the rocks. These drove their flocks into a valley that was so deep and dangerous that it was a wonder that they could make their way at all. The islanders were naturally sure-footed to a wonderful degree, but several of them fell from the crags and were killed. It was hard work for the Portuguese, for the Canarians hurled stones and lances with sharp horn points at them with great strength and precision. The contest ended in the capture of seventeen Canarians, men and women. One of the latter was of extraordinary size for a woman, and they said that she was the queen of a part of the island. In retiring to the boats with their capture they were closely followed by the Canarians, and were obliged to leave the greater part of the cattle that they had had so much trouble in taking.

On their return to Gomera they thanked the island chieftain for the good service he had rendered them, and afterwards, when Piste, with some of the islanders, went to Portugal, they were so well received by the prince that he and some of his followers remained for the rest of their lives.

Now João de Castilha, having but little booty to carry back to Portugal, conceived the dastardly idea of capturing some of the Gomerans, in spite of the pledge of security. As it seemed too hideous a piece of treachery to seize any of those who had helped them so well, he removed to another port, where some twenty-one of the natives, trusting to the Portuguese, came on board the caravel and were straightway carried to Portugal. When the prince heard of it he was extremely angry, and had the Canarians brought to his house, and with rich presents sent them back to their own country.

Azurara, writing forty years after Jean de Béthencourt's retirement to France, gives the Christian population of the three islands of Lançarote, Forteventura and Ferro in his time as follows:—In Lançarote sixty men, in Forteventura eighty, and in Ferro twelve. They had their churches and priests.

In the Pagan islands the numbers were, in Gomera[1] about seven hundred men, in Palma five hundred, in Teneriffe six thousand bearing arms, and in the Great Canary five thousand fighting-men. These had never been conquered, but some of their people had been taken, who gave information respecting their customs.

The Great Canary was ruled by two Kings and a Duke, who were elected, but the real governors of the island were an assembly of Knights, who were not to be less than one hundred and ninety, nor so many as two hundred, and whose numbers were filled up by election from the sons of their own class. The people were intelligent, but little worthy of trust; they were very active and powerful. Their only weapons were a short club and the stones with which their country abounded, and which supplied them also with building materials. Most of them went entirely naked, but some wore

[1] Maciot, attempted, with the assistance of some Castilians, to subdue the island of Gomera, but without success.

petticoats of palm leaves. They made no account of the precious metals, but set a high value on iron, which they worked with stones and made into fishing-hooks; they even used stones for shaving. They had abundance of sheep, pigs, and goats, and their infants were generally suckled by the latter. They had wheat, but had not the skill to make bread, and ate the meal with meat and butter. They had plenty of figs, dragon's blood, and dates, but not of a good quality, and some useful herbs. They held it an abomination to kill animals, and employed Christian captives as butchers when they could get them. They kindled fire by rubbing one stick against another. They believed in a God who would reward and punish, and some of them called themselves Christians.

The people of Gomera were less civilized. They had no clothing, no houses. Their women were regarded almost as common property, for it was a breach of hospitality for a man not to offer his wife to a visitor by way of welcome. They made their sisters' sons their heirs. They had a few pigs and goats, but lived chiefly on milk, herbs, and roots, like the beasts; they also ate filthy things, such as rats and vermin. They spent their time chiefly in singing and dancing, for they had to make no exertion to gain their livelihood. They believed in a God, but were not taught obedience to any law. The fighting-men were seven hundred in number, over whom was a captain with certain other officers.

In Teneriffe the people were much better off, and more civilized. They had plenty of wheat and vegetables, and abundance of pigs, sheep, and goats, and were dressed in skins. They had, however, no houses, but passed their lives in huts and caves. Their chief occupation was war, and they fought with lances of pine-wood, made like great darts, very sharp, and hardened in the fire. There were eight or nine tribes, each of which had two kings, one dead and one living, for they had the strange custom of keeping the dead king unburied till his successor died and took his place: the body was then thrown into a pit. They were strong and active men, and had their own wives, and lived more like men than some of the other islanders. They believed in the existence of a God.

The people of Palma had neither bread nor vegetables, but lived on mutton, milk, and herbs; they did not even take the trouble to catch fish like the other islanders. They fought with spears like the men of Teneriffe, but pointed them with sharp horn instead of iron, and at the other end they also put another piece of horn, but not so sharp as that at the point. They had some chiefs who were called Kings. They had no knowledge of God, nor any faith whatever.

In 1414 the exactions and tyranny of Maciot de Béthencourt had caused Queen Catherine of Castile to send out three war caravels under the command of Pedro Barba de Campos, Lord of Castro Forte, to control him. Maciot, although only Regent, for Jean de Béthencourt was still alive, ceded the islands to Barba and then sailed to Madeira, where he sold to Prince Henry these very islands of which he had just made cession to another. But as yet there still remained unconquered the Great Canary, Palma, Teneriffe, and the small islands about Lançarote, and, in 1424, Prince Henry had sent out a fleet under the command of Fernando de Castro, with two thousand five hundred infantry and a hundred and twenty horse, to effect the conquest of the whole of the islands; but the expense entailed thereby, combined with the expostulations of the King of Castile, caused him to withdraw for a time from the undertaking.

Subsequently, in the year 1446, he resumed his efforts at this conquest, but before taking any step he applied to his brother, Dom Pedro, who was then regent, to give him a charter prohibiting all Portuguese subjects from going to the Canary Islands, either for purposes of war or commerce, except by his orders. This charter was conceded, with a further grant of a fifth of all imports from those islands. The concession was made in consideration of the great expenses which the prince had incurred. Still Spain maintained its claims, and it was not till 1479, when, on the 4th of September, the treaty of peace was signed at Alcaçova, between Affonso V. of Portugal, and Ferdinand and Isabella of Castile, that the disputes of the two nations on this point were settled: and it was provided that "the conquests from Cape Non to the Indies, with the seas and islands adjacent, should remain in possession of the Portuguese, but the Canaries and Granada should belong to the Castilians."

CHAPTER X.

THE AZORES.

1431—1466.

At the beginning of the chapter on "Porto Santo and Madeira," allusion was made to a very remarkable Genoese map of the early date of 1351 in the Laurentian Library at Florence, on which the Madeira group was already laid down. On that same map the far outlying group of the Azores is also to be found. Nevertheless the effective discovery, colonization, and present names of those islands are due to Prince Henry.

There can be little doubt that the knowledge conveyed by that map was repeated on the one brought from Venice in 1428, by Dom Pedro, and enabled the prince to give directions to his navigators for the re-discovery of these islands. Thus, we find on the Catalan map of Gabriel de Valseca, dated 1439, the entire group laid down, accompanied by the following significant legend: "These islands were *found* [not *discovered*] by Diego de Sevill, pilot of the King of Portugal, in the year MCCCCXXXII."

As in 1439, the island of Santa Maria and the Formigas were all that had been re-discovered in Prince Henry's time, Valseca's word "found" would imply the *lighting on* the group, which he was able geographically to depict from other sources. In 1431, the Prince Henry had sent out Gonzalo Velho Cabral, a gentleman of illustrious family, in search of these islands. He then discovered the Formigas only, but in the following year, on the 15th of August, the Feast of the Assumption, he fell in with the island which, on the Italian maps, had been named Uovo, or the Egg, and named it accordingly Santa Maria. In all probability Diego de Sevill, the king's pilot, mentioned in Valseca's map, was the pilot in this expedition. Prince Henry resolved to colonize the island, and gave Cabral the rank of Captain Donatary, with full powers to collect, even from his own household, as many volunteers as he could, with all the requisites for that object. Cabral devoted three years to recruiting, and finally succeeded in taking out to the island a great number of men of rank and fortune.

Many years afterwards, a runaway negro slave, who had escaped to the highest mountain on the north of the island, perceived in the distance, on a clear day, another island, and he returned to his master with the news, which he hoped would secure him his pardon. After the fact had been verified, intimation thereof was transmitted to Prince Henry, and as it tallied with the information afforded by the ancient maps which he possessed, he commissioned Cabral, who happened at that time to be with him, to go in search of the new island. His first essay was fruitless, but the prince showed him that he had passed between Santa Maria and the island he was in search of, and in 1444 sent him out again. This time he was successful. Dom Pedro, who, with Prince Henry's acquiescence, interested himself much in the colonization of this island, gave it the name of San Miguel (or St. Michael, as we well know it by its oranges), from his own peculiar devotion to that saint.

The prince gave Cabral the command of this second island also, with instructions to colonize it, and a year having been spent in the needful preparations, the explorer returned thither on the 29th of September, 1445. In the previous voyage he had taken out with him some Moors belonging to the prince, for the purpose of tilling the soil, but on his return he found them in such a state of alarm from the earthquakes that were taking place in the island, that if only they had had a boat to escape in, they would certainly not have awaited his return. Moreover, the ship's pilot, who had accompanied him in both voyages, remarked, that, whereas in the former voyage he had seen a very lofty peak at the east end of the island and another at the west, that at the east only now remained.

It was at this time that the name of Azores was first given to these two islands of Santa Maria and San Miguel, from the circumstance that the explorers had found azores, or hawks, there, or, what is more probable, kites, which they may have taken for hawks. Prince Henry subsequently bestowed on the Order of Christ the tithes of the island, and one half of the sugar revenues.

The third island discovered in the Archipelago of the Azores, and on that account named Terceira or "the third," would seem to have been sighted by some sailors, probably returning from Cape Verde to Portugal, whose names were not deemed of importance enough to be attached to the discovery. Nor is the date of the discovery known, but it occurred between the years 1444 and 1450, and on some festival especially dedicated to our Blessed Lord, since it at first received the name of the Island of Jesu Christo, and bore for its arms the Saviour on the Cross.

The Flemings, however, claim for themselves the exclusive discovery, to which they give the date of 1445, as made by Josué van den Berge, a native of Bruges. This pretension is not corroborated, but rather disproved by contemporary evidence; for in a grant of the captaincy of the island on the 2nd of March, 1450, to one Jacques de Bruges, the sole reason given by the prince for making it was that Jacques came to him and stated, that as in the memory of man the Azores had been under the aggressive lordship of no one except the prince, and as the Island of Jesu, the third of these islands, was entirely uninhabited, he begged permission to colonize it. As he had no legitimate sons and only two daughters, the prince allowed the inheritance to descend to the female line. This unusual grant is readily explained by the fact that the new Captain Donatary was very rich, fitted out the armament and requisites for this rather distant colonization at his own expense, was a good Catholic, had married a noble Portuguese lady, and in all probability had entered the prince's service under the recommendation of his sister, the Duchess of Burgundy.

The islands of San Jorge and Graciosa, being within sight of Terceira, soon became participators in the colonization which had been brought to the latter. A Portuguese gentleman named Vasco Gil Sodrè, while on service in Africa, hearing of the newly colonized island of Terceira, went thither with all his family, but soon passed over to Graciosa, where he was joined by his brother-in-law, one Duarte Barreto, who went out with the rank of Captain Donatary of half of the island.

One of the companions of Jacques de Bruges, a wealthy and noble Fleming, named William van der

Haagen, whose northern name sounded so harsh to Portuguese ears, that they translated it into Da Silveira, which means the same thing, viz., "Hedges" or "Underwood," took from Flanders, at his own cost, two ships, full of people and artisans of different kinds, to make a trial of the island of San Jorge. Selecting a point of the island which they called the Topo, he founded the city which afterwards bore that name, but the comparative sterility of the island at a later period made him remove to Fayal, which had been discovered in the interval.

On what day or in what year the islands of Fayal and Pico were discovered, or who was the discoverer, no research has ever succeeded in finding. There is no doubt that the first colonizer and Captain Donatary was Jobst van Huerter, Lord of Moerkerke in Flanders, father-in-law of the celebrated Martin Behaim, from a legend on whose famous globe, made in 1492, and still preserved in the ancestral house in Nuremberg, we gather the following statement respecting the bestower of the captaincy:—

"The islands of the Azores were colonized in 1466, when they were given by the King of Portugal, after much solicitation, to his sister Isabel, Duchess of Burgundy. A great war was at that time being carried on in Flanders, accompanied by severe famine, and the duchess sent out to these islands a great number of men and women of all classes, with priests and everything requisite for the maintenance of religious worship. She also sent out several vessels laden with materials for the cultivation of the soil and for building houses, and during ten years she continued to send out means of subsistence. In 1490 there were some thousands of souls there who had come out with the noble knight, Jobst van Huerter, Lord of Moerkerke in Flanders, my dear father-in-law, *to whom and his descendants these islands were given by the Duchess of Burgundy*. In them grows the Portuguese sugar. There are two crops in the year, for there is no winter. All food is cheap, and there would be abundance of subsistence for a large population."

This statement is not exactly correct, for whereas King Duarte had in 1433 made a grant to Prince Henry of the newly discovered islands, this grant was transmitted by bequest of the latter to his nephew and adopted son Dom Fernando, and confirmed by Affonso V., by a charter dated at Evora, December 3rd, 1460.

At the same time it is reasonable to infer that the extraordinary expenses incurred by the Duchess of Burgundy, Van Huerter, and other Flemings in colonizing these islands, would secure to them privileges and powers that would give some show of plausibility to Behaim's statement, that the islands had been given by the King of Portugal to the Duchess of Burgundy.

Some years after Jobst van Huerter had undertaken the colonization of Fayal, he obtained the commission of the captaincy of Pico, which island, though lying at only a league's distance from Fayal, is supposed not to have been discovered for many years later than it. This is quite possible, for we have seen that it was some time before the dark spot observed from the island of Porto Santo was made out to be the important island of Madeira, though only at one league distant.

Equal obscurity rests on the date of the discovery of the islands of Flores and Corvo, as well as on the discoverer. It is only known that they were first conceded to a lady of Lisbon, named Maria de Vilhena. When the Fleming Willem van der Haagen, *alias* Da Silveira, went from San Jorge to Fayal, it was by invitation from his compatriot Jobst van Huerter, who had been now four years established there, and promised to give him part of the island. It happened, however, that Silveira became so popular by his virtues and distinguished personal qualities, that Van Huerter, under the influence of jealousy, broke his promise on the pretence that the lands he had referred to had been already given away. Silveira thence passed to Terceira, where he grew great quantities of corn and woad for dyeing blue, which he exported to Flanders. Returning from a visit to his native country by way of Lisbon, he became the guest of Dona Maria de Vilhena, who proposed to him that he should go out and colonize her two islands of Flores and Corvo, and rule over them in her name. This offer he accepted, but after a trial of seven years, found himself a loser both in property and position; he therefore once again betook himself to his original locality at the Topo in the island of San Jorge, where he realized great wealth from his corn plantations, and became the ancestor of some of the most noble families in the Atlantic islands.

A tradition which we look for in vain in any Portuguese or Spanish historical document of the fifteenth or sixteenth centuries, has been widely disseminated in almost every work which speaks of the discovery of America, to the effect that an equestrian statue pointing with its right hand to the west, was discovered by the Portuguese in the island of Corvo. A Portuguese writer of the seventeenth century, Manoel de Faria y Souza, thus describes it: "On the summit of a mountain called Corvo was found the statue of a man on horseback without saddle, bare-headed, the left hand on the horse's mane, the right pointing to the west. It stood on a slab of the same stone as itself; beneath it, on a rock, were engraved some letters in an unknown language." M. Boid, who resided a long time in the Azores, speaking of Corvo in his work entitled " Description of the Azores," London, 1835, 8vo, explains how a natural phenomenon has given rise to this fable. He says, " Among a great number of absurdities dealt in by the poor and superstitious inhabitants they gravely assert that the discovery of the New World is due to their island, because a promontory which stretches far into the sea towards the north-west, *presents the form* of a person with his hand stretched out towards the west." They say that " it was the will of Providence, that this promontory should have this extraordinary form in order to indicate to European navigators the existence of another world, and that Columbus understood and interpreted this sign, and threw himself into the career of Western discovery." We can thus understand how the grotesque configuration of a volcanic rock should have given rise to a story of an equestrian statue, which learned men have not hesitated to attribute to Carthaginians and Phœnicians, who, we know but too well, were very little inclined to point out the road of discovery to rival nations.

CHAPTER XI.

CADAMOSTO.

1455—1456.

WE now reach the period of a very important voyage, made by a Venetian gentleman named Alvise Cadamosto, under the auspices of Prince Henry. This young adventurer, though only twenty-two years of age, had already made one voyage to Flanders on a trading expedition, and his object being, as he expressly declares, to acquire wealth, a knowledge of the world, and, if possible, fame, he determined to repeat his venture. On the 8th of August, 1454, he set sail in one of the galleys belonging to the Republic, under the command of a Venetian cavalier, named Marco Zeno.

Contrary winds detained the vessel off Cape St. Vincent, near which Prince Henry happened to be at the time, at a village named Reposeira, which being a retired and quiet spot, well suited for his studies, was a favourite residence of his. When the prince heard of their arrival, he sent his own secretary, Antonio Gonsalves, and the Venetian consul, Patricio de' Conti, with samples of Madeira sugar, dragon's blood, and other products of the newly-discovered countries which he had colonized, and commissioned them to assure the Venetians that great things were to be done by those who would make the voyage. All this awakened in Cadamosto a strong desire to go, and he inquired what conditions the prince made with those who undertook the adventure. He was told that either the adventurers were to equip and freight a caravel at their own expense, and on their return pay the prince a fourth part of the produce, and retain the remainder themselves; or the prince would supply the caravel and furnish it with every necessary, in which case the adventurers were to retain only the half of the produce, the prince, in the event of failure, being at the expense of the entire outlay. Cadamosto was, however, assured that the voyage could scarcely fail of realizing great profits. He then had an interview with the prince, who received him with great kindness, confirmed all that had been told him, and easily persuaded him to undertake the voyage.

Having made inquiry as to the nature and quantity of the merchandise and provisions he would require, Cadamosto made the arrangements necessary for his new undertaking, and the Venetian galleys went on their way to Flanders. The prince kept Cadamosto with him at Reposeira, till he had fitted out for him a new caravel of ninety tons burthen. The sailing captain was Vicente Diàs, of whom we have heard already. They set sail on the 22nd of March, 1455, and at midday of the 25th reached the island of Porto Santo.

He found the island, which thirty-seven years before was uninhabited, tolerably well peopled, producing sufficient wheat and oats for the use of the inhabitants, and abounding in goats, wild boars, and rabbits, which last were innumerable. The island produced dragon's blood, excellent honey and wax, and the coast abounded in fish.

They left Porto Santo on the 28th of March, and the same day arrived at Machico, one of the ports of Madeira, where they landed. Cadamosto found four settlements on the island, named Machico, Santa Cruz, Funchal, and "Camara dos Lobos." There were inhabitants elsewhere, but these were the principal localities. The island could furnish about eight hundred armed men, and of that number one hundred mounted. Cadamosto describes the fertility as so great that the island produced an average of nearly seventy thousand bushels of wheat yearly. The soil had at first yielded sixty fold, but at the time of his visit only thirty or forty, because the land had become impoverished, although well watered.

On eight or more small rivers which intersected the island they had set up saw-mills, which were kept constantly at work in cutting wood for making furniture of various kinds, which was sent to Portugal and elsewhere. Two kinds of wood used for this purpose were held in great esteem: the one a fragrant cedar like cypress, of which they made tables of great length and breadth, boxes and other articles; the other a yew, which was also very exquisite, and of a red colour.

The sugar canes, which the prince had imported from Sicily, and planted in the island, were producing so abundantly that twelve hundred gallons of sugar were made at one boiling, and the climate was so favourable that the quantity was likely to increase. White sweetmeats were made in great perfection. Honey and wax were produced, but in small quantities. The wines were extremely good, considering the infancy of the colony, and the vines which the prince had imported thither from Candia, flourished so luxuriantly, in consequence of the richness of the soil, that Cadamosto declared it was the most beautiful sight in the world. There were wild peacocks, some of which were white; no partridges, or other game, except quails, and wild boars on the mountains in great abundance. Many of the inhabitants were wealthy, for the whole country was like a garden. There were Friars Minors of the Observantine order, men of good and holy life.

From Madeira they sailed southward, touching at the Canary Islands. Thence they made their way for Cape Branco, on reaching which Cadamosto landed and made an expedition to a place named Hoden, about six days' camel-journey inland. It was not enclosed with walls, but was a place of resort for the Arabs and caravans trading between Timbuctoo and other places belonging to the negroes, and the western parts of Barbary. The inhabitants of this place lived on dates and barley, which they had in abundance. Their drink was camels' milk. The people were Mahometans, and had no settled habitations, but travelled in great numbers, with long trains of camels, conveying brass and silver and other things from Barbary to Timbuctoo, and the country of the Blacks, and bringing back in exchange gold and malaguette pepper.

About six days' journey from Hoden, there was a place named Tegazza (which signifies a chest of gold), whence rock-salt was obtained in great quantities, and carried by the Arabs and Tawny Moors on the backs of camels to Timbuctoo, and thence to Melli, in the empire of the negroes, where it was sold in loads of two or three hundred mitigals[1] each, in exchange for gold.

The gold taken to Melli was divided into three parts. The first was sent by caravan to a place called Kukia on the road to Cairo; the two others to Timbuctoo, and thence

[1] The mitigal or miscal is equal to about a drachm and a half.

to Tunis; the other part to Hoden, and thence to Oran in Barbary within the straits, and to Fez, Marocco, Arzilla, Saffi, and Messa without the straits. It was taken hence by Italian merchants, in exchange for a variety of merchandise. The greatest advantage which the Portuguese obtained from the country of the Tawny Moors was the gold which was yearly sent from Hoden to the island of Arguin, and which they got by barter with the negroes.

The Tawny Moors used no coin, but in some of the inland towns the Arabs used cowries for small purchases; these were brought from the Levant to Venice, and sent thence to Africa. The gold was sold by the mitigal, as in Barbary. The women were brown, and had little petticoats brought from the country of the negroes, which some wore without any other dress. Those who had the longest breasts were considered the most beautiful, and so anxious were they for this distinction, that girls of seventeen or eighteen submitted to have a cord drawn tightly round each breast, so as to break them, and make them hang down; and by frequently pulling these cords, they made them grow so long that they sometimes reached the navel. These people were good horsemen, like the Moors, but they could not keep many horses, on account of the barrenness of the land and the great heat, and those they had did not live long. There were no rains, except in August, September, and October. The locusts, which were of a finger's length, and of a red and yellow colour, sometimes rose in the air in such numbers that for ten or twelves miles nothing else could be seen on the earth or in the air, and nothing remained undestroyed wherever they passed. These creatures came only once in three or four years, or the country would have become unfit for habitation.

Cadamosto now came to the Senegal, which he describes as more than a mile wide at the mouth, and very deep. The flux and reflux of the tide extended more than sixty miles up the river, as Cadamosto learned from Portuguese who had ascended it in their caravels. In entering the river it was necessary to go with the tide to avoid the sand-banks at the mouth.

Cadamosto was surprised to find so great a difference between the inhabitants on the two sides of the river. On the south side the people were very black, stout, and well made, and the country verdant, woody, and fertile; while on the north side, the men were thin, tawny, and short, and the country dry and sterile.

The first kingdom of the negroes bears the same name as the river, the Senegal, and the people are called Jaloffs. The country is quite flat as far as Cape Verde, which is the highest land on the whole coast, and is four hundred miles from Cape Branco. The King of Senegal was named Zucholin; he was about twenty-two years of age. The succession was not hereditary, but the chiefs chose a king from among their number, who remained on the throne as long as he pleased them. The king had no fixed revenue, but the chiefs made him presents of horses and cattle, and different kinds of vegetables and grains. The principal part of his wealth, however, was got by pillage. He carried off the neighbouring people for slaves; some to cultivate the land, and some for sale to the Tawny Moor and Arab merchants; in exchange for horses and other merchandise, besides the traffic with the Christians, since the trade was opened with them. Each negro was allowed as many wives as he pleased.

The king had never less than thirty, who were honoured according to the rank of their fathers. These wives were distributed by tens and twelves in different villages, where each had a house to herself, with women to wait upon her, and slaves to cultivate the land assigned her by her lord. They also had cows and goats, with slaves to keep them. When the king visited them, he took no provision with him for himself or his retinue. At sunrising, each wife at the place where he arrived prepared for him food and delicacies, and after the king had stayed his appetite, the remainder was distributed among his followers; but they were so numerous, that there were always some left unsatisfied. The king travelled in this way from place to place, to visit all his wives in succession, and in consequence his children were very numerous. As soon as he knew one of his wives to be pregnant, he left her; which custom was observed by all his chieftains.

These negroes professed Mahometanism, but were not so strict as the white Moors. The chiefs having most intercourse with the Tawny Moors or Arabs, paid more attention to religion than the people, but since they had become acquainted with Christians, they had less respect for Mahometanism.

The common people wore nothing but goats' skins made in the shape of breeches. The chiefs wore shirts of cotton, spun by the women. The width of the cloth was only a hand's-breadth; they did not know how to make it wider, and were obliged to sew several pieces together to make it the required width. These shirts reached half way down the thigh, and had wide sleeves which covered half the arm. Besides this they had hose of the same cloth, which reached from the waist to the instep, and were exceedingly broad, some of them containing thirty or even forty hands'-breadths of cloth, which hung in many folds, like a sack in front, and dragged on the ground behind. The women wore nothing above the waist. Whether married or not, they had only a short petticoat reaching from the waist to the middle of the leg. Both sexes went bare-foot, and wore nothing on their heads. Their hair was well-dressed, and fastened up tastefully, though it was very short. The men worked like the women, at spinning, washing, &c.

The climate was very hot, their January being warmer than April in Italy, and later in the season the heat became insupportable. It was the custom to wash three or four times a day, so that the people were extremely clean in their persons, but the reverse in their food. Though they were very stupid and awkward in matters that they were not accustomed to, they showed considerable skill in those they had been used to. They were great talkers and great liars, but so hospitable that the poorest would give food and lodging to strangers, looking for no reward. They were often at war among themselves or with their neighbours. They fought on foot, the heat preventing them from keeping war-horses. The same cause prevented their wearing armour. They used round shields, covered with the skin of an animal and called danta, which was very difficult to pierce. Their offensive arms were azagays, or light darts, having barbed iron points, which they threw with admirable skill, and inflicted very dangerous wounds; and a kind of scimitar, which they got from the negroes of Gambra; they had iron in their country, but did not know how to work it. They had also a kind of javelin. Their wars were very deadly, because, their bodies being unprotected, all their blows took effect. They were a bold and savage people, with no fear of death, which they infinitely preferred to flight. They knew nothing of navigation, and never saw a ship till the coming of the Portuguese. Those who lived on the banks of the river, or on the seashore, had canoes made of one piece of wood, the largest of which could contain only three or four men, and which they used for fishing and other purposes. They were the finest swimmers in the world.

After having passed the river Senegal, Cadamosto reached the country of Budomel, which is about fifty miles further. Budomel was the title of the prince, but it gave the name to the country, as in Europe we should say the territory of such a count or such a lord. The country is flat all along the coast. Cadamosto, having heard that the prince was a courteous and honourable man, stopped here. He had on board the caravel some Spanish horses, much valued by the negroes, linen cloths, Moorish silks, and other merchandise. Having anchored in the bay called the Palma de Budomel, he sent his interpreter on shore, to give notice of his arrival and make proposals of commerce.

The following day the negro prince appeared with a retinue of fifteen horse and a hundred and fifty foot soldiers. He invited the Portuguese to land, and Cadamosto came on shore in a sloop, and was very well received by the prince, to whom he offered seven horses in harness, and other merchandise to the value of about three hundred ducats. The payment was to be made at the house of the prince, which was twenty-five miles inland, and Cadamosto was invited to receive it himself, and to be the prince's guest for some days. Before setting out Budomel presented him with a young girl twelve or thirteen years old, to serve, he said, in his cabin; she was very black, and on that account was considered very beautiful. The prince also furnished him with horses and all things necessary for the journey. When they were within four miles of his house he consigned him to the care of one of his nephews named Bisboror, the chief of a neighbouring village, who received him into his house and entertained him honourably.

It was now November. Cadamosto remained there twenty-eight days, and made frequent visits to the prince, which gave him excellent opportunities of observing the customs of the country. He had still more opportunity of doing this when he was obliged to return to Senegal by land; the weather was so stormy that he could not return to the ships without danger, and in consequence he sent them to the entrance of the river, and made the journey himself on horseback. In order to communicate with his caravel, and send orders to his men to meet him at Senegal, he had to put the swimming powers of the natives to the test. He says the vessel was three miles out at sea, and it appeared impossible to execute his commission on account of the violence of the waves breaking on the sand-banks, but in spite of this the negroes were eager in offering their services to carry his letter on board. He asked two of them what he should give them for the enterprise, and they only asked two mavulgies of tin apiece, the mavulgi being worth something less than a penny. "I cannot describe," says Cadamosto, "the difficulty they had to pass the sand-banks in so furious a sea. Sometimes I lost sight of them, and thought they were swallowed up by the waves. At last one of the two could no longer resist the force of the water, turned his back on the danger, and returned to the shore. The other, more vigorous, after battling for more than an hour with the wind and the waves, passed the bank, carried my letter to the ship, and brought me the answer. I dared hardly touch it, looking upon it as a wonderful and sacred thing. And thus I learned that the negroes of Budomel are the best swimmers in the world."

The negro kings and chiefs had neither cities nor forts, their richest habitations were but miserable villages. The Prince Budomel's authority depended chiefly on the respect the negroes had for his riches, so little was the subordination to rank understood. Personal merit, strength, sense, justice, courage, and good looks also produced an effect, and Budomel possessed these advantages. He had assigned to him, for himself and his wives, a certain number of villages, which he visited in succession. The one in which Cadamosto stayed contained between forty and fifty houses covered with thatch, built close to each other in a round, encompassed by a ditch and screens of large trees, with two or three passages for entrance; each house had an enclosed court.

Budomel had nine wives in this place, and more or less in his other villages. Each wife had five or six young girls for her service, with whom their lord was permitted to live as with his wives, who did not consider this an injury, as it was the custom. Jealousy was a common vice among them, and it was an insult to a negro to enter the house of his wife; even his sons were excluded. Budomel had always about two hundred negroes in attendance upon his person, when one left, another supplying his place; besides which there were always a number of people who came to attend his court. Between the entrance of his house and his own private apartment there were seven courts, and in the midst of each was a large tree, to shelter those who waited for an audience. In these courts his retinue were distributed, according to their rank and employments: those in the courts nearest the prince being the most distinguished. Few, however, dared approach the person of the prince; the tawny Moors and the Christians had almost the exclusive privilege of entering his apartment, and speaking to him. He maintained great state towards his subjects, and showed himself only for one hour in the morning, and again for a short time in the evening near the door of the outermost court.

He required great ceremony when giving audiences to his subjects. However high the rank of a suitor, he had to take off his garments, with the exception of a covering round the middle, and when he entered the last court he threw himself on his knees, with his forehead on the earth, casting sand over his head and shoulders. Even the prince's relatives were not exempt from these humiliations. The suppliant remained a long time in this posture, sprinkling himself with sand. He approached his lord on his knees, still throwing sand on his bowed head; when about two paces from him, he stopped and offered his petition. The reply was given as shortly as possible, and with scarcely a glance towards him. Cadamosto witnessed this scene several times, and accounts for the excess of submission by the excess of fear; the negroes knew that their tyrants could carry off their wives and children, and sell them for slaves at their pleasure, and they trembled before them, and feared them more than God himself, with Whose name, indeed, they were scarcely acquainted.

Bumodel was so gracious to Cadamosto, that he allowed him to enter his mosque at the hour of prayer. The Tawny Moors and Arabs, who were his priests, were summoned to attend, and Budomel performed his orisons in the following manner. Standing up, he raised his eyes towards heaven, then walked forward two steps, uttered a few words in a low tone, and prostrated himself on the ground, which he kissed respectfully. In all this he was followed by the Tawny Moors, and the rest of his retinue. He continued in prayer about half an hour, repeating the same ceremonies ten or twelve times. Having finished, he turned to Cadamosto, asked him what he thought of it, and desired him to give him some idea of the Christian religion. Cadamosto had the courage to tell him, in the presence of the priests, that the Mahometan religion was false, and that the Catholic was the only true faith. This enraged the priests, but Budomel only laughed, and said that the Christian faith must be good, because God alone could have bestowed such riches and knowledge as the Christians possessed. He added that he thought the Mahometan religion was good also, and that the negroes must have a better chance of salvation than the Christians, because God being a just master, and having given the Christians so many advantages in this world that they had a paradise here, it followed that great compensation awaited the negroes in the next world, and they might expect their paradise there. Budomel showed much good sense and reflection in his remarks, and took pleasure in conversing about religion. Cadamosto thought he would easily have been induced to embrace Christianity, had he not been afraid of offending the people. His nephew told Cadamosto this, and took great delight himself in conversing on the subject.

The table of Budomel was supplied in the same manner as that of the King of Senegal. The negro chiefs ate lying upon the ground, without ceremony, and no one might eat with them but the Moors, whom they looked upon as instructors. The common people ate in companies of ten or twelve, round a copper full of meat, in which they all put their hands. They ate little at a time, but had frequent meals.

The climate was so hot that they could not grow wheat, rye, barley, oats, or vines, for there was no rain for nine months, that is, from October to June. However, they had millet, large and small, and two kinds of beans, very fine, both red and white. They sowed in July to reap in September, and this was the rainy season when the rivers overflowed and fertilized the land; and thus all the work of agriculture was done in the three months.

Their drinks were water, milk, and palm-wine, which was distilled from a tree found in abundance in the country, but not the same that produces the date, though it is like it. This wine, which was called *mignol*, was distilled into calabashes from two or three openings in the trunk of the tree: from morning till night a tree would not fill more than two calabashes. This liquor had a good flavour, and without any mixture was as intoxicating as wine. Cadamosto says that the first day it was as good as the best European wine, but daily it lost its flavour, till it became sour. It was, however, more wholesome on the third or fourth day than the first; for in losing some of its sweetness, it became purgative. There was a kind of oil used by the natives to flavour their food, the ingredients of which Cadamosto was unable to discover. It had the scent of violets, the taste of olives, and the colour of saffron, evidently palm oil, and not a bad description of it. There was also a tree which produced little red beans, with black specks, in great abundance.

The country abounded with animals, and there were a prodigious number of serpents, some venomous, and some so large that they would swallow a goat whole. Cadamosto was told by the negroes that these creatures went in great numbers to the mountainous parts of the country, which also abounded in white ants. The ants by a wonderful instinct built houses for these terrible neighbours with earth, which they carried in their mouths. The negroes being great magicians, had recourse to charms on all occasions, especially to defend themselves against serpents. Cadamosto relates an anecdote which he had from a Genoese, a trustworthy man, who told him that the year before he had been in the country of Budomel and was staying in the house of his nephew Bisboror. Once at midnight he was awakened by hisses all round the house, and saw his host rise and give orders to two negroes to bring his camel. The Genoese asked where he was going so late, and was only told that he was going on business, and would soon return. He came back early in the morning, and the Genoese, curious to know the end of the adventure, renewed his questions. "Did you not hear at midnight," said Bisboror, "hissings all round the house? It was surrounded by serpents, and if I had not employed charms to make them return to their own place, they would have destroyed much cattle." The

Genoese was greatly surprised, but Bisboror told him that his uncle could do much more wonderful things. When he wanted to obtain venom to poison his arrows, he had a large circle formed, into which he charmed all the serpents in the neighbourhood; and when he had selected the most venomous, he killed them with his own hands, and let the others go. He then mixed their venom with the seed of a certain plant, which made a poison so powerful that a wound from a weapon dipped in it was fatal in a quarter of an hour. The Genoese added that Bisboror offered to show him some charms, but he had no taste for such things, and declined having anything to do with them.

There were no domestic animals nor sheep in Senegal, but there were oxen and goats. The cattle were thinner than in Europe, and red was a rare colour among them, the usual colours being black, white, or a mixture of both. There were great numbers of beasts of prey; lions, panthers, leopards, wolves, and other wild animals. The wild elephants went in herds; they were of great size, as the tusks imported into Europe proved.

Cadamosto saw no other beasts than those here mentioned, but there were a great number of birds, especially paroquets, which the negroes hated because they destroyed their millet and vegetables. They said that there were several kinds, but Cadamosto only saw two; one like those of Alexandria, but a little smaller; the other much larger, with the head brown, and the rest of the body mingled with green and yellow. He took many of both kinds, but lost a number of them on the voyage home. The caravel which accompanied him took a hundred and fifty more, which sold for half a ducat each in Portugal. These birds build their nests very cleverly: they collect a quantity of reeds and twigs, and make them into the shape of a ball, with a hole for the entrance; these they hang from the slenderest branches they can find, as a protection from serpents, the weight of these creatures preventing them from attacking the nests in such a position. There were great numbers of the birds called Pharaoh's chickens (the Egyptian vulture), which came from the East. They were dark birds, and marked with black and white spots.

During Cadamosto's sojourn with Bisboror, he went to a market or fair, which was held on Thursday and Friday in a meadow near, and which was attended by numbers of both sexes from five or six miles round. Those who lived at a greater distance had other similar markets. The poverty of the people was shown by their merchandise, consisting of cotton in small quantities, nets and cotton cloths, vegetables, oil, millet, wooden bowls, and palm mats. Sometimes they brought a little gold, but in very small quantities. They had no money, and all the traffic was by barter. The people who came from the interior were very much astonished at the whiteness of Cadamosto's skin, and the fashion of his dress. He wore a Spanish dress of black damask; his mantle, being of wool, greatly surprised them, as they have no wool in their country; and some of them rubbed his hands with saliva to find out if they were painted white. His object in going to these markets was to see if any quantity of gold was brought there.

Horses were valued by the negroes in proportion to their rarity. The Arabs and Tawny Moors imported them from Barbary and the countries bordering upon Europe, but the extreme heat soon killed them; besides, the beans and millet, which were their only food, made them so fat that it became a disease. A horse with its harness was worth from nine to fourteen slaves, according to its beauty. When a chief purchased a horse, he went to the sorcerers, who lighted a fire of dried herbs, over the smoke of which they held the horse's head by the bridle, and repeated their charms. They anointed him with the best oil, shut him up for eighteen or twenty days, so that no one might see him, and tied round his neck certain charms folded square, and covered with red leather, and having done this the master believed him to be secured from danger.

The negro women were very gay, especially the young ones, and very fond of singing and dancing. Their time for dancing was by moonlight.

Nothing caused so much astonishment to the natives as the discharges of artillery from the caravel. Cadamosto caused a cannon to be fired when some of the negroes were on board, the noise of which terrified them extremely, but they were still more frightened when they were told that one discharge of this dreadful machine would kill a hundred of them. After they had recovered from their fright, they declared that so destructive an engine could only be the work of the devil. They were greatly pleased with the sounds of the bagpipe, and thought it was an animal which sung the different tunes. Cadamosto, amused with their simplicity, placed the instrument in their hands, and when they saw that it really was a work of art, they thought it must be made by divine skill, for they had never heard such sweet sounds. The most simple instruments about the vessel excited their admiration, and they thought the eyes painted on the prow of the vessel were real eyes, by which it saw its way through the water. They repeated incessantly that the Europeans must have much more skilful sorcerers than theirs, and little inferior to the devil himself, for travellers by land found it difficult enough to keep the right road from one place to another, while they, in their vessels, could find their way on the sea, however distant they might be from the land.

Though the country abounded in honey, the negroes had no idea of making any use of the wax, and Cadamosto greatly surprised and delighted them by making some honeycomb, drained of the honey, into candles before their eyes. "The white people," they exclaimed, "know everything." They had two kinds of musical instruments—the one was a sort of Moorish drum, and the other a kind of violin with two strings, played with the fingers, but there was little music to be got out of them.

After this long sojourn in Budomel's country, Cadamosto resolved, after buying some slaves, to proceed on his way to double Cape Verde, and make further discoveries. He remembered to have heard from Prince Henry that beyond Senegal there was another river called the Gambia, from which a quantity of gold had already been brought, and that no one could go there without amassing great riches. With this inviting prospect he took leave of Budomel, and again set sail. One morning he came in sight of two vessels, which proved to belong, the one to Antonio Uso di Mare, a Genoese gentleman, and the other to some Portuguese in the service of Prince Henry. They were going together towards the coast of Africa, with the intention of passing Cape Verde and making new discoveries. Cadamosto, whose objects were the same, joined company; they sailed together towards the south, keeping sight of land, and the day following they came to the Cape.

Beyond the Cape was a gulf; the coast was low, and covered with fine large trees, which were always green, the fresh leaves supplying the place of those that fell, without the trees ever becoming bare, as in Europe. They grew so close to the sea, that they seemed to be watered by it. The prospect was so beautiful that Cadamosto declared that he had never seen anything to compare to it. The land was watered by several small rivers, but as it was impossible for the vessels to enter, they could not take in water.

Beyond the little gulf, the coast was peopled by two nations of negroes, the Barbacins and the Serrers, both independent of the King of Senegal. They had no distinctions of rank among them, but only of riches and personal qualities. They were idolaters, lawless, and very cruel. They fought with poisoned arrows, the least scratch of which that fetched blood caused instant death. They were very black, and very well made. The country was full of wood, lakes, and rivers, and could only be approached through very narrow defiles, which had helped them to preserve their independence. The Kings of Senegal had often tried to conquer them, but had always been foiled by the difficulties of the country.

Advancing along the coast with a favourable wind, they discovered the mouth of a river, about a bow-shot in width and very shallow (the Joal?). They gave it the name of Barbacins. This river is sixty miles from Cape Verde. Continuing to follow the coast they arrived at the mouth of another river as large as the Senegal (the Joombas), which was so beautiful, with the trees growing down to the water's edge, that they determined to send one of their negro interpreters on shore. Each ship had some on board whom they had brought from Portugal; slaves that had been taken in the first voyages, who having learned the language, had come out as interpreters with the promise that they should be made free. They drew lots to find which of the three ships should send to the shore, and it fell to that of the Genoese. He despatched an armed barque, with orders to his people not to land till the interpreter had obtained information respecting the government and riches of the country. They set him on shore, and when they had put off to a little distance, saw several negroes advance to meet him, who had been waiting in ambush. After some questioning, which the men in the boat could not hear, they attacked and killed him, before the others could come to his rescue. The boat returned to the ships with the news, and the commanders thinking that people who had shown themselves so cruel to one of their own countrymen would be still more barbarous to strangers, continued their course along the coast, which increased in beauty and verdure the further they went, but was very flat and low.

At length they came to the mouth of a very large river, at the narrowest part not less than three or four miles wide, and the ships could enter it with safety. The next day they learned that this was the much desired Gambia. They sent on the smallest caravel, well equipped with men and arms, to sound the river, and find out whether the larger vessels could follow. Finding that at the shallowest it was four feet deep, they resolved to send sloops well armed with the caravel, with instructions that if the negroes came to attack them, they were to return without fighting, because, their object being to establish commerce, they could only do this by gaining the confidence of the people. Two miles up the river the sloops found twelve and sixteen feet of water. The banks of the river were extremely beautiful and covered with magnificent trees, but, as they proceeded, it became so winding that they did not care to go further. On their way back, they saw, at the entrance of a small river which ran into the large one, three canoes made each of a single piece of wood. Though the men in the sloops were strong enough to defend themselves, they rowed back with great speed, in accordance with their orders, and when they reached the caravel and had got on board, they saw the blacks about a bow-shot behind. The negroes were about twenty-five or thirty in number, and seemed much surprised at the sight of the caravel. They stayed some time to satisfy their curiosity; but made no reply to the signs made to them, and at last departed as they had come.

The following day, at three in the morning, the two caravels which had remained at the mouth of the river, took advantage of wind and tide being in their favour, to enter the river and rejoin their companions. They had scarcely gone three or four miles, one after the other, when they perceived that they were followed by a great number of canoes, but could not understand where they came from. Seeing this, they turned upon the negroes, and a battle appearing inevitable, covered themselves as well as they could as a protection against the poisoned arrows. The canoes surrounded the prow of Cadamosto's ship, which was in advance of the rest. There were fifteen of them, containing about a hundred and fifty

negroes, all tall, well-made men. They had on shirts of
white cotton, and white hats with a plume, which gave
them a warlike air. At the prow of each canoe was a
negro on the look-out, with a round shield that seemed
made of leather. When close to the caravel, they remained with their oars raised, looking at it with admiration, till the other caravels came hastening up at the
sight of danger. As soon as they came quite near, the
negroes laid down their oars, and took to their bows,
from which they discharged a heavy shower of arrows.
The three caravels remained stationary, but fired off
four cannon, which astonished the negroes so much that
they threw down their bows, and looked on all sides in
the greatest terror for the cause of so frightful a sound.
When the noise ceased they again took courage, and
resumed their bows, coming within a stone's throw of
the ships, and bearing the fire of the crossbow-men very
bravely. One of them was killed by a shot from the son
of the Genoese gentleman, but they continued their
attack till a great number had been slain, without the
loss of a single man on board the caravels. When the
negroes became aware of their loss, and found their
canoes likely to sink, they threw themselves on the
smallest caravel, which was badly armed, and attacked
it violently. Cadamosto seeing their intention, placed
the smaller vessel between the other two, and gave
orders for a general discharge of artillery. Though they
took care not to fire on the canoes, the noise and the
agitation of the water so terrified the negroes, that they
fled in disorder. The three caravels were then made
fast to each other, and by means of a single anchor
remained as firm as a vessel in the greatest calm.

During several days following, Cadamosto sought

occasion to convince the natives that he had no intention of hurting them. The interpreters persuaded the men in the canoes to approach within bowshot, and asked them why they attacked strangers who only wished to make conditions of peace and commerce with them, as they had already done with the people of Senegal, and who had come from a far distant land with presents from the King of Portugal to them. They asked the name of their country and river, and invited them to come to the vessels and make exchanges of merchandise, according to their own will and pleasure. To all this the negroes replied, that they had heard of the arrival of the white people at Senegal, and that they despised their neighbours of Senegal for entering into any treaty with the Christians, who, they believed, lived on human flesh, and only bought negroes to devour them. They declared their intention to kill the Christians if possible, and take their spoil to their sovereign, who was three days' journey inland. Their country was called Gambia, and the large river had a name which Cadamosto could not remember. The wind having risen, during this conference, the caravels took advantage of it to bear down upon the negroes, who escaped to the shore, and thus ended the encounter.

The commanders then consulted whether they should sail further up the river, in the hope of finding some more hospitable people, but the sailors were so anxious to return home, that they declared they would not go on. The commanders were obliged to submit, fearing a mutiny. On the following day they set out on their homeward voyage and sailed towards Cape Verde on their way to Portugal.

The next year Cadamosto, in company with the Genoese

Uso di Mare, undertook a second voyage, with the view of following up his discoveries in the country of Gambia, which had been frustrated before by the barbarity of the natives and the opposition of the Portuguese sailors. Prince Henry warmly approved of the expedition, and fitted out a caravel in his own name to accompany them.

The three ships set out from Lagos in the beginning of May, and without stopping went on to Cape Branco, which they doubled, and then put out into the open sea.

On the third day two men from the mast-head saw two large islands, at which there was great rejoicing, for they believed them to be hitherto unknown, and hoped to find them inhabited. They made for them, and having found good anchorage, sent on shore a skiff with men well armed to explore, but they found no sign of habitation. The next day, to make quite sure, Cadamosto sent ten men, armed with crossbows, with orders to ascend a mountain and see if there were any sign of habitation, or if there were any other islands within sight. They saw no dwellings of any kind, but they could see three other islands, one toward the north, and two in a southward direction. They thought they could see islands in the west, but so far off that they could not distinguish them, and Cadamosto did not care to spend the time required to go to them, as he thought they would be all alike wild and uninhabited.

The three caravels then weighed anchor and went to one of the other islands, which appeared covered with trees, and finding the mouth of a river, they anchored there in order to get water for the ships. Some of the sailors went up the river a good distance in the sloop, and found some small lakes of salt, fine and white, which they brought into the vessel in great quantity. They found also a great many turtles, larger than a shield. The sailors salted a good number, which proved very useful in their voyage. At the mouth of the river and further up, they found fish in incredible numbers and great variety.

They remained two days to refresh themselves, agreeing to name the first island they had found Boavista, because it was the first they had discovered. The larger one they named Santiago, because they came to anchor there on the feast of St. James and St. Philip. These were the Cape Verde Islands.

They again set sail and came in sight of land at a place called Spedegar, and followed the coast till they came to The Two Palms, a place situated between Cape Verde and the River Senegal. Without any further difficulty they proceeded on their way to the River Gambia, which they entered without interruption. They sounded the river for about ten miles, the few negroes that they saw not daring to approach. They then anchored one Sunday near an island, where they buried one of the sailors, who had died of a fever, and as he was much beloved and lamented, they named the island after him, S. André. They now continued their course up the river, followed by some canoes at a distance. Cadamosto sent interpreters to them to tell the negroes they might come on board in safety. The interpreters showed them stuffs and toys which had been brought for the purpose, and offered to give them some if they would come on board.

At length overcoming their fears, they came to the caravel, and one of the negroes was able to talk with Cadamosto's interpreter. They were very much astonished at everything they saw on board the caravel, and especially with the sails, for they had only been accustomed to use oars. The dress and colour of the Europeans amazed them, their own dress being only a white cotton shirt. Cadamosto received them with great kindness, and asked them the name of their country and of their prince, to which they replied that their country was called Gambia, and that their prince was named Farisanguli; that he lived about ten days' journey from the river, between the south and south-west; that he was a vassal of the Emperor of Melli, who was chief of all the negroes; that there were many other princes who lived nearer, and that if Cadamosto wished it, they would take him to one named Batti Mansa (*i.e.* King Batti, Mansa being the Mandingo for king). This offer was thankfully accepted, and the caravel proceeded up the river, according to the direction of the negroes, till they reached the residence of this prince, which Cadamosto believed to be about sixty miles from the river's mouth.

When they had cast anchor, Cadamosto sent one of the interpreters with the negroes to Batti Mansa, bearing a very handsome Moorish dress as a present, and charged with a message to the effect that they had come from the Christian King of Portugal, to make a treaty with him. The messengers were favourably received by Batti Mansa, who sent some of his people to the caravel. A treaty was made, and European goods were exchanged for slaves and gold, but the quantity of gold was not at all equal to the expectations raised by the accounts given by the people of Senegal, who being very poor themselves, thought their neighbours richer than they were. The negroes valued their gold as highly as the Portuguese did, but showed how much they admired the European trifles by their willingness to give a large price for them. The Portuguese remained there eleven days, during which many negroes came on board, some only from curiosity, others to sell their merchandise, cotton cloths, white and striped nets, gold rings, &c. They also brought baboons and marmots, civet and skins of the civet cat, all which they sold very cheap. Others brought fruits, especially dates, which the sailors found very good, but which Cadamosto would not touch, fearing they were not wholesome.

Every day the caravels were visited by negroes differing in race and language, both men and women, who came and went in their canoes with the utmost confidence. They only used oars and rowed standing, having always a second in the boat to steer with his oar. The oars were in the form of a half-lance, between seven and eight feet long, with a round board like a trencher at the end; with these they managed their canoes very skilfully, keeping close to the coast, not venturing far for fear of being taken by the neighbouring people and sold for slaves.

At the end of eleven days, they resolved to return to the river's mouth, as fever began to show itself among them. Cadamosto had not failed to make his observations on the religion and customs of the people. They were generally idolaters, and superstitious with regard to charms and enchantments; but they believed in a God, and there were some Mahometans among them, who travelled about, and traded with other countries. There was but little difference between the food of these people and that of the natives of Senegal, except that they ate dogs' flesh, which Cadamosto had never seen done elsewhere. They dressed in cotton, which they had in abundance, while the natives of Senegal, where cotton was scarce, often wore nothing at all. The women dressed like the men, but for ornament tattooed their skins when they were young with a hot needle. The heat of the climate was extreme, and was greater on the river than on the sea, on account of the vast numbers of trees which grew on the banks and kept the air confined. As an instance of the size of these trees, Cadamosto mentions one which measured seventeen fathoms round; the trunk was pierced and hollowed out in many places, but the foliage was green, and the branches spread out so as to afford an immense shade. There were others still larger, showing that the country was wonderfully fertile and well watered.

There were great numbers of elephants, which the natives did not know how to tame. While the caravels were at anchor, these elephants came out of the neighbouring wood, down to the banks of the river. Some of the sailors got into the skiff, but before they could reach the bank, the elephants saw them and went back to the wood. These were the only living elephants that Cadamosto saw. A negro chief named Guumi Mansa, who lived near the mouth of the river, showed him a small one that he had killed after a hunt of two days. The negroes hunted on foot with bows and poisoned darts or javelins. They hid behind the trees, and sometimes climbed up into them, and from their hiding-places threw their poisoned weapons at the animals, leaping from tree to tree in pursuit, and the elephants being large and unwieldy were struck many times before they could escape or defend themselves. They never dared attack an elephant in the open country, for however active a man might be, he could not hope to outrun him. But the elephant never

attacks a man unless in self-defence, being naturally
gentle and docile.

The tusks of the little elephant which Cadamosto saw
dead were not more than three palms long, one-third of
the length being buried in the jaw; this showed it was
quite a young one, for the full-grown animals have tusks
from ten to twelve palms long. Young as this one was,
it had as much flesh as five or six oxen. The negro
chief presented Cadamosto with the best part, and gave
the rest to the hunters. Cadamosto's portion was taken
to the caravel to be cooked, as he was curious to taste
the flesh of an animal so new to him, but he found it
hard and disagreeable; however, he had some salted to
take home to Prince Henry on his return. He sent on
board the caravel one of the feet and a part of the trunk,
with some of the skin, which was black and very coarse;
all of which with the salted flesh he presented to the
prince, who received them as great curiosities.

The chief also gave him another elephant's foot, which
measured three palms and a finger each way, and a tooth
twelve palms in length, which were afterwards presented
by the prince to his sister the Duchess of Burgundy.

In the river Gambia and other rivers of the country,
Cadamosto saw the hippopotamus, which had not been
seen by Christians before, except on the banks of the Nile.
He saw also bats three palms long or more, a number of
birds, different from those of Europe, and a multitude of
fishes, also differing from the European, but almost all
very good to eat.

The sickness of the men now compelled them to leave
the country of Batti Mansa. They descended the river,
and being well-furnished with provisions, determined to
go further along the coast. The current of the Gambia

carried them far beyond the mouth of the river, and the land stretched south-south-west, in the form of a cape (Cape St. Mary).

Seeing breakers at four miles distance, they stood out to sea, to escape the sand-banks and rocks, and so they coasted along for three days.

On the fourth day they came to the mouth of a very large river, but somewhat smaller than the Gambia, with banks covered with trees of extraordinary size and beauty. Two armed sloops, with interpreters, were sent on shore to reconnoitre, which returned with the information that the river was called Casa Mansa, from the name of a negro chief, who resided thirty miles up it and was then at war with a neighbouring chief. The distance from the Gambia was about a hundred miles. They departed the following day, and about twenty miles further on came to a cape to which they gave the name of Capo Roxo, from the red colour of the earth. They next came to the mouth of a river, about a bow-shot in width which they did not enter, but gave it the name of Rio de Santa Anna (the Cacheo). Further on they found another river of the same size, which they named S. Domingo (the Rio de Jatte), which was about fifty-five or sixty miles from Cape Roxo.

A day's journey beyond, they came to the mouth of a river, so wide that they thought it was a gulf; they were some time crossing, for it was twenty miles over. The south bank was covered with beautiful trees, and when they arrived there, they discovered some islands out at sea. They then cast anchor, resolving to gain more information before they went on. The following day two canoes approached the caravels, the largest containing about thirty negroes, and the other sixteen. All on board the caravels took to their arms, expecting an attack, but the negroes raised a piece of white linen fastened to an oar, in sign of peace. The Portuguese replied in the same manner, and the negroes came on board Cadamosto's caravel, where they showed great surprise at everything they saw, for all was new to them, the whiteness of the men, the form of the vessel, the masts, the sails, and cordage, &c. It was a great disappointment to find that the interpreters were no longer of use, for they did not understand the language of the natives. This induced Cadamosto to think of turning back, as they could not get any further information, and to this the other commanders agreed. During their stay, which lasted two days, one of the negroes gave bracelets of gold in exchange for other things, without speaking a word, only making use of signs.

They named the river, Rio Grande. From the extreme breadth of its mouth it would seem to have been the river Jeba. The north star appeared to them very low. They also found that the tides were different here from anything they had observed in other countries. Instead of the flux and reflux being as usual six hours each, the tide here rose in four hours, and took eight to subside; and so great was its impetuosity, that three anchors scarcely sufficed to keep each caravel steady, and they set sail with great danger, for the force of the sea was greater than that of the wind, though all the sails were set.

In returning to Portugal, Cadamosto visited two large islands and some small ones, which they saw about thirty miles from the main land, low and covered with fine trees. The large islands, the Bissagos, were inhabited, but the language of the people was unknown to the interpreters, so they made a very short stay, and steered homewards, arriving safely in Portugal after a good voyage.

About this time, either in 1456 or 1457, the prince fitted out the Picanço at Lagos, and appointed Diogo Gomez captain, with two other caravels also under his command, and with orders to proceed as far as they could. After passing the Jeba and the Rio Grande they encountered such strong currents in the sea, that no anchor could hold, and the other captains, believing that they were at the extremity of the ocean, were so alarmed that they begged Gomez to return. In the middle of the current the water was very clear and the natives came from the shore and brought cotton-cloth, elephants' teeth, and a quart measure of Malaguetto pepper in grain and in its pods as it grew. This gave great pleasure to the Portuguese. The current, however, increased so much that they were compelled to put back.

At length they made their way to the Gambia, which they entered with the wind and tide in their favour, and came to a small island in the middle of the river, where they remained that night. In the morning, further in, they saw many canoes full of men, who fled at sight of them, for it seems they were the same who had slain Nuño Tristam and his men. The next day, however, they saw some people on the right hand side of the river, by whom they were received in a friendly manner. Their chief was Frangazick, the nephew of Farisanguli, already mentioned. There Gomez received from the negroes one hundred and eighty pounds weight of gold, in exchange for cloths, necklaces, &c. They told the Portuguese that the negroes on the left shore would not hold intercourse with them because they had slain the Christians. The chief had a certain negro, named Bucker, who was well acquainted with the whole country of the negroes, and whom Gomez asked to go with him to Cantor, a large town five hundred miles up the river and near its southern bank, promising to give him a mantle and shirts, and every necessary. He made also a similar promise to his chief, which he kept. They ascended the river, and sent one of the captains with his caravel into a certain harbour, named Ollimansa. The other remained in Nomimansa, and Gomez went up the river as far as Cantor, whence he sent out Bucker to make known to the people of the country that he had come thither for the purpose of exchanging merchandise. As soon as the report was spread that Christians were in Cantor, the natives came together from all quarters, from Timbuctoo in the north, and from Mount Gelu in the south. There came also people from Kukia, a great city surrounded by a wall of baked tiles, where there was abundance of gold, and caravans of camels and dromedaries crossed over thither with merchandise from Carthage or Tunis, from Fez, from Cairo, and from all the land of the Arabs, in exchange for the gold. They said that the gold was brought from the mines of Mount Gelu, on the opposite side of the range called Sierra Leone. They said that that range of mountains began at Albafur, and ran southwards, which pleased Gomez much, because all the rivers, large and small, descending from those mountains (which had been as yet observed) ran westward; but they told him that other very large rivers ran eastward from them, and that near that city was a certain great river, named Emiu, and that there was also a great lake, but not very broad, on which were many canoes, like ships, and that the people on the opposite sides were in constant warfare with each other, those on the eastern side being white men. The chief of the negroes, they said, was named Sambegeny, and the lord of the eastern part Semanagu, and a short time before these two had had a great battle, in which Semanagu was the conqueror. A certain Arab of Tlemsen, named Admedi, told Gomez that he had been present at the battle. When Gomez afterwards related all these things to the prince, the prince told him that a merchant in Oran had written to him two months before respecting this engagement between Semanagu and Sambegeny, a fact which supplies an incidental proof of the perseverance with which the prince pursued his inquiries respecting the interior tribes between the Mediterranean and the West Coast of Africa. Gomez further questioned the negroes at Cantor as to the road which led to the gold country, and asked who was the lord of it. They told him that the king's name was Bormelli, and that the whole land of the negroes on the right side of the river was under his dominion, and that he lived in Kukia. They said further, that all the mines were his and that before the door of his palace was a mass of gold just as it was taken from the earth, so large that twenty men could scarcely move it, and that the king always fastened his horse to it, and kept it as a curiosity on account of its being found just as it was, and of so great size and purity. The chiefs of his court wore in their nostrils and ears ornaments of gold. They said also, that the parts to the east were full of gold-mines, and that the men who went into the pits to get the gold did not live long, on account of the impure air. The gold sand was afterwards given to women to wash the gold from it.[2]

[2] The mountainous country of Bouré on the Tankisso, an affluent of the Joliba, is doubtless here referred to. It contains many very abundant

This journey of nearly five hundred miles up the Gambia to Cantor more than four hundred years ago is most remarkable, for, with the exception of Hecquard's passage through Cantor in 1850, the visits to that country through all that long period have been of the most cursory and incidental character.

At length Gomez' men became worn out with the heat, and he returned in search of the other two caravels. In the one which had remained in Ollimansa, they found nine men had died, the captain, João Gonzalo Alphonso, very ill, and all the rest of his men sick, except three. They found the other caravel fifty leagues lower down towards the ocean, and in it five men had died. They immediately withdrew and made for the sea, and Gomez went to the place where he had hired the negro traveller, and gave him what he had promised him.

Gomez here heard of the great chief, Batti Mansa, and desiring to make peace with him, sent Bucker to him. That chieftain invited him to a great wood on the bank of the river, and brought with him an immense throng of people armed with poisoned arrows, azagays, and swords and shields. Gomez went to him, carrying some presents and biscuit, and Portuguese wine, for they had no wine except what was made from the date palm, and in return Batti Mansa gave him three negroes, one male and two female, and he was pleased and extremely gracious, making merry with Gomez and swearing by the

---

gold-mines. The gold of Bouré circulates throughout the whole interior, and finds its way to the French and English settlements on the coasts; while Jenné, which was formerly considered as the country most plentifully supplied with this precious metal, has none except what is brought from this rich tract. See Caillié's "Travels through Central Africa to Timbuctoo." London, 1830. Vol. i. p. 284.

one only God that he would never again make war against
the Christians, but that they might travel safely through
his land and interchange their merchandise.

He also sent him some elephants' tusks, one of them
very large, which was carried by four negroes aboard
the ship. Gomez afterwards went to Batti Mansa's
abode, which was surrounded by many habitations made of
seaweed covered with straw, and remained there three
days. Batti Mansa gave him several parrots and six
ounces' skins, and ordered that an elephant should be
killed and its flesh carried on board the caravels.

Here Gomez learned the fact that it was Nomimansa,
the chief of that promontory, who had done all the mischief
that had been done to the Christians, and on this account
he stood in great dread of them. But Gomez took great
pains to make peace with him and sent him many
presents by his own men in his own canoes, which had
been despatched to fetch salt, which was plentiful there,
and of a red colour. When Gomez reached the mouth
of the river, Nomimansa several times sent men and
women to try whether he would do them any harm,
but he always gave them a friendly reception. When
the chief heard this, he came to the river side with a
great retinue, and sitting down on the bank, sent for
Gomez, who approached him in his best fashion with all
ceremonious respect. A Mahommedan sheikh then put
questions to Gomez respecting the God of the Christians, which he answered according to the best of his
understanding, and retorted with questions respecting
Mahomet. What Gomez said pleased the chief so much
that he ordered the sheikh to quit his dominions within
three days, and springing to his feet, declared no one, on
pain of death, should dare ever again to utter the name of

Mahomet, for that he only believed in the one only God, and that there was no other God but He, whom his brother, the Prince Henry, said that he believed in. Calling the Infant his brother, he desired that Gomez should baptize him, and so said also all his chiefs and his women likewise. He himself declared that he would have no other name than Henry, but his chiefs took other names, such as Jacob, Nuño, &c., as Christian names. Gomez remained that night on shore with Nomimansa and his chiefs, but did not venture to baptize them, because he was a layman.

On the next day, however, he invited the king, with his twelve principal chiefs and eight of his wives, to come to dine with him on board the caravel, which they all did unharmed, and he gave them fowls and meat cooked after the Portuguese fashion, and wine, both white and red, as much as they pleased to drink; and they said to each other that no nation was better than the Christians.

Afterwards, when they were on shore, he repeated his request that Gomez would baptize him; but he answered that he had not received authority from the supreme pontiff. He told him, however, that if he so desired, he would convey his wishes to the prince, who would send a priest to baptize them. He immediately dictated a letter to the prince requesting him to send a priest, to inform him respecting the faith, and begged the prince also to send him a falcon for hunting, for he wondered greatly when Gomez told him that the Christians carried a bird on the hand which caught other birds. He wished him besides to send two rams, and sheep, and ganders and geese, and a pig, as well as two men who would know how to construct houses and make a survey of his city. All these requirements Gomez promised that the prince would fulfil. At Gomez' departure he and all his people lamented, so great was the friendship which had sprung up between them.

Gomez then pursued his way to Portugal, and when nearing Cape Verde saw two canoes put out to sea. He sailed between them and the land, and came up to them, and in one of the canoes counted thirty-eight men. Meanwhile the interpreter came to him, and whispered, that that was Beseguiche, lord of that land, well known as a man of evil disposition. Gomez made them come into the caravel, gave them to eat and drink, and a double portion of presents, and pretending that he did not know the chief, said to him by way of trying him, "Is this the land of Beseguiche?" He said "Yes." Gomez replied, "Why is he then so malignant against the Christians? It would be better for him to make peace with them, and that both might interchange merchandise, and that he might have horses, &c., as Burbruck in Budomel, and other lords of the negroes did. Tell him that I have taken you in this sea, and for love of him have set you free to go on shore." He much rejoiced, and Gomez told them to go into their canoes, which they did, and as they all stood in their canoes, Gomez said to the chief, "Beseguiche, Beseguiche, do not think that I did not know thee. It was certainly in my power to do with thee whatever I wished, and since I have acted kindly by thee, do thou do likewise with our Christians," and so they went their way. They then sailed for Portugal, and came to Lagos, where the prince at that time was, who rejoiced greatly at their arrival.

It so happened that for two years no one went back to Guinea because King Alphonso was gone, with a fleet of three hundred and fifty-two ships, to Africa, and took the powerful city of Alcaçar El Seguer, for which reason the prince, being fully occupied, gave no attention to Guinea.

But after the prince's return Gomez reminded him of what King Nomimansa had said, so that he should send to him all those things which had been promised. This the prince did, and sent thither a relation of the cardinal's, the Abbot of Soto de Cassa, that he should remain with that chief and instruct him in the faith. The remainder of the Cape Verde Islands were soon after discovered by some mariners in the service of Prince Fernando, when they received their collective name from the cape off which they lay. The king ceded them to that prince on the 19th of September, 1462. The first colonized was Santiago.

CHAPTER XII.

THE DEATH OF PRINCE HENRY.

1457—1460.

At this time King Affonso, energetic and warlike, occupied himself with those conquests on the north coast of Africa which gained for him the surname of "the African."

In 1454 Constantinople fell into the hands of the Turks, and the pope summoned all the princes of Europe to a general crusade against the infidels. As King Affonso's limited exchequer would not enable him to contend against the Turks unless the pope's appeal were warmly responded to by other sovereigns; he declared his intention to proceed to Africa to avenge the injury done to Portugal by the Moors in the person of Prince Fernando. His first thought was to attack Tangier, but remembering its strength, and how much it had cost the Portuguese on a former occasion, he fixed on Alcaçar Seguer, as the place to be attacked.

On the 30th of September, 1458, Affonso sailed from Setuval with a fleet of ninety sail, and on the 3rd of October landed near Sagres, where Prince Henry gave him a magnificent reception. The fleet consisted of two hundred and twenty sail, and on the 16th of October twenty-five thousand men disembarked, though not without some opposition and loss, off Alcaçar. The artillery and implements for the siege were promptly landed, and that same evening the order was given to invest the town. A portion of the ramparts was soon broken down, and at midnight Prince Henry, having constructed a battery in a favourable position, brought to bear a large piece of ordnance, a few shots from which made a considerable breach in the wall. The Moors, who, it must be acknowledged, had hitherto offered a brave and troublesome resistance, were overcome with fear at this result, and sent to propose terms of surrender. Prince Henry replied that "the king's object was the service of God, and not to take their goods or force a ransom from them. All that he required was that they should withdraw with their wives and children and effects from the town, but leaving behind them all their Christian prisoners." They begged for time to reflect, which was prudently refused, with a threat that if the town had to be taken by main force, all would be put to the sword. On this the Moors submitted, and sent the king hostages for the suspension of the conflict.

On the morrow they withdrew from the city unmolested, under the prince's warrant for their safety. The Portuguese entered in triumph, the mosque was consecrated, and thanks were offered for the conquest. Duarte de Menezes was appointed governor of the place, and the king, who then assumed the title of Lord of Alcaçar, withdrew by sea to Ceuta.

In a short time the King of Fez brought a large force to lay siege to Alcaçar. Affonso had at first intended to march from Ceuta to the assistance of the place, but soon found that it was necessary to raise more men in Portugal, if he was effectually to relieve the besieged. A letter was shot into the town to tell the governor his plans, and an answer was shot back, saying that Menezes was failing in provisions and stores. This letter, which was written in French, unfortunately fell into the Moorish camp, and the King of Fez, availing himself of the condition of the Portuguese, offered favourable terms if the governor would surrender. Dom Duarte not only refused, but to show how little he feared the Moors, had the boldness to offer the king his scaling-ladders, if he chose to accept them. After some further attempts, the King of Fez withdrew for the purpose of raising fresh troops, and on the 13th of November returned with thirty thousand cavalry, and a vast force of infantry and artillery. The siege had now lasted fifty-three days, when, on the 2nd of January, 1459, the Moors were obliged to retire with immense loss. When Dom Duarte saw that the siege was about to be raised, he sent a message to the king, recommending him to try a little longer before he quite gave it up.

King Affonso now perceiving the advantage which would result from this place having a mole for the mooring of small craft, sent out twenty-six vessels, laden with materials, masons, and labourers. Dom Duarte commenced the construction of the mole on the 12th of March, and it was finished by the end of July, in spite of the continued hindrances offered by the Moors to the progress of the work.

We have no public act of Prince Henry to record between his return from Alcaçar and his death on Thursday, the 13th of November, 1460, with the exception of the donation, on the 18th September, 1460, of the ecclesiastical revenues of Porto Santo and Madeira to the Order of Christ, and of the temporality to the king and his successors.

We have already seen that he carried into effect the promises which had been made on his behalf to Nomimansa, the king of the Barbaçins, by his faithful navigator, Diogo Gomez. It would seem that that loyal servant was about his master's person at the time of his death, inasmuch as, by the king's command, he remained constantly near the prince's remains till they were removed from Lagos to their last resting-place in Batalha. It is therefore a satisfaction to be able to give the old sailor's own account of the matter in his own language.

"In the year of our Lord 1460," he says, "Prince Henry fell ill in his town on Cape St. Vincent, and of that sickness he died on Thursday, the 13th of November, of the same year. And the same night on which he died, they carried him to the church of St. Mary in Lagos, where he was buried with all honour. At that time King Affonso was in Evora, and he, together with all his people, mourned greatly over the death of so great a prince, when they considered all the expeditions which he had set on foot, and all the results which he had obtained from the land of Guinea, as well as how much he had laid out in continuous warlike armaments at sea against the Saracens in the cause of the Christian faith.

"At the close of the year King Affonso ordered me to be sent for, for, by the king's command, I had remained constantly in Lagos near the body of the prince, giving out whatever was necessary to the priests, who were occupied in constant vigils and in divine service in the church. And the king ordered that I should look and examine if the body of the prince was decomposed, for it was his wish to remove his remains to the most beautiful monastery called Santa Maria de Batalha, which his father, King João I., had built for the Order of Friars

Preachers. When I approached the body of the deceased, I found it dry and sound, except the tip of the nose, and I found him clothed in a rough shirt of horse-hair. Well doth the Church sing, 'Thou shalt not give thine holy one to see corruption.' That my Lord the Infant had remained a virgin till his death, and what and how many good things he had done in his life, it would be a long story for me to relate.

"The king then issued a command that his brother Dom Fernando, Duke of Beja, and the bishops and nobles should go and convey the body to the aforesaid monastery of Batalha, where the king would await its arrival.

"And the prince's body was placed in a large and most beautiful chapel which King João his father had built, and where lie the bodies of the king and his queen Philippa, the prince's mother, together with his five brothers, the memory of all of whom is worthy of praise for evermore. There may they rest in holy peace. Amen."

On the face of the tomb, on the south side of the Founder's Chapel,[1] which contains the mortal remains of Prince Henry, and which is in a line with those of his brothers, Dom Pedro, Dom João, and the Constant Prince, are three escutcheons. On the first are sculptured Prince Henry's own arms; on the second the cross,

[1] The following remark from the pen of our late distinguished ecclesiologist, Dr. Mason Neale, will give some notion of the beauty of the noble specimen of Christian architecture which King João erected at Batalha, and in which he and his family are entombed. He says, "It were worth all the trouble of a trip to Portugal for any one to come to Batalha to revel in the inexhaustible beauty of this superb monument of the taste of bygone days." It is not unlikely, from the friendly intercourse that existed between Portugal and England, that Don Manoel conceived the idea of imitating Henry VII.'s chapel in the Capella Imperfeita.

THE TOMB OF PRINCE HENRY.

In the Monastery of Patalha.

Page 183.

device, and motto of the Order of the Garter, the riband of which had been conferred on him by King Henry VI., in 1442-3,[2] and on the last the cross of the military order of Christ. Over the tomb is a recumbent statue of the prince in full armour, with a kind of turban bound round the head. This is protected by a sort of canopy worked in minute sculpture. On the frieze of the tomb, intertwined with ilex boughs, is the prince's well-known motto, " Talent de bien faire," and below the frieze, in a single line, the following inscription : " Aqui jaz o muito alto e muito honrado senhor o Ifante dom anrique governador da ordem da cavallaria de no . . . . . . om Joham e rainha philipa, que aquy jazem nesta capella cuias almas deos por sua mercee aja o qual se finou em . . . . . . na era de mil e . . . . . ." The first of the gaps here marked has arisen from a fault in the stone. The other two, which should contain the date, seem to show that the tomb was prepared during the prince's lifetime, and that, after his death, the day, month, and year of his decease were neglected to be inserted.

The following is Azurara's description of Prince Henry :—" He was large of frame and brawny, and stout and strong of limb. His naturally fair complexion had by constant toil and exposure become dark. The expression of his face at first sight inspired fear in those who were not accustomed to him, and when he was angry, which rarely happened, his look was very formidable. Stout of heart and keen in intellect, he was extraordinarily ambitious of achieving great deeds. Neither luxury nor avarice ever found a home with him. In the

[2] His Excellency the late Count de Lavradio informed me that he had traced the identical collar of Prince Henry to its then holder as a Knight of the Order, the late Earl of Clarendon.

former respect he was so temperate that after his early youth he abstained from wine altogether, while the whole of his life was reputed to have been passed in inviolate chastity. As for his generosity, the household of no other uncrowned prince formed so large and excellent a training school for the young nobility of the country. All the worthies of the kingdom, and still more foreigners of renown, found a general welcome in his house, and there were frequently assembled in it men of various nations, the diversity of whose habits presented a curious spectacle. None left that house without some proof of the prince's generosity. His self-discipline was unsurpassed; all his days were spent in hard work, and it would not readily be believed how often he passed the night without sleep, so that by dint of unflagging industry he conquered what seemed to be impossibilities to other men. His wisdom and thoughtfulness, excellent memory, calm bearing, and courteous language, gave great dignity to his address.

"He was constant in adversity, and humble in prosperity, and it was impossible for any subject of any rank to show more obedience and reverence to the sovereign. This was especially noticeable in his conduct to his nephew Don Affonso, even at the beginning of his reign. He never entertained hatred or ill-will towards any, however serious the offence they might have committed against him. So great was his benignity in this respect, that the wise-acres said that he was deficient in retributive justice, although in other matters he was very impartial. No stronger example of this could be shown than his forgiveness of some of his soldiers who deserted him in the attack on Tangier, when he was in the utmost danger. He was devoted to the public interests of the kingdom, and took great pleasure in trying new plans for the general welfare at his own expense. He gloried in feats of arms against the enemies of the Faith, but earnestly sought peace with all Christians. He was universally beloved, for he did good to all and injured none. He never failed to show due respect to every person, however humble, without lowering his own dignity. A foul or indecent word was never known to issue from his lips.

"He was very obedient to all the commands of Holy Church, and attended all its offices with great devotion, and they were celebrated with as much solemnity and ceremony in his own chapel as they could be in any cathedral church. He held all sacred things in profound reverence, and took delight in showing honour and kindness to all who ministered in them. Nearly one half of the year he passed in fasting, and the hands of the poor never went empty away from his presence. His heart never knew what fear was, except the fear of committing sin. Assuredly," continues Azurara, " I know not where to look for a prince that shall bear comparison with this one."

Such was the exalted character of the man whom we honour as the *originator of continuous modern discovery*. In the prefatory chapter to this work, where the prince's purpose was spoken of, a passing allusion was made to his dignity as the son of a king, and there was an especial object in the mention of that reality. All modern discovery found its origin in one great event— the rise of the powers which bordered on the Atlantic; and this rise, although slow, was identical with the strengthening of the respective monarchies. At the close of the middle ages, the kings were, in all these countries, the real centres of their nations, whilst in the "Roman Empire" many contending claims existed, but no general government. This difference had long been in favour of the East as far as commerce and navigation were concerned. But now the balance began to turn to the other side. The Hanseatic confederacy, powerful as it might be, was but a confederacy; and Venice, however magnificent, was but a city. The really modern states of Western Europe had the germs of quite another force and power within them.

The first discoveries of the Portuguese were originated by that exuberant regal power which was free to leave the paternal realms, and to extend itself beyond the Mediterranean in wars against the infidels. This movement also received a new intensity by the emigration of the able seamen of Italy, Germany, and the Netherlands to the rising states along the Atlantic. Under the liberal inducements of Prince Henry, men of these three nations held prominent positions in the early naval exploits of the Portuguese. But not Portugal only rose by their talents; the newly united kingdoms of Castile and Aragon, England, and France received with avidity the offers of service of the most gifted men of those nations which had held the sway of the sea.

It is a notable fact, and one that greatly redounds to the honour of Italy, that the three Powers, which at this day possess almost all America, owe their first discoveries to the Italians: Spain to Columbus, a Genoese; England, to the Cabots, Venetians; and France, to Verazzano, a Florentine: a circumstance which sufficiently proves, that in those times no nation was equal to the Italians in point of maritime knowledge and extensive experience in navigation.

It is, however, remarkable, that the Italians, with all their knowledge and experience, have not been able to acquire one inch of ground for themselves in America, a failure which may be ascribed to the penurious mercantile spirit of the Italian republics, to their mutual animosities and petty wars, and to their contracted and selfish policy.

Indeed, it may be said that it was principally to the efforts of Italians and Hanseatics that the dominion of the waters was lost to Italy and the Hanse Towns, and passed to the nations of the West. Nor can this be deplored or ascribed to ingratitude; the new regal powers, such as Portugal, disposed of better means to carry out extensive plans of discovery, to make the first and necessary sacrifices, and to pursue one purpose, with that unremitting earnestness which is so seldom found in republics. Nor were they inapt pupils in the practical development of nautical knowledge. Cadamosto, himself a Venetian, and well acquainted with the progress of navigation in the Mediterranean, declares that the caravels of Portugal were the best sailing ships afloat.

Furthermore, their geographical situation along the Atlantic made them also, beyond comparison, fitter for these endeavours than the old masters of what are merely inland waters compared with the mighty oceanic seas. Nevertheless for the prosecution of these endeavours the knowledge of the latter was of the utmost value.

During the long period in which Prince Henry was continuing his maritime explorations he did not cease to cultivate the science of cartography. In this he was warmly seconded by his nephew King Affonso V. We have, unfortunately, nothing to show as the result of the cartographical labours of the geographer Mestre Jayme, whom the prince had procured from Majorca, to superintend his school of navigation and astronomy at Sagres, whither he had also brought together the most able Arab and Jewish mathematicians that he could obtain from Morocco or the Peninsula; but at his instance the king caused to be made in Venice the finest specimen of mediæval map-making that the world has ever produced, and which exists at the present day. The discovery that beyond Cape Verde the coast trended eastward, inspired the king with new energy, for he assumed therefrom that it would soon lead to India. He thought it possible that in that direction the meridian of Tunis, and perhaps even that of Alexandria, had been already passed. He gave names to rivers, gulfs, capes, and harbours in the new discovery, and sent to Venice draughts of maps on which these were laid down, with a commission for the construction of a mappemonde on which they should be portrayed.

It was to the Venetian Fra Mauro of the Camaldolese Convent of San Miguèl de Murano, that this commission was entrusted. King Affonso V. spared no expense, and Fra Mauro paid the draughtsmen from twelve to fifteen sous a day, while from 1457 to 1459 he himself gave all possible pains to perfecting his task. The practised draughtsman Andrea Bianco was called to take a part in its execution. At length this magnificent specimen of mediæval cartography was completed, and by desire of the king despatched to Portugal, in charge of the noble Venetian Stefano Trevigiano, on the 24th April, 1459. In the same year, on the 20th of October, the drawings and writings, and a copy of the mappemonde, were enclosed in a chest and sent to the abbot of the convent, from which it would seem that Fra Mauro was then dead. It is to be presumed that while elaborating the mappemonde for King Affonso he made at the same time a copy which he intended to leave to the convent. In the convent library still exists the register of Receipts and Expenditure of the convent, written by the Abbot, afterwards Cardinal, Maffei Gerard, in which is a note of the current cost of the map.[3]

On this map, which preceded by forty years the rounding of the Cape of Good Hope by Vasco da Gama, we see clearly laid down the southern extremity of Africa, under the name of "Cavo di Diab." North-east of Cavo di Diab, are inscribed the names of "Soffala" and "Xengibar." This southern extremity is separated from the continent by a narrow strait. An inscription on Cape Diab states that in 1420 an Indian junk from the East doubled the Cape in search of the islands of men and women (separately inhabited by each), and after a sail of two thousand miles in forty days, during which they saw nothing but sea and sky, they turned back, and in seventy days' sailing reached Cavo di Diab, where the sailors found on the shore an egg as big as a barrel, which they recognized as that of the bird Crocho, doubtless the roc or rukh of Marco Polo, a native bird of Madagascar.

It is matter of history that the Arabs who traded on the east coast of Africa were prevented, by the force of

---

[3] A photograph copy of this planisphere, of the size of the original, and the finest existing, having been made by Signor Naya, of Venice, under the express supervision of my friend Mr. Rawdon Brown, is now in the Department of Maps and Charts in the British Museum.

the current, from venturing southward of the Cape, afterwards named by the Portuguese the Cabo dos Corrientes. It could only, therefore, be by communication with the natives, or from some daring expedition such as that recounted by Fra Mauro, that the form of the southern extremity of Africa could have been learned. The Indian junk, after being carried westward by the Great Lagulhas stream, might, after passing forty days in the Atlantic, return by the southern connecting current, which, reinforced by the west wind in more southern latitudes (between 37° and 40°), brings back a portion of the waters of the Atlantic eastward into the Indian Ocean.

It is more remarkable that the Camaldolese geographer makes no mention of the sources from which he derived his information. He does not mention the names of the most renowned voyagers, not even that of his own countryman, Cadamosto, whose recent discoveries he was made acquainted with by direct communication. The unfortunate Doge, Francesco Foscari, states in a letter that "when he considered the success of Cadamosto's voyage, and witnessed the plan and commencement of Mauro's work, he trusted that Prince Henry would therein find new inducements to continue his explorations." But the sums expended by the prince on his maritime expeditions were so large, that not only were his own revenues exhausted, as well as the profits derived from commerce with the African coast, but he died heavily involved in debts, which were partly paid by his nephew and adopted son, Dom Fernando, and partly by Dom Manoel, the son of Fernando, while Duke of Beja. The Duke of Braganza, Dom Fernando I., in a declaration or codicil, dated 8th of November, 1449, declares that Prince Henry owed him, in 1448, nineteen thousand three hundred and ninety-four and a-half golden crowns, somewhat under £70,000, for the payment of which he had pledged his lands and goods, and in his will the duke states that this debt was further increased by sixteen thousand and eighty-four golden crowns, nearly £60,000 more.

But we have already seen that the prince did not confine his expenditure or his patronage to the development of geographical knowledge. Having already in 1431 purchased residences for the University of Lisbon, which had previously been obliged to rent its house-room, he, by a deed dated 25th March, 1448, established the chair of Theology in that University, and subsequently confirmed it by a charter dated from the Villa do Infante, at Sagres, the 22nd of September, 1460. He ordered that every Christmas-day twelve silver marks should be given to the lecturer in that science out of the tithes of the island of Madeira. These important services gained for him the honourable designation of *Protector of the studies of Portugal*, in like manner as the maritime expeditions won for him the epithet of the Navigator.

On 24th of July, 1840, in the reign of Dona Maria II., at the instance of His Excellency the late Marquis de Sá da Bandeira, then Minister of Marine and since Prime Minister of Portugal, a monument to Prince Henry, prepared in 1839, was finally erected at Sagres.

The monument consists of one piece of marble, twelve palms and a half high, embedded in the wall over the inner gate of the principal entrance of the fort of Sagres. On the upper part of the monument is sculptured, in semi-relief, the escutcheon of the prince, with an armillary sphere on the right, and a ship in full sail on the left. The lower part of the monument contains two panels with an inscription on the one below the sphere in Latin, and another on the one below the ship in Portuguese, of which the following is a translation :—

SACRED FOR EVER.

IN THIS PLACE

the Great Prince Henry, son of John I., King of Portugal, having undertaken to discover the previously unknown regions of West Africa, and also to open a way by the circumnavigation of Africa to the remotest parts of the East, established at its own cost his Royal Palace, the famous School of Cosmography, the Astronomical Observatory, and the Naval Arsenal, preserving, improving, and enlarging the same till the close of his life with admirable energy and perseverance, and to the greatest benefit of the kingdom, of literature, of religion, and of the whole human race. After reaching by his expeditions the eighth degree of north latitude, and discovering and planting Portuguese Colonies in many islands of the Atlantic, this great Prince died on the 13th of November, 1460. Three hundred and seventy-nine years after his death, Maria II., Queen of Portugal and the Algarves, commanded that this monument should be erected to the memory of the illustrious Prince, her kinsman, the Viscount de Sá da Bandeira being Minister of Marine. 1839.

To the kindness of His Excellency the Marquis de Sá da Bandeira, I am indebted for the accompanying plan of the promontory of Sagres, which was taken at the time by Captain Lourenço Germack Possollo, to whose able management the erection of the monument was entrusted.

On this plan will be seen the site of the present small fort, which was erected in 1793, and the traces of the few ancient walls and ruins that remain. The hard granite rock of which the promontory consists is hollowed out at

PLAN OF THE FORT AND PROMONTORY OF SAGRES.

Taken by Captain Lourenço Germack Possollo on the occasion of the erection of a Monument to Prince Henry in July 1840, under the auspices of his Excellency the Viscount (now Marquis) de Sá da Bandeira, then Minister of Marine, by whom the Copy from which the present reduction is made was kindly communicated to the Author.

Copied in the "Archivo Militar" by J. C. Bou de Souza in 1863.

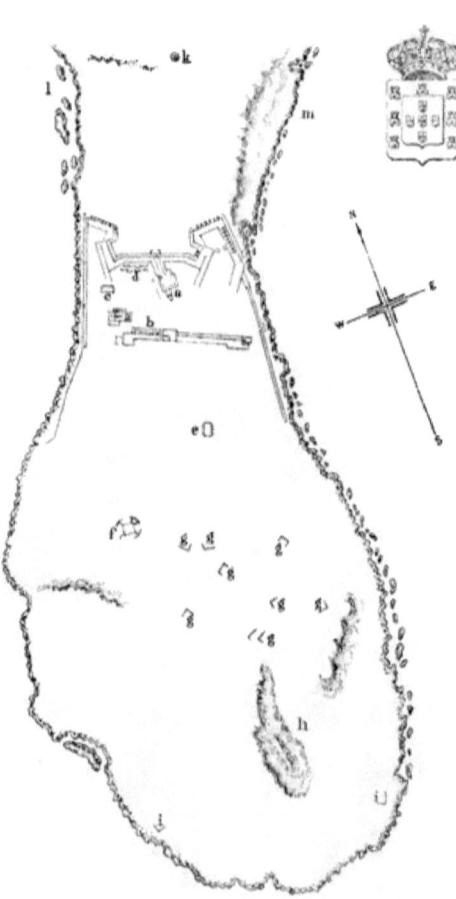

REFERENCES.

a Tower now serving as a hay-loft, below which is the entrance to the Forts and in which above the doorway inside is placed the Monument to the Prince.

b Old walls brought into the Construction of the new residences

c Remains of the original Mother Church.

d Remains of the Barracks destroyed in 1750.

e St. Leo.

f Powder Magazine built on the ruins of a circular edifice probably the Observatory built by Prince Henry.

g g Traces of walls entirely razed to the ground.

h An excessively deep Cavern communicating with the Sea.

i i Batteries at the edge of the Promontory.

k A Pedestal on which formerly stood a Cross. It is here that the Promontory commences.

l Bay of Beliche

m Bay of Sagres.

Scale of Half an English Mile.

its base into a natural arch, and there are holes worn through to the surface, through which in time of storms from the south-west, the sea drives the air with terrific force, and expels to a considerable height any objects which may be in the way. On some occasions the sea-water is driven through these holes in great quantity, and falls down on the surface of the earth in the form of rain. This salt-water shower, which will sometimes extend to a distance of nearly two miles, goes far to destroy the very few traces of vegetation which are to be found on this desolate and sterile spot.

CHAPTER XIII.

THE STORMY CAPE.

1460—1487.

The death of Prince Henry produced the effect that might have been expected. The progress of discovery received for the time a check when the presiding genius was removed from the scene of action. In the main the tendencies of King Affonso were rather towards conquest in Mauritania, and the support of his pretensions to the throne of Castile, than to the prosecution of discoveries on the west coast of Africa. Nevertheless the " talent de bien faire " had left behind it its impress in its example and its benefits, and we are not without something to record in the way of discovery, between the death of the prince in 1460, and that of his nephew, King Affonso V., in 1481. Indeed in the year following the death of the prince, the king was induced, by the great traffic in gold at the island of Arguin, to build a fort there to insure its safety. Its construction and commandership were committed to Soeiro Mendez, a gentleman of his household, to whom and to his heirs the king, by deed of July 26th, 1464, made a grant of the governorship-in-chief of the fortress.

Cadamosto had reached the Rio Grande, and from his pen we have an account of the exploration of more than six hundred miles yet further south by a gentleman of the king's household, named Pedro de Cintra, whom the king sent out in 1461-62 in command of two armed caravels. De Cintra first went to the two large inhabited islands, the Bissagos, discovered by Cadamosto in his second voyage, at the mouth of the Rio Grande, on one of which they landed. In the miserable straw-thatched hovels in the interior they found some wooden figures, which led them to think that the blacks were idolaters, but as they were unable to hold any conversation with them, they returned to the ship and proceeded on their voyage. After sailing forty miles, they reached the mouth of a large river, about three or four miles in breadth, called Beseque, from the name of the chief who lived at its mouth. A hundred and forty miles further on they came to a cape, which they called Cape Verga. The hills were lofty, and eighty miles beyond they came to another cape, which the sailors all agreed was the highest they had ever seen. It was covered with beautiful green trees, and had at its summit a point shaped like a diamond. In honour of Prince Henry, and in remembrance of his residence at Cape Sagres, the Portuguese gave it the name of "Cape Sagres of Guinea." The people worshipped wooden images in the shape of men, to which at meal-times they offered food. They were tawny rather than black, and had figures branded on their faces and bodies. They had no clothes, but simply wore pieces of the bark of trees in front of them. They had no arms, for they had no iron in their country. They lived on rice, honey, and vegetables, such as beans and kidney-beans, of a finer and larger kind than those of Europe. They had also beef and goats' flesh, but in no great abundance. Near the cape were two little islands, one about six miles distant, the other eight, but too small to be inhabited.

They were thickly covered with trees. On the adjacent river, the Pongas, the natives used very large canoes, each carrying from thirty to forty men, who rowed standing, without rowlocks. They had their ears pierced with holes all round, and wore in them a variety of gold rings. Both the men and women had the cartilage of their noses pierced and a ring passed through it, like the buffaloes in Italy; but these they took off when they ate.

About forty miles beyond Cape Sagres they found another river, which they called the San Vicente, about four miles broad at the mouth, and some five miles further they came to another river, called Rio Verde, yet broader at the mouth than the San Vicente. The country and coast were very mountainous, but there was good anchorage everywhere. Four-and-twenty miles from this cape was another, which they called Cape Ledo, or "Joyous," on account of the beauty and verdure of the country. Further on was a lofty mountain range extending fifty miles, covered with fine trees, at the end of which, at about eight miles out at sea, were three little islands, the largest about ten or twelve miles in circumference. These they called the Selvagens, and the mountain they called Sierra Leona, on account of the roaring of the thunder, which was constantly being heard on its cloud-enveloped summit.

Thirty miles beyond Sierra Leona they found a large river, three miles broad at its mouth. They called it Rio Roxo, or Red River, because passing through a red soil, it assumed that colour. Beyond was a cape, also of red colour, which they named Cabo Roxo; and about eight miles out to sea, an uninhabited island, which for the same reason they called Ilha Roxa. From this island (which is about ten miles from the Rio Roxo) the north star seemed to be about the height of a man above the sea. Beyond Cabo Roxo they discovered a gulf, into which flowed a river, and this they named Santa Maria das Neves,[1] "St. Mary of the Snows." They saw it on the 2nd of July, the visitation of the Blessed Virgin. On the other side of the river was a point, and opposite that, a little way out at sea, a small island. The gulf was full of sandbanks, running ten or twelve miles along the coast. The sea broke here with great violence, and there was a very powerful current, both at the ebb and flow of the tide. They called this island Ilha dos Bancos, on account of these sandbanks.

Twenty-four miles beyond this island was a great cape, which they called Cabo de Santa Anna, because it was discovered on St. Anne's day, the 26th of July. Sixty miles beyond they found another river, which they called Rio das Palmas, on account of the many palms which grew on its banks; but its mouth, though of considerable breadth, was full of sandbanks, which made it very dangerous. This was the character of the coast the whole distance between Cabo de Santa Anna and this river. About sixty miles further they discovered another small river, which they called Rio dos Fumos, because when they discovered it they could see nothing on land but smoke. Four-and-twenty miles beyond this river, they discovered a cape jutting out into the sea, which they called Cabo del Monte, because beyond it they saw a very lofty mountain. Coasting thence for sixty miles, they saw another small cape, not very high, but similarly capped by a hill. This they called Cabo Mesu-

[1] There would appear to be some blunder here, as the feast of St. Mary of the Snows is on the 5th of August, which would not accord with the chronology of the voyage.

rado. Here they observed a great number of fires, lighted by the blacks in consequence of their getting sight of the ships, the like of which they had never seen before. Sixteen miles beyond this cape, there was a wood of fine trees, reaching down to the sea. This they called the Bosque de Santa Maria, or St. Mary's Grove.

The caravels came to anchor beyond this wood, but no sooner had they arrived than some little canoes, with two or three naked men in each, came towards them, some of them having the remains of what seemed to be human teeth hanging on their necks. One of them they captured in order to bring him into communication with other blacks in Portugal, that they might gain information respecting his country, but nothing of importance could be gathered from him. He was subsequently sent back to his own country with clothes and other presents. Cadamosto informs us that no other ship had returned from that coast up to the period of his departure from the Peninsula, on the 1st of February, 1463.

In 1469, King Affonso V. rented the trade of the African coast to Fernam Gomez, for five hundred cruzados a year, for five years, reserving the ivory trade only to the crown, and stipulating for the discovery of a hundred leagues of coast annually. This stipulated exploration was to commence at Sierra Leona, the point reached by Pedro de Cintra and Sociro da Costa, who were the latest previous discoverers. The latter, who had already distinguished himself as one of the first explorers from Lagos, subsequently discovered the river which received his name, but which is now known as the Great Bassam or Assinie River. The explorers selected by Fernam Gomez were João de Santarem, and Pedro de Escobar, both knights of the king's household.

The pilots were Martin Fernandez and Alvaro Esteves, the latter having at that time the highest repute as a navigator in the whole kingdom.

In 1470, they discovered the coast afterwards named La Mina, where so large a trade in gold-dust was carried on, and, as is generally believed, had managed to run along the whole of the coast of the kingdom of Benin, and on the 21st of December, St. Thomas's Day, sighted a lofty island covered with wood, to which they gave the name of that apostle. On the 1st of January, 1471, they are supposed to have come upon a smaller island, to which they gave the name of Anno Bom, or Good Year, in memory of the happy omen that it was discovered on New Year's Day. And in truth a good year it was, for in that same month of January they made the first traffic in gold on the Gold Coast, in the village of Sama, between Cape Three Points and La Mina, whither they were carried by the currents and breezes from the South, after having sighted the terra firma of Cape Lopo Gonsalves. In this same voyage they discovered the Ilha do Principe, and as they originally gave the island the name of Santo Antão, or Saint Anthony, we may infer that it was discovered on the 17th of January, which is the day of that saint's commemoration. It afterwards received the name of Ilha do Principe, because the king's eldest son had assigned to him, as his appanage, the duty on the sugars grown in the island. It is also supposed, but is not quite certain, that the Ilha Formosa, or Beautiful island, discovered by Fernam do Pó, a gentleman of the king's household, whose name it afterwards received, was discovered in this voyage. It will have been noticed that in previous voyages, when islands at a distance from the mainland, as for example

Porto Santo and the Cape Verde Islands, had been discovered, it had been through the vessels being driven on them by storms; but in the present case we have islands, one, S. Thomé, more than fifty, the other, Annobon, more than eighty leagues distant from the mainland, discovered without the interference of any storm whatever, of which we are informed. The reasonable inference seems to be that the navigators used their newly-improved nautical instruments to good purpose, and were able to leave the coast with impunity, which their predecessors were not in the position to do, for want of being able to take the altitude. In this same year 1471, *for the first time within the memory or even the knowledge of man the equinoctial line was crossed from North to South.* As Cape Lopo Gonsalvez, now Cape Lopez, was the first locality, south of the equator, to have a geographical name attached to it, it may fairly be inferred that this was the name of the navigator who first crossed the line.

The last of the explorers, during the reign of King Affonso V., was a knight of his household named Sequeira, who discovered Cape St. Catherine, two degrees south of the equator.

Fernam Gomez acquired great wealth by this traffic, so that he was able to render good service to the king in his wars in Morocco. When his contract expired in 1474, the king conferred on him a coat-of-arms argent, three negroes' heads collared or, and with rings in their noses and ears. He also gave him the surname of Mina, in commemoration of his important discovery.

On the death of Affonso V., his son and successor, João II., entered with zeal into the views of his predecessors and of his great uncle Prince Henry. Before he came to the throne, a part of his revenues had been derived from the African trade, and the fisheries connected therewith, so that he had every inducement to prosecute its extension. With this view he not only ordered the completion of the fort of Arguin, which had been commenced years before, but resolved on the construction of another, on a larger scale, at S. Jorge da Mina. The gold traffic had at first been carried on at a place called Saama, discovered in 1472, by João de Santarem and Pedro de Escover, in the service of Fernam Gomez, already mentioned; but San Jorge de Mina was now selected for its superior convenience.

That the fort might be constructed the most expeditiously, both for preventing objections and saving his people from exposure to the dangers of the climate, the king took the precaution to have the stones cut and fashioned in Portugal. With these, and bricks, and wood, and other needful materials, he loaded ten caravels and two smaller craft. He sent out also provisions sufficient for six hundred men, one hundred of whom were officers to superintend the work. The command of this fleet was given to Diogo de Azambuja.

It set sail on the 11th December, 1481, and stopping only to conclude a favourable treaty with Bezeguiche, already mentioned, they reached La Mina on the 19th of January, 1482. On the following morning they suspended the banner of Portugal from the bough of a lofty tree, at the foot of which they erected an altar, and the whole company assisted at the first mass that was celebrated in Guinea, and prayed for the conversion of the natives from idolatry, and the perpetual prosperity of the church which they intended to erect upon the spot.

By good luck they found there a small Portuguese

vessel, the captain of which, João Bernardes, was engaged in traffic with the natives, and him they made interpreter between Caramansa, the chief of the place, and Azambuja. The interview took place with the greatest ostentation possible on both sides, a kind of rivalry in which, as may be supposed, the negro prince had a very sorry chance of producing any very imposing effect. Azambuja appeared in a tunic of brocade, with a collar of gold and precious stones, and his captains were all in gala attire, while Caramansa, who was no less ambitious of making a good display, was habited, like the rest of his people, in the best vestments with which nature had provided them. With their skins anointed and glistening till their native blackness was made blacker still, they considered their toilette perfect, although their only garment was an apron of monkeys' skin or palm leaves. To this extreme simplicity, however, Caramansa himself was in so far an exception that his arms and legs were adorned with bracelets and rings of gold, and round his neck was a collar from which hung small bells, and some sprigs of gold were twisted into his beard, so that the curls were straightened by the weight.

Azambuja then addressed the chieftain in the name of King João, commending to him the Christian religion, and promising that if he would recognize it and be baptized, the King of Portugal would regard him as a brother, and make with him an alliance, offensive and defensive, against their common enemies, and enter into a treaty for the interchange of the products of their respective countries. With this view he proposed, with the chieftain's permission, to found a permanent establishment in his country which should serve as a place of security against their enemies, as a refuge to the Portuguese who visited the coast, and also as a storehouse for their merchandise. Caramansa, who was very shrewd for a negro, after some hesitation, gave his consent. On the following day Azambuja put the work in hand, but no sooner was it commenced than the negroes showed signs of an intention to interrupt it. Fortunately mischief was prevented by Azambuja's learning that this arose from displeasure that the requisite presents had not as yet been offered to the chieftain. The oversight was soon remedied, and the work was set about with so much activity that in twenty days the fort was in a condition to repel an attack. Azambuja also built a church on the site where on his arrival he had erected an altar. Both the church and the fort were dedicated to St. George. In the former, a daily mass was established in perpetuity for the soul of Prince Henry, and to the latter the king conceded the privileges of a municipality. Azambuja took up his abode there, with a garrison of sixty men, and sent back the rest to Portugal with gold and slaves and other articles of merchandise.

Hitherto the Portuguese in making their explorations had contented themselves by setting up crosses by way of taking formal possession of any country; but these crosses soon disappeared, and the object in setting them up was frustrated. They would also carve on trees the motto of Prince Henry, "Talent de bien faire," together with the name which they gave to the newly-discovered land. In the reign of King João, however, they began to erect stone pillars surmounted by a cross. These pillars, which were designed by the king, were fourteen or fifteen hands high, with the royal arms sculptured in front, and on the sides were inscribed the names of the king and of the discoverer, as well as the date of the discovery, in Latin and Portuguese. These pillars were called Padrãos.

In 1484, Diogo Cam, a knight of the king's household, carried out with him one of these stone pillars, and passing Cape St. Catherine, the last point discovered in the reign of King Affonso, reached the mouth of a mighty river, on the south side of which he set up the pillar, and accordingly called the river the Rio do Padrão. The natives called it Zaire. It was afterwards named the Congo, from the country through which it flowed. Diogo Cam ascended the river to a little distance, and fell in with a great number of natives, who were very peacefully inclined, but although he had interpreters of several of the African languages, none of them could make themselves understood. He accordingly determined to take some of the natives back with him to Portugal, that they might learn the Portuguese language and act as interpreters for the future. This was easily managed, and without any violence, by sending Portuguese hostages to the King of Congo, with a promise that in fifteen months the negroes should be restored to their country. He took with him four of the natives, and on the voyage they learned enough Portuguese to enable them to give a fair account of their own country and of those which lay to the south of it. King João was greatly gratified, and treated the negroes with much kindness and even munificence, and when Diogo Cam took them back the following year, the king charged them with many presents for their own sovereign, accompanied by the earnest desire that he and his people would embrace the Christian religion. Up to the year 1485, João II. used the title of King of Por-

tugal and the Algarves on this side the sea and beyond
the sea in Africa,[2] but in this year he added thereto that
of Lord of Guinea.

In this remarkable voyage Diogo Cam was accompanied by the celebrated Martin Behaim, the inventor of
the application of the astrolabe to navigation, of whom
we have already had to speak.

As Diogo Cam had faithfully fulfilled his promise to
return with his charges to Congo within the fifteen
months, he was received with great welcome by the natives,
and by their king. He then proceeded further south,
and planted two pillars surmounted by crosses, one
named St. Augustine, in 15° 50′ south, and the other at
a point which they called the Manga das Areas, or Sleeve
of Sands, in 22°, now called Cape Cross by the English.
The cross is still in good preservation, only part of one
of the arms being gone. It is here that the country of
the Cimbebas terminates, and that of the Hottentots
begins. Cam thus traversed more than two hundred
leagues beyond the Congo, landing occasionally, and
taking some of the natives for the sake of the language.

On his return he was received by the King of Congo
with marked affection, and had the happiness of inspiring
him with a great desire to receive instruction in the tenets
of the Christian religion. For this purpose, he not only
requested that priests might be sent out from Portugal,
but he himself despatched one of his own subjects, named
Caçuta, with some youths to urge this request. On their
arrival, the king and queen stood sponsors for Caçuta,
who received the king's name of João for his Christian

---

[2] This arose from the name of Algarb being given by the Moors to the
Prince of Fez, while the southernmost province of Portugal bore the same
name.

name, with the surname of Silva, from his other godfather Ayres da Silva, the king's chamberlain. The whole of the little embassy were baptized before their return to Africa, in the year 1490, and thus originated the diffusion of Christianity in those benighted countries.

The expedition which took them back consisted of three ships under the command of Gonzalo de Sousa, but this commander died at Cape Verde, and was succeeded by his nephew Ruy de Sousa. On their arrival in Congo, they were warmly received by an aged uncle of the king, named Mani Sono, who very soon received baptism, and was named Manuel. His son was also baptized, and took the name of Antonio. This was the first baptism that was administered in those heathen countries. It took place on Easter-day, the 3rd of April, 1491. Twenty-five thousand men were present at the ceremony. The king was fifty leagues away at the time, but when he heard of it he testified his approval by bestowing on his uncle a large increase of territory, and he ordered the idols to be destroyed throughout his dominions. Indeed, so zealous was he for the maintenance of reverence for everything sacred, that on one occasion when some of his people made a disturbance at the door of the church which the Portuguese had constructed of boughs, he would have had them put to death but for the intercession of the priests. The king's residence was at Ambasse Congo, about twenty leagues from the sea-coast, where he received Ruy de Sousa. When at two leagues from the city he was met by a chieftain, accompanied by a great host of men formed in procession, who to the noise of trumpets and kettle-drums, barbarously constructed, sang the praises of the King of Portugal, three or four singing a verse, and the whole body joining in the chorus. The king sat on a throne of ivory, raised on a lofty wooden platform, so that he could be seen from all sides. From his waist upwards, his black and glittering skin was uncovered. Below that he wore a piece of damask which had been given him by Diogo Cam. On his left arm was a bracelet of copper, and from the shoulder hung a dressed horse's tail, which was a symbol of royalty. He had a cap on his head resembling a mitre, made of palm leaves so skilfully that it had the appearance of stamped velvet. Ruy de Sousa made his obeisance to him in the Portuguese fashion, which the king returned in his; that is, he put his right hand on the ground as if to take up dust; he then passed his hand first over Sousa's breast, and then over his own, which was the greatest courtesy he could show him. He not only gave permission to build a church, but ordered one of his chieftains to provide materials and labourers, so that no time might be lost. The first stone was laid on the 3rd of May, and the work proceeded so rapidly that the church was completed on the 1st of June. It was dedicated to the Holy Cross, and afterwards became the Cathedral Church of a bishopric. The king himself received baptism in presence of a hundred thousand men, who were brought together both by curiosity and the preparations for a war with some rebels, who had done great mischief in his territory. He took the name of João, and the queen that of Leonora, from the Portuguese sovereigns. After the ceremony he proceeded to the battle, and with more than eighty thousand men in the field, won an easy victory over the rebels. When they returned the king's eldest son was baptized, and took the name of Affonso.

The king's second son, however, named Panso Aquitimo, not only rejected the Christian religion, but excited others to do the same. One great ground of dissatisfaction was that the Church forbad them to have more than one wife, and at this the king himself took offence, and relaxed from his original fervour, even so far as to leave the crown to his second son, to the prejudice of the eldest. At the death of the old king, however, Affonzo recovered his right by force, and, firm to the religion of his adoption, zealously developed the Christian faith throughout his dominions, and sent his children and grand-children to Portugal to be educated, and two of these young princes afterwards received consecration as bishops.

In the course of a century from this time, the Portuguese having become well established in Congo, we find one of their countrymen, Duarte Lopes, going on a mission from the King of Congo to Pope Sixtus V. and Philip II., King of Spain and Portugal, for the purpose of representing the deplorable condition of Christianity in the country at that time, and begging for missionaries. In Rome Lopes recounted by command of the pope to Felipe Pigafetta, his Holiness' chamberlain, all that he had learned from his countrymen during the nine years he had been in Africa (1578-87), and this narrative, under the title of "Description of the kingdom of Congo," was published by Pigafetta at Rome, in 1591, 4to. In this rare work is a map, of which is a reduction annexed, showing that the two great equatorial lakes, Victoria Nyanza and Albert Nyanza, with their possible southern feeder, Lake Tanganyika, the positive existence of which has only been made known to us in recent years by our noble explorers, Burton, Speke and Grant, Sir Samuel Baker, &c., were actually laid down and described from information gathered in Africa by a Portuguese three hundred years ago. But though so laid down and described, these three

MAP
(DATE OF 1578-1587)
Showing the
EQUATORIAL LAKES
VICTORIA & ALBERT NYANZA,
the latter fed by
LAKE TANGANYIKA,
AS DELINEATED IN
DUARTE LOPEZ'
"CONGO"
Edited by F. Pigafetta,
ROME 1591.

great facts, of such vital importance to the question of
the discovery of the sources of the Nile, slept and
remained unrepeated by geographers during all those
centuries, until our brave adventurers unfolded the truth
from absolute personal observation.

The single fact of the map exhibiting, as none of its
predecessors or successors had done, these three important
lakes so recently discovered, would be sufficient to justify
us in hoping for enlightenment on points which have not
yet been established by satisfactory modern observation,
and, in fact, vague and strange as its delineation will
appear to eyes accustomed to more systematic cartography, it does contain several other items of information
which have been wanting in subsequent maps, until they
had become matters of fact substantiated by recent
explorations.

On it is laid down for the first time the great empire
of Monomoezi, or Uniamuezi, occupying in a remarkably
striking manner a position between the easternmost of
the two equatorial lakes and another vast lake to the
south-west, exactly corresponding with the true position
of that country between the Victoria Nyanza and Lake
Tanganyika. In the north-east is the Lago Barcena
corresponding with Lake Dembea, with an affluent of the
White Nile issuing from it,—a fact by no means unworthy
of notice, even though the indistinctness of the delineation leaves us in doubt whether the Atbara or Bar-el-
Azreh may be intended: moreover, the name of Barsena
still survives in another affluent of the White Nile. Nor
is it without significance that north-westward of the
Lake Colue, which answers to the Victoria Nyanza, there
occurs the word Barimboa, closely expressing Baringo,
the name of the water north-west of that great lake.

P

The following is the description of the Nile Region as derived from Duarte Lopes :—

"The Nile does not rise in the country of Bel Gian, *i. e.* Prester John (the Emperor of Abyssinia), nor in the Mountains of the Moon, nor, as Ptolemy writes, from two lakes lying east and west of each other, with about four hundred and fifty miles between them. For in the latitude in which he places these two lakes lies the kingdom of Congo and Angola on the west; and on the east are the empire of Monomotapa and the kingdom of Sofala, the distance from sea to sea being twelve hundred miles. In this region Lopes stated that there was only one lake, on the confines of Angola and Monomotapa. It is one hundred and ninety-five miles in diameter, as he learned from the people of Angola on the west, and those of Sofala and Monomotapa on the east; and while they give us a full account of this, they mention no other lakes, whence we may conclude that there is no other in that latitude. It is true that there are two lakes, not lying east and west, but north and south of each other, and about four hundred miles apart. Some of the natives think that the Nile, issuing from the first lake, flows underground and again appears; but Lopes denies this. The first lake is in 12° S. lat., and like a shell, and surrounded by very lofty mountains, the highest of which on the east are called Cafates, and on both sides are mountains from which saltpetre and silver are dug. The Nile flows thence four hundred miles due north, and enters another very great lake, which the natives call a sea. It is larger than the first, for it is two hundred and twenty miles across, and lies under the equinoctial line. Respecting this lake very certain information is given by the Anzichi, near Congo. They say that there are people on it who sail in great ships, and who write and have weights and measures, such as they have not in Congo. Their houses were built of stone and lime, and equalled those of the Portuguese, whence it might be inferred that Prester John was not far off. From this second lake the Nile flows seven hundred miles to the island of Meroe, and receives other rivers, the principal of which is the river Colues, so named because it issues from a lake of that name on the borders of Melinde, and when the Nile reaches Meroe it divides into two branches, and embraces a high land named Meroe, to the right of which, on the east, is a river named Abagni that rises in the Lake Barcena and crosses the empire of Prester John till it reaches that island."

But to return: while the teaching of the doctrines of

Christianity was thus successful in Congo, it was far otherwise in the kingdom of Benin, which lay between Congo and the Fort of St. Jorge da Mina. At about the same time that Diogo Cam was returning for the first time under such propitious circumstances from Congo, one João Affonso de Aveiro was commissioned by the King of Benin to convey an ambassador to the King of Portugal, with a request that he would send missionaries to teach his people the Christian religion. His real object, however, was much more to strengthen his hands against his enemies than to secure the blessings of Christianity. The mission accordingly languished, and the unwholesomeness of the locality caused many deaths, amongst the earliest to succumb being Aveiro himself. The negro ambassador, however, had informed King João that eastward of Benin, some three hundred and fifty leagues in the interior, lived a powerful monarch named Ogane, who held both temporal and spiritual dominion over all the neighbouring kings, and that the King of Benin on his own elevation to the throne sent him an embassy with rich presents, and received from him the investiture and insignia of sovereignty. These latter consisted of a staff and cap of shining brass by way of sceptre and crown, with a cross of brass. Without this ceremony the kings were not held to be legitimized. The ambassadors never saw this monarch during the whole term of their stay at his court. Only on the day of audience he showed one of his feet, which they kissed with reverence as something holy. At their departure a cross of brass was thrown over the neck of each in the name of the king, and this liberated the wearer from all slavery, and was to him as an ennobling order of chivalry.

The story tallied so remarkably with the accounts of Prester John which had been brought to the peninsula by Abyssinian priests, that the king was seized with an ardent desire to get enlightened upon this subject, for he plainly saw how immensely his double object of spreading Christianity and extending his commerce by opening the road to the Indies would be furthered by an alliance with such a sovereign. It was the idea of the geographers of the time that the sources of the Senegal and the Nile were very near to each other. The king therefore gave orders that as soon as the fortress at the mouth of the Senegal was completed the ascent of the river should be made as far as its source; but he little foresaw the difficulties of such an undertaking. He nevertheless determined that both by sea and land the attempt should be made to reach the country of Prester John.

By sea he sent, in August, 1486, two vessels of fifty tons respectively, under the command of Bartholomeu Dias and João Infante. A smaller craft which carried the provisions, was commanded by Pedro Dias, Bartholomeu's brother. Of this voyage, however, we shall speak more fully after that we have described the measures which the king adopted with the view of finding, if possible, the country of Prester John by the East. The first persons whom he sent out with this object were Father Antonio de Lisboa and one Pedro de Montarryo; but when they reached Jerusalem they found that without knowing Arabic it would be useless to continue their voyage, and therefore they returned.

On the 7th of May, 1487, however, the king despatched two men who were not wanting in that respect, viz., Pedro de Covilham and Affonso de Payva. They went by Naples and Rhodes to Alexandria and Cairo, and so to Aden, where they separated with an agreement to meet at a certain time at Cairo. They left Lisbon for Naples, where their bills of exchange were paid by the son of Cosmo de Medicis; and from Naples they sailed to the island of Rhodes. Then crossing over to Alexandria, they travelled to Cairo as merchants, and proceeding with the caravan to Tor on the Red Sea, at the foot of Mount Sinai, gained some information relative to the trade with Calicut. Thence they sailed to Aden, where they parted; Covilham directed his course towards India, and Payva towards Suakem in Abyssinia, appointing Cairo as the future place of their rendezvous.

At Aden, Covilham embarked in a Moorish ship for Cananor, on the Malabar coast, and after some stay in that city, went to Calicut and Goa, being the first of his countrymen who had sailed on the Indian Ocean. He then passed over to Sofala, on the eastern coast of Africa, and examined its gold-mines, where he procured some intelligence of the island of St. Lawrence, called by the Moors the Island of the Moon, now known as Madagascar.

Covilham had now heard of cloves and cinnamon, and seen pepper and ginger; he therefore resolved to venture no further until the valuable information he possessed was conveyed to Portugal. With this idea he returned to Egypt; but found on his arrival at Cairo, where he met with messengers from King João, that Payva had died a short time before. The names of these messengers were Rabbi Abraham of Beja, and Joseph of Lamego; the latter immediately returned with letters from Covilham, containing, among other curious facts, the following remarkable report:—" *That the ships which sailed down the coast of Guinea might be sure of reaching* the termination of the continent, by persisting in a course to the south; and that when they should arrive in the eastern ocean, their best direction must be to inquire for Sofala, and the Island of the Moon." Rabbi Abraham and his companion, having already visited the city of Baghdad and the island of Ormuz, had made themselves acquainted with many particulars respecting the spicetrade. This alone was sufficient to recommend them to the patronage of João II., and they accordingly were employed by him to seek Covilham and Payva at Cairo, with additional directions to go to Ormuz and the coast of Persia, in order to improve their commercial information.

Covilham eagerly embraced this opportunity to visit Ormuz, and having attended Abraham to the Gulf of Persia, they returned together to Aden, whence the latter hastened to give King João an account of their tour, and Covilham embarked for Abyssinia to complete that part of his voyage which the death of Payva had hitherto frustrated.

Crossing the Straits of Babelmandeb, he landed in the dominions of the Negus. That prince took him with him to Shoa, the residence of the court, where he met with a very favourable reception. He at length became so necessary to the prince, that he was compelled to spend the remainder of his life in Abyssinia. He married in that country, and from occupying highly important posts, amassed a considerable fortune. He passed thirty-three years of his life in Abyssinia, and died there. From his letter to King João, already quoted, it will be seen that to him is to be assigned the honour of the theoretical discovery of the Cape of Good Hope, as that of the practical discovery will presently be shown to belong to Bartholomeu Dias.

Meanwhile, in the year 1488, the king had fitted out a considerable armament with the view of founding another station at the mouth of the Senegal, similar to that of San Jorge da Mina, but this project met with very different success. It so happened that the Prince of the Jaloffs, a man whose vicious habit of life made the cares of ruling irksome, had to a certain extent abandoned the government to his uterine brother, named Bemoi, and in so doing had slighted the claims of his two brothers, the sons of the late king. Bemoi, who was a man of talent and energy, strengthened himself against the princes, his rivals, by forming a close alliance with the Portuguese, to whom he never failed to show every possible attention and kindness. All went on well till the death of the king, who was assassinated at the instigation of his brothers. Bemoi now found himself engaged in open warfare, and naturally appealed for help to his allies. King João promised him every help if only he would become a Christian and be baptized, and for this purpose sent out ambassadors with presents and accompanied by missionaries. Bemoi promised to do what was required of him, but objected that it was highly inexpedient, during a civil war, to make a change which would naturally alienate even many of his own partisans, but he engaged that, if he should obtain quiet possession of the kingdom, he would not only embrace Christianity, but would make the whole nation do the same. A year thus passed, during which the commerce was seriously interrupted by the war, and the Portuguese merchants complained to King João, who, finding that Bemoi did not embrace Christianity, ordered all his subjects under heavy penalties to leave him and return to Portugal. Bemoi became alarmed, and sent a nephew of his in company with the Portuguese, with a collar of gold and a hundred picked slaves as a present to the king, in the hope of securing his assistance. There was not time, however for him to receive the answer, for he was beaten and with difficulty escaped to the fortress of Arguin, whence he embarked for Portugal, with twenty-five of his most faithful adherents.

When the king heard of his arrival he had him conducted to the palace of Palmella, where he was treated with the greatest magnificence until he should make his public entry into Lisbon. On that occasion his passage through the streets was an ovation, and he was received with the greatest pomp, both by the king and queen at separate palaces, each surrounded by a numerous court of ladies and grandees. For a long time Bemoi had been receiving instruction in the tenets of Christianity; so that the king's anxiety was gratified by his spontaneous request, that he and his companions might be admitted by baptism into the Christian Church. He was baptized in the queen's palace, by the Bishop of Ceuta, on the 3rd of December, 1489, and received the king's name of João. On the following day the king dubbed him knight, and gave him for arms, gules, a cross or, between the five escutcheons of Portugal.

Meanwhile the king equipped twenty caravels, well provided with men, and provisions, and munitions of war, and everything requisite for the construction of a fortress, together with a number of missionaries for the conversion of the heathen. Unhappily for the fulfilment of the king's desires, the command was entrusted to Pedro Vaz da Cunha, a man of brutal nature, who, in a moment of spleen at finding the foundations of the new fortress laid in an unhealthy position, in which it would be his duty for some time to reside, stabbed Bemoi to death upon an empty pretence that he had plotted treason against him. Not only the negroes, but the Portuguese themselves were horrified at this act of baseness, which caused the king much pain. He contented himself, however, with leaving Da Cunha to his remorse, which would probably be but a trivial punishment to so heartless a coward.

But it is time we revert to that most important expedition of which Bartholomeu Dias was the commander, and which set sail for the south in 1486. It was fitting that a Dias should be the first to accomplish the great task which it had been the ruling desire of the life of Prince Henry to see effected. It was a family of daring navigators. João Dias had been one of the first who had doubled Cape Bojador, and Lorenzo Dias was the first to reach the Bay of Arguin, while Diniz Dias was the first to reach the land of the Blacks and even Cape Verde, to which he gave its name. The expedition of Bartholomeu started about the end of August, and made directly for the south. Passing the Manga das Areas where Diogo Cam had placed his furthest pillar, they reached a bay to which they gave the name of Angra dos Ilheos. Here Dias erected a pillar, which was broken some eighty years ago. The point is now called Dias Point or Pedestal Point. From seaward is seen what looks like two conical shaped islands, on the highest of which stood the cross. These hillocks stand out dark from the surrounding sand, and probably gave rise from their tint to the name of Serra Parda, or the Dark Hills, in which Barros places this monument. Proceeding southward, Dias reached another point, where he was delayed five days in struggling against the weather, and the frequent tacks that he had to make induced him to call it

Angra das Voltas, or Cape of the Turns or Tacks. It is called Cape Voltas, and forms the south point of Orange River. From this they were driven before the wind, for thirteen days, due south, with half-reefed sails, and of course out of sight of land, when suddenly they were surprised to find a striking change in the temperature, the cold increasing greatly as they advanced. When the wind abated, Dias, not doubting that the coast still ran north and south, as it had done hitherto, steered in an easterly direction with the view of striking it, but finding that no land made its appearance, he altered his course for the north, and came upon a bay where were a number of cowherds tending their kine, who were greatly alarmed at the sight of the Portuguese, and drove their cattle inland. Dias gave the bay the name of Angra dos Vaqueiros, or the Bay of Cowherds. It is the present Flesh Bay, near Gauritz River. He had rounded the Cape without knowing it.

It is a fact specially worthy of notice that in this voyage an entirely different system was adopted with respect to the natives than had prevailed hitherto. Instead of capturing the negroes that they chanced to find on the coast, they had orders to leave on the shore at intervals negroes and negresses well dressed and well affected towards Portugal, to gather information respecting Prester John, to speak in praise of the Portuguese from experience of kindnesses received, and to infuse a desire to contract alliances with them. In accordance with these instructions two negroes had been restored at Angra do Salto (the Bay of the Capture), so called from Diogo Cam having captured them at this place. They had left also a negress at Angra dos Ilheos (Angra Pequeña), and another at Angra das Voltas. An unfortunate event, however, occurred which neutralized the effect of this well-intended plan. In proceeding eastward from Flesh Bay, Dias reached another bay, to which he gave the name of San Bras, where he put in to take water. In doing this he met with determined opposition from the natives, who threw stones at his men. They were thus compelled to resort to their own weapons in self-defence, and an unfortunate shot from an arblast struck one of the Caffres dead, and thus the favourable impressions which had been looked for from a pacific system of procedure were nullified by an act of violence which they would gladly have avoided. Continuing east, Dias reached a small island in Algoa Bay, on which he set up another pillar with its cross, and the name of Santa Cruz, which he gave to the rock, still survives; and as they found two springs in it, many called it the Penedo das Fontes. This was the first land beyond the Cape which was trodden by European feet, and here they set on shore another negress.

The crews now began to complain, for they were worn out with fatigue, and alarmed at the heavy seas through which they were passing. With one voice they protested against proceeding farther. Dias, however, was most anxious to prosecute the voyage. By way of compromise he proposed that they should sail on in the same direction for two or three days, and if they then found no reason for proceeding farther, he promised they should return. This was acceded to. At the end of that time they reached a river some twenty-five leagues beyond the island of Santa Cruz, and as João Infante, the captain of the second ship, the *S. Pantaleon*, was the first to land, they called the river the Rio do Infante. It was the river now known as the Great Fish River.

Here the remonstrances and complaints of the crews compelled Dias to turn back. When he reached the little island of Santa Cruz, and bade farewell to the cross which he had there erected, it was with grief as intense as if he were leaving his child in the wilderness with no hope of ever seeing him again. The recollection of all the dangers that he and his men had gone through in that long voyage, and the reflection that they were to terminate thus fruitlessly, caused him the keenest sorrow. He was, in fact, unconscious of what he had accomplished. But his eyes were soon to be opened. As he sailed onwards to the west of Santa Cruz he at length came in sight of that remarkable cape which had been hidden from the eyes of man for so many centuries. In remembrance of the perils they had encountered in passing that tempestuous point, he gave to it the name of Cabo Tormentoso, or Stormy Cape, but when he reached Portugal and made his report to João II., the king, foreseeing the realization of the long-coveted passage to India, gave it the enduring name of Cape of Good Hope.

The one grand discovery which had been the object of Prince Henry's unceasing desire was now effected. The joy of the homeward voyage was, however, marred by a most painful incident. Dias had, by way of precaution, left behind him, off the coast of Guinea, the small vessel containing the supplies of provisions. He now went in search of it, it being nine months since they had parted company. When they reached it, they found three men only surviving out of the nine that had been left, and one of these, named Fernando Colaço, a scrivener from Lumiar, near Lisbon, was so weakened by illness that he died of joy when he saw his companions. The cause of the loss had been that, while the Portuguese were holding friendly communication with the negroes, the latter were seized with a covetous desire to possess some of the articles which were being bartered, and as a short means of obtaining them killed the owners. Not to return empty-handed, Dias put in at St. Jorge da Mina, and received from the commander, João Fogaza, the gold which he had taken in barter. He then proceeded to Lisbon, which he reached in December, 1487, after an absence of sixteen months and seventeen days.

In that voyage he had discovered three hundred and fifty leagues of coast, which was almost as much as Diogo Cam had discovered in his two voyages. This great and memorable discovery was the last that was made in the reign of King João II.

CHAPTER XIV.

RESULTS WESTWARD.

1470—1507.

"It was in Portugal," said Ferdinand Columbus, the son and biographer of the most illustrious navigator that the world has seen,—"it was in Portugal that the admiral began to surmise, that, if the Portuguese sailed so far south, one might also sail westward, and find lands in that direction."

The period of Christopher Columbus' sojourn in Portugal was from 1470 to the close of 1484, during which time he made several voyages to the coast of Guinea in the Portuguese service. While at Lisbon he married Felipa Moniz de Perestrello, daughter of that Bartholomeu Perestrello to whom we have already seen that Prince Henry had granted the commandership of the island of Porto Santo.

For some time Columbus and his wife lived at Porto Santo with the widow of Perestrello, who, observing the interest he took in nautical matters, spoke much to him of her husband's expeditions, and handed over to him the papers, journals, maps, and nautical instruments which Perestrello had left behind him.

Las Casas, in his "History of the Indies," tells us distinctly that Columbus derived much information from Perestrello's maps and papers, and adds that, "in order to acquaint himself practically with the method pursued by the Portuguese in navigating to the coast of Guinea, he sailed several times with them as if he had been one of them." Las Casas says that he learned this from the admiral's son Diego, adding that "some time before his famous voyage Columbus resided in Madeira, where news of fresh discoveries was constantly arriving, and this," he says, "appeared to have been the occasion of Christopher Columbus coming to Spain, and the beginning of the discovery of this great world (America)."

"It was not only," says Ferdinand Columbus, "this opinion of certain philosophers, that the greater part of our globe is dry land, that stimulated the admiral; he learned also from many pilots, experienced in the western voyages to the Azores and the island of Madeira, facts and signs which convinced him that there was an unknown land towards the west. Martin Vicente, pilot of the King of Portugal, told him that at a distance of four hundred and fifty leagues from Cape St. Vincent, he had taken from the water a piece of wood sculptured very artistically, but not with an iron instrument. This wood had been driven across by the west wind, which made the sailors believe, that certainly there were on that side some islands not yet discovered. Pedro Correa, brother-in-law to the admiral, told him, that near the island of Madeira he had found a similar piece of sculptured wood, and coming from the same western direction. He also said that the King of Portugal had received information of large canes having been taken up from the water in these parts, which between one knot and another would hold nine bottles of wine, and Herrera declares that the king had preserved these canes, and caused them to be shown to Columbus.

The colonists of the Azores related, that when the wind blew from the west, the sea threw up, especially in the islands of Graciosa and Fayal, pines of a foreign species. Others related, that in the island of Flores they found one day on the shore two corpses of men, which had broad faces, different from those of Christians. The transport of these objects was attributed to the action of the west winds. The true cause, however, was the great current of the Gulf, or Florida stream. The west and north-west winds only increase the ordinary rapidity of the ocean current, prolong its action towards the east, as far as the Bay of Biscay, and mix the waters of the Gulf stream with those of the currents of Davis' Straits and of North Africa. The same eastward oceanic movement, which in the fifteenth century carried bamboos and pines upon the shores of the Azores and Porto Santo, deposits annually on Ireland, the Hebrides, and Norway, the seeds of tropical plants, and the remains of cargoes of ships which had been wrecked in the West Indies.

While availing himself of these sources of information, Columbus studied with deep and careful attention the works of such geographical authors as supplied suggestions of the feasibility of a short western passage to India. Amongst these, the "Imago Mundi" of Cardinal Pierre d'Ailly was his favourite, and it is probable that from it he culled all he knew of the opinions of Aristotle, Strabo, and Seneca, respecting the facility of reaching India by a western route. Columbus' own copy of this work is now in the cathedral of Seville, and forms one of the most precious items in the valuable library, originally collected by his son Ferdinand, and bequeathed to the cathedral on condition of its being constantly preserved for public use. It contains many marginal notes in his own handwriting, but of comparatively little importance.

The suggestions derived from these works were corroborated by the narratives of Marco Polo and Sir John Mandeville, whose reports of the vast extent of Asia eastward led to the reasonable inference that the westward passage to the eastern confines of that continent could not demand any considerable length of time. The natural tendency of his thoughts to nautical enterprise being thus fostered by the works that he studied, and by the animating accounts of recent adventurers, as well as by the glorious prospects which the broad expanse of the unknown world opened up to his view, we find that in the year 1474 his ideas had formed for themselves a determined channel, and his grand project of discovery was established in his mind as a thing to be done, and done by himself. The combined enthusiasm and tenacity of purpose which distinguished his character, caused him to regard his theory, when once formed, as a matter of such undeniable certainty, that no doubts, opposition, or disappointment, could divert him from the pursuit of it.

It so happened that while Columbus was at Lisbon, a correspondence was being carried on between Fernando Martinez, a prebendary of that place, and the learned Paolo Toscanelli of Florence, respecting the commerce of the Portuguese to the coast of Guinea and the navigation of the ocean to the westward. This came to the knowledge of Columbus, who forthwith despatched by an Italian then at Lisbon a letter to Toscanelli, informing him of his project. He received an answer in Latin, in which, to demonstrate his approbation of the design of Columbus, Toscanelli sent him a chart, the most important features of which were laid down from the descriptions of Marco Polo. The coasts of Asia were drawn at a moderate distance from the opposite coasts of Europe and Africa, and the islands of Cipango, Antilla, &c., of whose riches such astonishing accounts had been given by this traveller, were placed at convenient spaces between the two continents.

While all these exciting accounts must have conspired to fan the flame of his ambition, one of the noblest points in the character of Columbus had to be put to the test by the difficulty of carrying his project into effect. The political position of Portugal, engrossed as it was with its wars with Spain, rendered the thoughts of an application for an expensive fleet of discovery for the time worse than useless, and several years elapsed before a fair opportunity presented itself for making the proposition.

At length about the year 1480, Martin Behaim rendered the astrolabe useful for the purposes of navigation, and shortly afterwards Columbus submitted to the King of Portugal his proposition of a voyage of discovery westward.

The king seemed inclined to make a trial of the scheme, but some of his councillors, who were enemies of the Genoese, and at the same time loth to offend the king, suggested a plan which suited their own views, but which was as short-sighted as it was dishonest. Their design was to procure from Columbus a detailed account of his plan that it might be submitted to the council, and then, under the false pretext of conveying provisions to the Cape Verde Islands, to despatch a caravel on the voyage of discovery. King João, deviating from his general character for prudence and generosity, yielded to their insidious advice, and their plan was acted upon; but the caravel which was sent out, after keeping on its westward course for some days, encountered a storm, and the crew, possessing none of the lofty motives of Columbus to support their resolution, returned to Lisbon, ridiculing the scheme in excuse of their cowardice. So indignant was Columbus at this unworthy manœuvre, that he resolved to offer his services to some other country, and towards the end of 1484 he left Lisbon secretly with his son Diego.

It is not difficult to understand why the King of Portugal should not very eagerly have fallen in with the proposition of Columbus. Nearly seventy years of continued effort on the part of the Portuguese to realize the great onception of Prince Henry afforded substantial proof of their conviction of the soundness of that conception. Many years before Columbus proposed to reach India by the sea, Prince Henry had finished a life which had been spent in aiming at the same result by another route. That route, therefore, though by no means free from great dangers, was identified with their hopes in the future as well as their predilections in the past. What wonder that they refused to resign a course so hopeful, comparatively so simple, and so essentially their own, in favour of a project replete with danger, and which they regarded as the chimera of a visionary?

The interval till 1492 was spent in a succession of appeals to the Spanish court, and in contending against all the vexatious variety of obstacles that ignorance, envy, or a pusillanimous economy could suggest.

At length, having overcome all obstacles, Columbus set sail with a fleet of three ships on the 3rd of August, 1492, on his unprecedented and perilous voyage. The ordinary difficulties which might be expected to occur in so novel and precarious an adventure were seriously aggravated by the alarming discovery of the variation of the needle, as well as by the mutinous behaviour of his crew; and his life was upon the point of being sacrificed to their impatience, when the fortunate appearance of land, on the morning of the 12th October, converted their indignation into compunction, and their despondency into unbounded joy.

The following is an extract from the Diary of Columbus, describing the event:—

"Thursday, October 11th [1492] sailed W.S.W. Had much sea [more than they had had in the whole voyage]. Saw some pardelas and a green rush close to the ship. The sailors of the caravel Pinta saw a reed and a stick, and they picked up another small bit of wood, carved apparently with an iron tool, also a piece of cane, some other fragments of land vegetation and a small board. The sailors of the caravel Nina also saw some signs of land, and a small piece of wood covered with dog-roses. At these indications they drew in their breath and were all full of gladness. That day they made twenty-six leagues before sunset. After sunset, sailed the original course to the westward, made twelve miles an hour, and by two o'clock after midnight they had made ninety miles, i. e. twenty-two leagues and a half; and as the caravel Pinta was the best sailor and was in advance of the admiral, she found the land and made the signals that the admiral had commanded. The land was first seen by a sailor named Rodrigo de Triana; for at ten o'clock at night, the admiral while standing on the quarter-deck saw a light, although it was so indistinct that he would not say with certainty that it was land; but he called to Pero Gutierrez, the king's groom of the chambers, and told him there was a light in sight, and desired him to look out, and so he did, and saw it. He also spoke of it to Rodrigo Sanchez of Segovia who had been sent out as supervisor by the king and queen; but he not being in a good position for seeing, saw nothing. After the admiral had mentioned it, it was observed once or twice. It was like a small wax candle, which was lifted up from time to time, which few would take to be a sign of land, but the admiral held it for certain that land was close by. After the Salve, which all the sailors were in the habit of saying and singing in their own fashion, while they were all assembled, the admiral begged and admonished them to keep a good look-out for land from the bows, and promised an immediate present of a silk doublet to him who should first call out that he saw land, besides the reward that had been promised by the sovereigns; viz. an annuity of ten thousand maravedis to him who first saw land. At two o'clock after midnight the land appeared at two leagues' distance. They struck all sail except the storm square-sail, without topsails; and they lay to until Friday the 12th of October, when they reached a small island of the Lucayos [the Bahamas] which was called in the Indian language Guanahani. Presently the people came towards us. They were quite naked. The admiral went on shore in an armed barge and took possession of the island for the king and queen."

Columbus named this island San Salvador, in honour of the Saviour. For centuries it was supposed to be identical with Cat Island, but it has been recently proved to be Watling's Island, to the south-east of Cat Island.

In this first voyage the discovery was made of the islands of St. Salvador, Santa Maria de la Concepcion, Exuma, Isabella, Cuba, Bohio, the Archipelago off the south coast of Cuba, called by Columbus the Jardin del Rey, or King's Garden, the islands of St. Catherine and Hispaniola. On this latter Columbus erected the fortress of La Navidad, and established a colony. He set sail on his return voyage on the 16th January, 1493, and, after suffering severely from a storm and a wearisome struggle with the trade-winds, arrived on the 15th of March at the little port of Palos, from whence he had sailed on the 3rd of August in the preceding year. His reception in Spain was such as the grandeur and dignity of his unrivalled achievement deserved, and his entrance into Barcelona was scarcely inferior to a Roman triumph.

The description of his voyage, which he had addressed to the Spanish sovereigns through their treasurer, caused so much excitement, that numerous editions of it were issued in the same year (1493) from the various great printing cities of Europe; and the narrative, embodied in *ottava rima* by the Florentine poet, Giuliano Dati, was sung about the streets to announce to the Italians the astounding news of the discovery of a new world.

It is not my duty here to lead the reader through details of the explorations made by Columbus in his four voyages. It has been my purpose to show the correctness of my assertion in the first chapter, that "while this vast achievement of Columbus was the link that united the old world with the new, the explorations instituted by Prince Henry of Portugal were in truth the anvil on which that link was forged." It was an event in which all humanity was concerned, but one which was recompensed with the basest ingratitude even from those most closely and beneficially interested in it.

The seductive adulation of the court and the people shown for the moment to Columbus, did not divert his thoughts from the preparations for a second expedition. A stay of six months sufficed to make all ready for this purpose, during which period a papal bull was obtained which fixed the famous line of demarcation, determining the right of the Spanish and Portuguese to discovered lands; which line was drawn from the north to the south pole, at a hundred leagues west of the Azores and Cape de Verde Islands; the discoveries to the westward were to belong to Spain, and those to the eastward to Portugal.

On the 25th of September, 1493, Columbus sailed westward, taking his departure from Cadiz with a fleet of three large ships of heavy burthen, and fourteen caravels, and after a pleasant voyage reached the island of Dominica on the 2nd of November. In this voyage he discovered the Caribbee Islands, Jamaica, an archipelago named by Columbus the Queen's Gardens, and supposed to be the Morant Keys, Evangelista or the Isle of Pines, and the island of Mona.

He sailed with his fleet finally for Spain on the 28th of April, 1496, and after working his way for nearly two months against the whole current of the trade-winds,—during which provisions became so reduced, that there was talk of killing, and even eating, the Indian prisoners,—he reached the bay of Cadiz on the 11th of June. The emaciated state of the crew when they disembarked, presenting so mournful a contrast with the joyous and triumphant appearance which they were expected to make, produced a very discouraging impression upon the opinions of the public, and reflected a corresponding depression upon the spirits of Columbus himself. He was reassured, however, by the receipt of a gracious letter from the sovereigns, inviting him to the court; a letter the more gratifying to him that he had feared he was fallen into disgrace. He was received with distinguished favour, and had a verbal concession of his request to be furnished with eight ships for a third voyage.

It was not, however, till the 30th of May, 1498, that he set sail from San Lucar, with six of the eight vessels promised, the other two having been despatched to Hispaniola with provisions in the beginning of the year. In the course of this voyage the crews suffered intensely from the heat, having at one time reached the fifth degree of north latitude, but at length land was descried on the 31st of July,—a most providential occurrence, as but one cask of water remained in the ship. The island they came to formed an addition to Columbus' discoveries; and as the first land which appeared consisted of three mountains, united at their base, he christened the island, from the name of the Trinity, La Trinidad. It was in this voyage that he discovered Terra Firma, and the islands of Margarita and Cubagua. On reaching Hispaniola, he had the mortification to find the colony in a state of organized rebellion. He had scarcely, by his active and at the same time politic conduct, brought matters to a state of comparative tranquillity, when a new storm gathered round him from the quarter of the Spanish court. The hatred of his ancient enemies availed itself of the clamour raised against him by some of the rebels who had recently returned to Spain, and the king and queen, wearied with reiterated complaints, at length sent out a judge to inquire into his conduct; who, on the day after his arrival, seized on the government before he had even seen Columbus, and took possession of all his property, public and private, even to his most secret papers. No sooner did the admiral himself arrive, than he was put in chains, and thrown into confinement. In this shackled condition he was conveyed, in the early part of October, from prison to the ship that was to convey him home; and when Andreas Martin, the master of the caravel, touched with respect for the years and great merit of Columbus, and deeply moved at this unworthy treatment, proposed to take off his irons, he declined the offered benefit, with the following magnanimous reply: "Since the king has commanded that I should obey his governor, he shall find me as obedient to this, as I have been to all his other orders; nothing but his command shall release me. If twelve years' hardship and fatigue; if continual dangers and frequent famine; if the ocean first opened, and five times passed and repassed, to add a new world, abounding with wealth, to the Spanish monarchy; and if an infirm and premature old age, brought on by these services, deserve these chains as a reward, it is very fit I should wear them to Spain, and keep them by me as memorials to the end of my life." This in truth he did, for he always kept them hung on the walls of his chamber, and desired that when he died they might be buried with him.

His arrival in Spain in this painful and degraded condition produced so general a sensation of indignation and astonishment, that a warm manifestation in his favour was the immediate consequence. His reception at the Alhambra was gracious and flattering in the highest degree; ample restitution and rewards were promised him, and he had every sanction for indulging the fondest hopes of returning in honour and triumph to St. Domingo, but his reappointment was postponed from time to time with various plausible excuses.

It is possible that the delay manifested by the sovereigns in redeeming their promise might have continued until the death of Columbus, had not a fresh stimulant to the cupidity of Ferdinand been suggested by a new project of discovering a strait, of the existence of which Columbus felt persuaded, from his own observations, and which would connect the New World which he had discovered with the wealthy shores of the East. His enthusiasm on the subject was heightened by an emulous consideration of the recent achievements of Vasco da Gama and Cabral, the former of whom had in 1497 found a maritime passage to India by the Cape, and the latter in 1500 had discovered for Portugal the vast and opulent empire of Brazil. The prospect of a more direct and safe route to India than that discovered by Da Gama, at length gained Columbus the accomplishment of his wish for another armament; and finally, on the 9th of May, 1502, he sailed from Cadiz on his fourth and last voyage of discovery.

Favoured by the trade-winds, he made a gentle and easy passage, and reached Martinique on the 15th of June. After staying three days at this island, he steered northwards, touched at Dominica, and from thence directed his course, contrary to his own original intention and the commands of the sovereigns, to St. Domingo.

But we must not follow him through the remainder of this voyage which was a most unhappy one. Its toils and perils were aggravated to Columbus by extreme bodily suffering and by the treatment he received from the king's emissaries at San Domingo. It closed by his reaching Jamaica, where he would in all probability have perished but for the energy and zeal of a devoted friend, named Diego Mendez. This brave man with only one Spaniard and six Indians crossed the sea from Jamaica to San Domingo, a distance of more than a hundred and twenty miles, in an open canoe, in order to procure a vessel laden with provisions in which Columbus might return in safety to Spain. In commemoration of this great feat he left orders in his will that on his tomb a canoe should be sculptured and headed with the single word "Canoa."

On the 12th of September, 1504, Columbus set sail for Spain; but from beginning to end this his last voyage was the most disastrous one. The ship in which he came home sprung her mainmast in four places in one tempest, and in a subsequent storm the foremast was sprung, and finally, on the 7th of November, Columbus arrived, in a vessel as shattered as his own broken and care-worn frame, in the welcome harbour of San Lucar.

It is impossible to read without the deepest sympathy the half-suppressed complaints which are uttered in the course of the veteran navigator's touching letter to the sovereigns describing this voyage. These murmurings were wrung from the manly spirit of Columbus by sickness and sorrow, and though he was reduced almost to the brink of despair by the injustice of the king, yet do we find nothing harsh or disrespectful in his language to the sovereign. A curious contrast is presented to us. The gift of a world could not move the monarch to gratitude; the infliction of chains, as a recompense for that gift, could not provoke the subject to disloyalty. The same great heart which through more than twenty wearisome years of disappointment and chagrin gave him strength to beg and to buffet his way to glory, still taught him to bear with majestic meekness the conversion of that glory into unmerited shame.

The two years which intervened between this period and his death, present a picture of black ingratitude on the part of the crown to this distinguished benefactor of the kingdom, which it is truly painful to contemplate. We behold an extraordinary man, the discoverer of a second hemisphere, reduced by his very success to so low a state of poverty that in his prematurely infirm old age he is compelled to subsist by borrowing, and to plead, in the apologetic language of a culprit, for the rights of which the very sovereign whom he has benefited has deprived him. The selfish and cold-hearted Ferdinand beheld his illustrious and loyal servant sink, without relief, under bodily infirmity, and the paralyzing sickness of hope deferred; and at length, on the 20th of May, 1506, the generous heart which had done so much without reward, and suffered so much without upbraiding, found rest in a world where neither gratitude nor justice is either asked or withheld.

But injustice, unhappily, was not buried with Columbus in the tomb. It was but one twelvemonth after his death that an attempt was made, and only too successfully, to name the new world which he had discovered, after another who was not only his inferior, but his pupil in the school of maritime enterprise. In an obscure corner of Lorraine, at the little cathedral town of St. Dié, a cluster of learned priests, who had there established a printing-press under the auspices of René II., Duke of Lorraine, suggested to give to the newly-discovered continent the name of the Florentine, Amerigo Vespucci, whose nautical career did not commence till after Columbus had returned from his second voyage to the western hemisphere.

It took place in this wise. When Vespucci was at Seville in 1501, one Giuliano Giocondi, then resident at Lisbon, was sent to him by Dom Manoel, King of Portugal, to seduce him from the service of the King of Spain, in which mission Giocondi was successful. A letter, describing the voyage which he made in consequence, was translated from Italian into Latin by another member of the Giocondi family. This was no less than the celebrated Fra Giovanni Giocondi, of Verona, who had gained great renown as an architect at Venice, but was, at the time we speak of, engaged in the service of Louis XII., and built the bridge of Notre Dame at Paris, which is at present standing.

Now at the time that Fra Giocondi was thus engaged in Paris, a young man of great talent, named Matthias Ringmann, a native of Schlestadt, on the eastern side of the Vosges mountains, was also pursuing his studies in the French capital at the college of Cardinal Lemoine. Ringmann, better known in the literary world by the pseudonym of Philesius, was a great proficient in Latin versification, and when he returned to his native Alsace, he found the fiercest literary rivalry existing between two contiguous parties of students, the one known as the Swabians, the other as the Rhine-men. Among the latter Ringmann soon distinguished himself by the gracefulness, no less than the wit, of his versification. At the University of Fribourg, the party of the Swabians found a talented but discreditable supporter in a dissolute professor, named Jacob Locher, better known as Philomusus.

A pique occasioned by some able verses of Ringmann in defence of his own party, induced Locher to resort to a mode of retribution of the most brutal and disgraceful character. At the close of the year 1505, Ringmann, who was at the time but twenty-two, a beardless young man of inoffensive manners and far from strong in frame, happened to be on a visit to the Syndic Zasius at Fribourg. Locher, having heard that on a certain day Ringmann intended to proceed on his way through the Black Forest, secured the assistance of eight armed confederates, and awaited the arrival of his victim by the wall of the Carthusian Convent about two miles from Fribourg, which lay on his road. Totally free from suspicion, Ringmann came as was expected, and was forthwith seized by this troop of cowards, who untrussed him, and inflicted on his bare body a severe and ignominious flagellation. *This whipped and weakly youth was the originator of the name which now belongs to the whole of the vast western world.*

When in Paris, Ringmann had made the acquaintance of Fra Giovanni Giocondi. From Paris he carried back with him to Alsace that admiration for Vespucci and his achievements which no one in Paris, of whom we have as yet heard, was so likely to have instilled into him as Giocondi; and in August, 1505, he became the editor, at Strasburg, of an edition of Giocondi's translation of Vespucci's above-mentioned letter, in which there are not only a set of verses by himself, in laudation of Vespucci's discoveries in his so-called third voyage, but also a Latin epistle on the same subject, addressed to a friend. We thus find even at this early period an intellectual and earnest advocate of the glory of Vespucci existing in Alsace.

A short distance beyond the line which separated that province from Lorraine, stood the small cathedral city of St. Dié, on the banks of the Meurthe, within the dominions of René II., Duke of Lorraine, a prince who greatly distinguished himself by his encouragement of the arts and of literature. Duke René's secretary was Walter Lud, one of the Canons of the Cathedral. A zealous friend of literature, this worthy priest established a college at St. Dié under the Duke's auspices, and, as we have said, he there set up a printing-press. Ringmann became professor of Latin at the College, and corrector of the press in the printing-office; and in 1504 another important personage joined this little confraternity. This was Martin Waldseemüller, or, as he is better known by his Græco-latinized pseudonym, Hylacomylus, a native and student of Fribourg, who, going in the vintage season of that year, in conformity with an annual habit of his, to eat grapes in Lorraine, became so charmed with the society of his learned friends at St. Dié, that he made up his mind to take up his abode there, and become the teacher of geography at the college. On the 25th of April, 1507, *a year after the death of Columbus,* this latter member of the clique produced, from the St. Dié printing-press, it cannot be doubted, under the inspiration of Ringmann a little work entitled " Cosmographiæ Introductio," to which was appended a Latin translation of Vespucci's four voyages as described by himself. Not only was it from this publication that the world was, for the first time, made aware of four voyages made to America by Vespucci, and one of them involving absolute priority in the discovery of the continent of America, but in the text which preceded the narrative of those voyages, the name of America was now, for the first time, suggested for the newly discovered western world in the following words:—" And the fourth part of the world, having been discovered by Americus, may well be called Amerige, which is as much as to say, the land of Americus, or America."

And a few pages later he says, " But now these parts are more extensively explored, and as will be seen in the following letters, another fourth part has been discovered by Americus Vesputius, which I see no just reason why any one should forbid to be named Amerige, which is as much as to say, the land of Americus, or America, from its discoverer Americus, who is a man of shrewd intellect; for Europe and Asia have both of them taken a feminine form of name from the names of women."

We have seen the connexion of the Giocondi with Vespucci. We have seen also the connexion of Ringmann with the work of Fra Giovanni Giocondi, and the interest taken by him in the glory of Vespucci. He has infused into the little circle of St. Dié a similar interest, and, certes, the question of a claim to the glory of having discovered a new world and of a right to confer on it a name, is one which might excite an interest in the most phlegmatic. But these men are possessed of a printing-press, and we can imagine the keenness of their pleasure in having the opportunity to set forth a subject which would throw so bright a reflection on the obscurity of their secluded valley. Well might Pico de Mirandola, who gave Ringmann a Greek MS. of Ptolemy to be edited by them, express his surprise that so learned a cluster of men should exist among those wild rocks.

In September of the same year appeared a re-issue at St. Dié of this same book, and in 1509 a new edition of it was issued from the printing-press of Johann Grüninger, of Strasburg. Now in this very same year, 1509, the name of America, thus proposed two years before, appears as if it were already accepted as a well-known denomination in an anonymous work, entitled "Globus Mundi," printed also at Strasburg in that year. This was three years before the death of Vespucci.

The first place in which we find the name of America, used a little further a-field, is in a letter dated Vienna, 1512, from Joachim Watt, Professor of Liberal Arts at the High School at Vienna, to Rudolphus Agricola, and inserted in the Pomponius Mela of 1518, edited by the former. The expression used is "America discovered by Vesputius." These men were all connexions of the same clique.

Thus subtly but surely was effected a great and irreparable injustice. No one can deny to Vespucci the credit of possessing courage, perseverance, and a practical acquaintance with the art of navigation; but he had never been the commander of an expedition, and had it not been for the great initiatory achievement of Columbus, we have no reason to suppose that we should ever have heard his name.

"To say the truth," as has been well remarked by the illustrious Baron von Humboldt, "Vespucci shone only by reflection from an age of glory. When compared with Columbus, Sebastian Cabot, Bartholomeu Dias, and Da Gama, his place is an inferior one. The majesty of great memories seems concentrated in the name of Christopher Columbus. It is the originality of his vast idea, the largeness and fertility of his genius, and the courage which bore up against a long series of misfortunes, which have exalted the admiral high above all his contemporaries."

CHAPTER XV.

RESULTS EASTWARD.

1487—1517.

MEANWHILE great things had been doing in the East. The grand discovery of Bartholomew Dias was not to remain fruitless, although it may fairly be wondered at that so long an interval should have been allowed to elapse between that discovery in 1487 and the realization of its advantages by Vasco da Gama ten years later. Some have even added to the reasonable inquiry, an unreasonable insinuation that the success of Columbus proved to be the effective stimulus to the second important expedition. No chimera was ever more untenable when examined by the light of facts and dates. Indeed the interval of five years between the two grand discoveries of Columbus and Da Gama is in itself sufficient to show that we must look elsewhere for an explanation of the delay. It will be remembered that before Dias had returned at the close of 1487, Payva and Covilham had been sent to Eastern Africa, and that from Cairo, in 1490, Covilham had sent home word to the king confirmatory of the fact that India was to be reached by the south of Africa. It happened, however, that in this same year, 1490, King John was seized with an illness so severe that his life was in the utmost jeopardy. So that the condition of the king's health and the personal anxieties accruing from the state of his kingdom, together with his domestic troubles, were of a nature to present serious obstacles to the development of those grander schemes which had been so vividly opened up to his ambition with respect to India, and thus it was that the momentous voyage of Bartholomeu Dias was the last that distinguished the reign of King John II. The king died on the 25th of October, 1495, in the fortieth year of his age and the fourteenth of his reign. His successor, King Manoel, received the name of "The Fortunate," from his good fortune in succeeding to the throne of a sovereign who had won for himself the designation of "The Perfect Prince." His first thought was to resume the distant maritime explorations which had already reflected so much honour on the far-sighted intelligence of their initiator, Prince Henry.

At length an experienced navigator of noble family was selected, in 1496, to attempt the passage to India by the newly-discovered southern cape of Africa. If we may trust an historian of good repute, and the holder of an important post in the royal archives, this selection was the result of a mere whim on the part of King Manoel. We are told by Pedro de Mariz, in his "Dialogos de Varia Historia," that the king was one evening at one of the windows of his palace, meditating on the possibility of realizing the grand projects of his predecessor John II., when Vasco da Gama happened to come alone into the court beneath the king's balcony. Without hesitation the king mentally resolved that he should be the chief in command of the fleet of the Indies.

The preparations for the enterprise were made by the king with the greatest forethought. Four vessels, purposely made small for the sake of easy and rapid movement, the largest not exceeding a hundred and twenty tons, were built expressly in the most solid manner, of the best-selected wood, well fastened with iron. Each ship was provided with a triple supply of sails and spars and rope. Every kind of needful store was laid in in superfluity, and the most skilful pilots and sailors that the country could furnish were sent out with Da Gama. The largest vessel, the "Sam Gabriel," he of course took under his own command. The captaincy of the "Sam Raphael," of one hundred tons, was given to his brother, Paolo da Gama; the "Berrio," a caravel of fifty tons, was commanded by Nicolao Coelho; and a small craft laden with munitions was given to the charge of Pedro Nuñez, a servant of Da Gama. It had been intended that Bartholomeu Dias should accompany the expedition, but he was subsequently ordered to sail for San Jorge da Mina, perhaps for political reasons, on a more profitable but less glorious mission. His pilot, however, Pero de Alemquer, who had carried him beyond the Stormy Cape, was sent out on board Vasco da Gama's ship, and the other two pilots were João de Coimbra and Pero Escobar.

It was on Saturday, the 8th of July, 1497, that Vasco da Gama started from Restello, an *ermida* or chapel which had been built by Prince Henry about a league from Lisbon, and in which he had placed certain friars of the Order of Christ, that they might receive confessions and administer the Communion to outward-bound or weather-bound sailors. Dom Manoel, who succeeded his uncle as Grand Master of the order, subsequently built on the spot the splendid Temple of Belem, or Bethlehem. As the first-fruits of the success of that important voyage, on which Da Gama was now

STATUE OF PRINCE HENRY.

Over the side gate of the Monastery at Belem.

Page 245.

starting, he transferred it to the Order of the Monks of St. Jerome. The whole building is erected on piles of pine wood. It is entered on the south side under a rich porch, which contains more than thirty statues. The doorway is double. Above the central shaft is a statue of Prince Henry in armour. (*See Engraving*.)

Without dwelling on such details of Da Gama's outward voyage as present no important novelty, we shall pass over four months, and on the 4th of November we shall find the little fleet anchored in the Bay of St. Helena, on the west coast of Africa, where for the first time they became acquainted with the Bosjesmans or Bushmen, that peculiar race allied to the Hottentots, but so different from the Caffirs. Here they landed in order to take in water, as well as to take astronomical observations with the astrolabe, newly invented by Behaim, for Da Gama mistrusted the observations taken on board, on account of the rolling of the vessel. The astrolabe he used was of wood, three hands-breadth in diameter, formed of three pieces like a triangle. They afterwards took out smaller ones of latten. So humbly began the art which has since produced such mighty results in navigation. While he was thus occupied, they perceived two negroes, one of whom they captured with very little difficulty, but were unable to make him understand them. They therefore sent him back to his people laden with presents, which had the effect of bringing them in crowds to beg for similar gifts. These people were yellowish in colour, small in stature, ill-formed, ugly, stupid, and stammering in their speech.

On the 16th of November they proceeded south, and on Wednesday, the 22nd of November, at noon, Da Gama sailed before a wind past the formidable cape,

to which King John II. had given the undying name
of Good Hope, in anticipation of the achievement which
was now about to be accomplished.

On Saturday, the 25th of November, he entered the
bay which Bartholemeu Dias had named San Bras, and
where the Portuguese had had a disagreement with the
natives. The latter were now amiable enough, and
exchanged with their visitors ivory bracelets for scarlet
caps and other articles. Their cattle were remarkable
for their size and beauty. A misunderstanding unhappily arose through unfounded suspicions on the part
of the natives, but Da Gama prudently withdrew his men
without bloodshed, and frightened the Hottentots by
firing his guns from the ships. In this bay Da Gama set
up a padrão or cross, but it was thrown down before his
eyes by the natives.

They left the bay of San Bras on Friday, December
8th. On Friday the 15th they sighted the island of
Santa Cruz in Algoa Bay, where Dias had left a padrão.
On the night of Sunday, the 17th, they passed the Rio do
Iffante, the extreme point of Dias's discovery, and here Da
Gama became seriously alarmed at the force of the current
that he encountered. Fortunately the wind was in his
favour, and on Christmas Day he gained sight of land, to
which, on that account, he gave the name of Natal.

On Wednesday, the 10th of January, 1498, they came
to a small river, and on the next day landed in the country of the Caflirs, where an entirely new race of men from
those they had hitherto seen met their eyes. With these,
formidable as they were with their large bows and iron-tipped azagays, Da Gama established such friendly relations that he called the country the Terra da Boa Gente,
or Country of the Good People, and the river he called

the Rio do Cobre, on account of the copper which the natives brought in exchange for linen shirts. The great Portuguese historian Barros confounds the Rio do Cobre, which appears to be the Inhambane, or Limpopo, with the Rio dos Reis, which the early maps make to debouch in Delagoa Bay, and is probably the river Manice.

On Monday, the 22nd of January, Da Gama reached a large river, where, to his great joy, he met with two richly dressed Mahometan merchants, who trafficked with the Caffirs, and from whom he gathered valuable information as to the route to India. Here he erected a pillar, which he named the padrão of Sam Rafael, and he called the river the Rio dos Bōos Signaes, or River of Good Signs (the Quilimane River). In an inferior sense the name was inappropriate, for here the scurvy broke out amongst the crew.

They set sail on Saturday, the 24th of January, and on the 10th of March anchored off the island of Mozambique. The people of the country told them that Prester John had many cities along that coast, whose inhabitants were great merchants and had large ships, but that Prester John himself lived a great way inland, and could only be reached by travelling on camels. This information filled the Portuguese with delight, for it was one of the great objects of these explorations to find out the country of Prester John. The ships of this country were large and without decks, not fastened with nails, but with leather. Their sails were made of matting of palm leaves, and the sailors had Genoese compasses to steer with, as well as quadrants and sea-charts. The viceroy of the island, whose name was Colytam,[1] came very confidingly on board the vessel

---

[1] Probably Colytam or Sultan.

with his suite, and the friendliest intercourse ensued; but it was afterwards discovered that treachery underlay this seeming good-will. In fact the new comers had at first been supposed to be Mahometans, but the mistake was soon discovered. A pilot whom the viceroy had given to the Portuguese misled them, and conducted them to a place for taking in water, where they found armed men hidden behind palisades, who endeavoured with slings to drive them from the water. These, however, were soon dispersed by the Portuguese guns.

On Saturday the 7th, they reached Mombaza, and were treated with great kindness by the king, who sent them presents, and offered to supply them with all that they might require. But having discovered a plot between the Moors of Mombaza and the pilots which he had brought from Mozambique, and being besides attacked by them in the night, Da Gama thought it wisest to continue his voyage, and on the 12th of April he set sail, though with little wind. The following morning, being about eight leagues' distance from Mombaza, they saw two barks at sea about three leagues to leeward of them, and made for them, wishing to find pilots. By evening they came upon one of them, but the other made for the shore. In the one they took were seventeen men, and gold and silver, and a quantity of maize and provisions, and a girl, the wife of an old man of rank, who was a passenger. On the Portuguese boarding, all in the vessel threw themselves into the water, and the former proceeded to pick them up in the boats. On Easter Day, the 15th of April, they reached Melinda, and their captives informed them that they would there find four ships belonging to Indian Christians, from whom they might procure Christian pilots, and every necessary in the way of meat and water, and wood, &c. On the Monday morning Da Gama sent the old man whom he had captured to the king, to tell him how happy he should be to enter into peaceful relations with him. After dinner the old man returned, attended by one of the king's household and an officer, with three sheep from the king and a message that it would give the king great pleasure to enter into peaceful relations with the captain, and that he would be happy to supply him with pilots or anything that his country might afford. Da Gama sent word that he would enter the harbour on the following day, and immediately sent to the king an overcoat, two sprigs of coral, three copper basins, a hat, some bells, and two pieces of striped cloth. On Tuesday the king sent Da Gama six sheep, and a good quantity of cloves, and cummin seeds, and ginger, and nutmeg, and pepper, and also sent word that he would come to see him on the following day. After dinner on Wednesday the king came out in his boat to the ships, and Da Gama in his boat went to meet him. The king proposed that they should interchange visits, but Da Gama replied that he was not permitted by his sovereign to land. The king asked the name of Da Gama's king, and ordered it to be written down, and said that if Da Gama would return that way he would send an embassy, or would write to his sovereign. The king then went round the ships, and was delighted with seeing the guns fired. He spent three hours on board, and when he departed left one of his sons and an officer in the ship, and took with him two of the Portuguese, to show them his palaces, and told Da Gama that since he would not come on shore that he should go along the coast the next day to see his horsemen ride. The king brought with him a close-fitting damask robe, lined with green satin, and a very rich head-dress, two chairs of bronze with their cushions, a round sunshade of crimson satin fastened to a pole, a sword in a silver scabbard, several trumpets, and two of a peculiar form made of elaborately carved ivory as high as a man, to be played at a hole in the middle. There were four ships here belonging to Indian Christians, who, when they came on board the first time, were shown by Da Gama an altar-picture, in which was the Virgin and Child at the foot of the cross, with the Apostles. The Indians immediately threw themselves on the ground in an attitude of prayer. These Indians warned Da Gama not to go on shore, nor place any faith in the joyous demonstrations that were made in his favour, for that they were not sincere. On Sunday, the 22nd of April, the king came on board, and Da Gama begged of him the pilots that he had promised. The king accordingly sent him a Christian pilot, and Da Gama gave up the hostage that he had retained. On the 24th of April they made sail for Calicut, under the guidance of their pilot, whose name was Malemo Canaca.

On Thursday, the 17th of May, 1498, Da Gama first sighted, at eight leagues' distance, the high land of India, the object of so many anxieties and of so many years of persevering effort. On Sunday, the 20th of May, he anchored before Calicut. On the following day some boats came out to them, and Da Gama sent one of the "degradados," or condemned criminals, on shore with them, and they took the man to two Moors of Tunis, who spoke both Spanish and Genoese, and the first salutation they gave him was as follows: "The devil take you for coming here. What brought you here from such a distance?" He replied, "We come in search of Christians and spices." They said, "Why does not the King of Spain, and the King of France, and the Signoria of Venice send hither?" He replied that the King of Portugal would not consent that they should do so, and they said he was right. Then they welcomed him, and gave him wheaten bread with honey, and after he had eaten, one of the two Moors went back with him to the ships, and when he came on board said, "Happy venture! happy venture! abundance of rubies! abundance of emeralds! You ought to give thanks to God for bringing you to a country in which there is such wealth." The Portuguese were utterly astounded at hearing a man at that distance from Portugal speak their own language. This Moor, whom Barros calls Monçaide, most probably Bou-said, proved very useful to Vasco da Gama, and went home with him to Portugal, where he died a Christian. Calicut, the wealthy capital of that part of the Malabar coast, was governed at that time by a Hindoo sovereign, named Samoudri-Rajah (the King of the Coast), a name which the Portuguese afterwards converted into Zamorin. Gama had the good fortune to gain an audience of this prince, by whom he was favourably received, but with very little ultimate success, in consequence of his not being provided with presents suitable for an Eastern sovereign. This unlucky circumstance, combined with the hatred of the Arab merchants, whose ships crowded the harbour and who regarded with apprehension any rivals in the rich trade of spices, was near producing fatal results.

Da Gama thought it his duty to establish a factory, at the head of which he placed Diogo Dias, the brother of the first discoverer of the Cape. At the instigation of the Arabs, Dias and his men were taken prisoners. By way of reprisal, Da Gama kept as hostages twelve

Hindoos who had visited his vessels; but when Dias and his comrades were allowed to return, he sent back only six of the Hindoos and retained the other six. When he set sail on Wednesday, the 29th of August, several vessels came to recover their countrymen. This Da Gama refused, and warned them to keep their distance, believing that their motives were treacherous. He told them at the same time that he meant to return as soon as possible, when they would know whether the Portuguese were thieves or not, as the Arabs had represented them to be. Whatever might have been the danger of Da Gama, and doubtless it was great from the hostility of the Arabs, this conduct was indefensible, for there appears no reason to doubt either the integrity or the goodwill of the Zamorin, inasmuch as the detention of Diogo Dias and his companions had been without his knowledge, and he himself not only discharged him, but sent by him a letter to Da Gama for the King of Portugal, written in Dias's own hand, to the following effect: "Vasco da Gama, a nobleman of your household, has visited my kingdom, which has given me great pleasure. In my kingdom there is abundance of cinnamon, cloves, ginger, pepper, and precious stones in great quantities. What I seek from thy country is gold, silver, coral, and scarlet." The only shadow of an excuse for Da Gama's retention of the six Hindoos was that he hoped to take them to Portugal, and bring them back again, when they might prove of the greatest assistance in establishing friendly relations between the two countries. That it was a genuine motive there can be little doubt, however harsh in its first conception, but, alas! he was ignorant that the caste of the poor captives would make them prefer death to their present position, and it can only be supposed that they speedily perished. They were becalmed about a league below Calicut, and at noon, on Thursday the 30th, they were beset by seventy boats crowded with people, whom they kept at bay with their artillery. The contest continued for an hour and a half, when fortunately a storm arose which carried them out to sea, and the boats finding themselves powerless returned, and Da Gama pursued his course. On Monday, the 10th of September, as they had but little wind, Da Gama put on shore one of the captives with letters to the Zamorin, written in Arabic by a Moor who had come with them. On the 15th they reached some islets about two leagues from the shore, and on one of them Da Gama erected a pillar, to which he gave the name of Santa Maria, for the king had ordered Da Gama to erect three columns, which he should name respectively Sam Rafael, Sam Gabriel, and Santa Maria. That of Sam Rafael had been erected at the Rio dos Bôos Signaes, that of Sam Gabriel at Calicut, and now the last, that of Santa Maria, was placed on this islet, and the group has since received the name of Santa Maria from the pillar erected there. The inhabitants were pleased at the idea of the pillar with its cross being set upon their island, as they were Christians, and were happy to meet with those of the same creed. Da Gama then continued his course northward, and putting in for water at a point of the coast opposite six little islands near Hog Island, he became aware of the proximity of two barks of unusual size. He hastened his men on board, and found from the look-out at the mast-head, that eight more such were becalmed at about six leagues' distance. When the wind arose he sailed straight for them, and they put in for shore. One of them, however, broke its rudder, and the crew landed in their boat, leaving the ship at the mercy of the Portuguese. The other seven were run aground, and received the Portuguese fire as they pulled ashore in their boats. These they found were vessels come in pursuit from Calicut.

Thence Da Gama still proceeded north, till on Sunday, the 23rd, he reached the little island of Anchediva, where they drove the "Berrio" and the "Sam Gabriel" ashore to caulk them, but the "Sam Rafael" remained afloat. One day, while they were on board the "Berrio," two large row-boats approached laden with men with trumpets, and drums, and banners. Da Gama found on inquiry that these were armed pirates, who introduced themselves on board vessels under the show of friendship, and once on board took possession if they found themselves strong enough. When, therefore, they came within gun-shot the "Sam Rafael" fired at them. They called out that they were Christians, but finding that Da Gama was not to be duped, they put in for shore, and were pursued for some time by Nicolao Coelho. On the following day came several with presents, asking to see the ships, but they were coldly received. Among them, however, came one man of forty years of age, who spoke Venetian perfectly, was well dressed in linen, with a handsome turban on his head and a cutlass at his side. He said that he came originally from the west when he was a boy, that he lived with a Moor who commanded forty thousand horsemen (in fact the Rajah of Goa), and hearing that Franks, or people from the west, were come, he had begged permission to come to pay them a visit, and his master sent word by him, that he would be happy to offer them ships or provisions, or anything else in his dominions which might be of service to them, or if they would take up their abode in his country he would be very pleased. Meanwhile Paolo da Gama made inquiries as to who the man was, and was informed that he was the owner of the vessels that had come out to attack him. When Da Gama learned this he had him flogged for the purpose of extracting the truth from him. He confessed that he knew that all the country was hostile, and that he had come on board to ascertain the state of the Portuguese defences. This man proved to be a Polish Jew, a native of Posen, whence a cruel persecution had driven his family in 1456 to Palestine. They afterwards migrated to Egypt, and he himself was born in Alexandria, whence he passed by the Red Sea to India. He joined his fortunes to the Portuguese, and as he was an experienced and intelligent man, Da Gama took him to Lisbon, where he embraced Christianity, and at his baptism received the name of Gasparo da Gama. He proved of great use to Da Gama on the homeward voyage, especially at Melinda, and was subsequently employed by King Manoel in different negotiations with India, was made a knight of the king's household, and received pensions and emoluments which afforded him an honourable livelihood.

Da Gama set sail westwards from Anchediva on Friday, the 5th of October. When they were some two hundred leagues away from land, this same man said that he thought the time was come for him to dissemble no longer, and confessed that while he was with the rajah his master, news was brought that the Portuguese were wandering along the coast at a loss to find their way back, and that a number of flotillas were trying to capture them; that his master then desired that an attempt should be made not only to learn what strength the Portuguese had for defence, but if possible to induce them to land, and that once landed he would capture them, and as they were courageous men, employ them in battle against his enemies in the neighbourhood, but he reckoned without his host.

The passage across to Africa lasted for three months all but three days, in consequence of the frequent calms and contrary winds. During this time thirty of the men died of scurvy, so that there were only left seven or eight to work each vessel, and if the voyage had lasted a fortnight longer there would not have been a soul left. The commanders were even thinking of putting back to India, but happily a favourable wind arose which brought them in six days in sight of land, which was almost as welcome to them as if it had been Portugal. This was on Wednesday, the 2nd of January, 1499. The next day they found themselves off Magadoxo, but they were in quest of Melinda, and did not know how far they were from it. On Monday, the 7th of January, they anchored off that town. The king sent to welcome them, and to say that he had been long hoping to see them. They spent here five happy days of rest and relief from disease and the peril of death, receiving princely proofs of kindness and hospitality from the king, who, at Da Gama's request, gave him an ivory trumpet to convey to the king his master, as also a young Moor, with a particular recommendation of him to the King of Portugal, to whom he specially sent him to show how much he desired his friendship.

On Friday, the 11th of January, they set sail, and on the evening of Friday, the 1st of February, they anchored off the Ilhas de Sam Jorge (St. George's Islands), in Mozambique, and on the following morning raised a pillar on the island in which they had first heard mass on their outward voyage, though it rained so heavily that they were unable to light a fire to melt the lead that was needed for fixing the cross, so that the pillar was left without it.

On Sunday, the 3rd of March, 1499, they reached the bay of San Bras, where they took a quantity of anchovies and salted down penguins and sea-wolves for their homeward voyage, and the wind being fair they doubled the Cape of Good Hope on Wednesday, the 20th of March. The survivors had recovered their health and strength, but were half numbed with the cold, which they attributed less to the actual cold of the climate than to their having come from a hot country.

Da Gama reached Lisbon at the end of August or beginning of September, and was received with great pomp by the court. His return from a voyage in which so mighty a discovery had been made was hailed with magnificent fêtes and public rejoicings, which by the king's order were repeated in all the principal cities throughout the kingdom. In that important voyage he had lost his brother, more than half of his crew, and half his vessels, but he brought back the solution of a great problem which was destined to raise his country to the very acme of prosperity.

In the year after Da Gama's return, at his recommendation, Pedro Alvarez Cabral, a scion of a noble house of Portugal, was charged with the command of an expedition to Calicut, with the view of establishing commercial intercourse with the rajah of that country. The expedition was a magnificent one. It consisted of thirteen ships formidably armed with artillery, but at the same time sumptuously provided with presents for the rajah,

s

and although sent out with a purely commercial object,
the boldest and most famous seamen of the period were
placed under the orders of Cabral. Among these were
Bartholomeu Dias, who fourteen years before had rounded
the Stormy Cape, Nicolao Coelho, the able companion of
Da Gama in 1497, and the talented interpreter Gasparo,
whom Da Gama had brought home with him from India.
To these were added men of administrative intelligence,
who might be able to treat with prudence on matters of
commercial policy, it being intended to establish a factory
on the coast of Malabar. Great as the importance of
this object was, it was the fate of the expedition to make
a discovery, before which even the results thus contemplated shrunk into insignificance. The expedition
sailed on the 9th of March, 1500. After thirteen days,
when off the Cape Verde Islands, one of the vessels, which
was commanded by Luis Pires, lost convoy, and after a
short delay the fleet proceeded without her. Various
have been the reasons assigned for the westerly course
which the expedition now took. According to Barros
the object was to avoid the calms off the coast of Guinea,
while others have asserted that the fleet was driven
westward by a storm. If, however, we take into consideration the intensity of the curiosity excited by the
recent discoveries in the New World, and the noble
emulation which such discoveries, made in the service
of a rival nation, would inspire in the minds of men,
who in another direction had gained so many laurels in
the career of maritime enterprise, we may fairly doubt
whether this south-westerly course was not pursued by
Cabral in the hope of lighting on some part of the new-
found western world. But whatever the inducement or
the cause, the result was such as to satisfy both hope

and curiosity. On Wednesday, the 22nd of April, Cabral perceived the rounded top of a mountain, on what he at first supposed to be an island, and as they were then in Holy Week or in the octave of Easter he gave the mountain the name of Monte Pascoal. It forms part of the chain of the Aymores, in Brazil.[2] To the country he gave the name of Vera Cruz, or, as it was afterwards called, Santa Cruz, which name it retained till the importation from it into Europe of the valuable dye-wood of the *ibirapitanga* caused it to be called Brazil, from the name which for centuries had been given to similar dye-woods imported from India. On the 23rd, Nicolao Coelho was despatched to examine the coast. On the 24th they anchored in the bay afterwards named Porto Seguro. On the 1st of May formal possession was taken of the country for Portugal, and a large cross was set up on the coast in commemoration of the event. The luxuriance of the vegetation, as well as the sociable demeanour of the natives, and their respectful bearing when witnessing the solemn celebration of mass, were matters of surprise and gratification to the discoverers. Cabral forthwith despatched Gaspar de Lemos to the king with the important news, which was described most admirably in a letter drawn up by Pedro Vaz de Caminha, the second secretary of the Calicut Factory, accompanied by an astronomical diagram by Mestre João, the physician of the expedition. By this means the first information of the discovery of Brazil was brought to Europe. Before

---

[2] Fortunate as Cabral was in this discovery, he had been anticipated in landing on the coast of Brazil, although at a widely different part of that coast. On the 20th of January of the same year, viz., forty-eight days before the departure of Cabral, Pinzon had discovered Cape St. Augustine.

the departure of the fleet an incident of importance occurred. One of the natives who had come on board the "Admiral," was struck with the brightness of a brass candlestick, and made signs to the effect that a similar metal was found in that country. Cabral accordingly left behind him two young *degradados*, or banished criminals, with orders to make themselves acquainted with the products and habits of the country, thus giving them the double chance of serving their nation and retrieving their own position. One of these subsequently became an able and respected agent of the colony which King Manoel lost no time in establishing. The fleet set sail on the 22nd of May, but the joy which had been awakened by their success was soon to be turned into mourning. The appearance of an immense comet produced an alarm which was only too unhappily realized. A fearful typhoon sunk four vessels, and the brave Bartholomeu Dias, whose great achievement had converted his Stormy Cape into a Cape of *Good Hope*, perished off that very cape which for him was still to be a Cape of Storms.

Cabral, notwithstanding, pushed on, and reached Quiloa on the 20th of July, whence proceeding to Melinda, he renewed with the sovereign of that country the alliance which had been based upon his friendly treatment of Da Gama. Thence he crossed to India, and anchored before Calicut on the 13th of September. Through the medium of his intelligent interpreter, Gasparo da Gama, he succeeded in laying before the Zamorin or rajah the objects of the embassy, which were favourably received. The splendid presents which he brought, and the formidable artillery with which he was protected, doubtless served to extinguish the recollection of the misunderstanding with

Da Gama. Permission to establish a factory on the coast was readily granted, and the rajah solemnly pledged himself to the terms of this new treaty of commerce, in which the future interests of Europe were so largely involved. The factory was peacefully established at Calicut under the direction of Ayres Correa, but within a short time the treachery of the Mohammedans showed itself, and Correa and more than fifty of the Christians were massacred. Cabral took ample revenge for this unprovoked injury, and forthwith betook himself to the King of Cochin, the enemy of the Rajah of Calicut, with whom, as well as the King of Cananor, he succeeded in establishing peaceful relations. Having laden his remaining vessels with a most valuable cargo, he set sail for Portugal. Near Melinda, however, one of the most richly freighted of the ships, commanded by Sancho de Tovar, foundered on a reef. The vessel was of two hundred tons burden, and laden with spices. The crew escaped with their lives, and they burnt the ship; but the King of Mombaza succeeded in recovering the guns, which he afterwards turned to account against the Portuguese. When they reached Cape Verde at the beginning of June, they fell in with a Portuguese flotilla of three ships, which had sailed from Lisbon on the 13th of May, for the purpose of making discoveries on the coast of Brazil, on board of which was Amerigo Vespucci.

In a letter addressed to Lozenzo di Pier Francesco de' Medici, dated from that cape on the 4th of June, and recently discovered by Count Baldelli Boni, Vespucci relates the story of Cabral's discoveries as communicated to him by the interpreter Gasparo. He further mentions how, by a curious coincidence, on that very day one of Cabral's ships, that of Pedro Dias, which had lost convoy in the terrible storm off the Cape in which his brother Bartholomeu Dias had perished a twelvemonth before, again joined the squadron to which it belonged. It had wandered as far as the mouth of the Red Sea, and worked its way back through incredible hardships. Before it made its appearance two vessels alone remained with Cabral out of the thirteen with which he had set sail. The three returned to Lisbon in company. Of the wealth brought back Vespucci gives the following account. He says there was an immense quantity of cinnamon, green and dry ginger, pepper, cloves, nutmegs, mace, musk, civet, storax, benzoin, porcelain, cassia, mastic, incense, myrrh, red and white sandal-wood, aloes, camphor, amber, canne (Indian shot, *Canna Indica*), lac, mummy,[3] anib,[4] and tuzzia (or Thuja, Indian cypress), opium, Indian aloes, and many other drugs too numerous to detail. Of jewels he knew that he saw many diamonds, rubies, and pearls, and one ruby of a most beautiful colour weighed seven carats and a half, but he did not see all.

They reached Lisbon on the 23rd of July, 1501, where, although Portuguese historians are silent on the subject, it may be inferred from the rewards subsequently conferred on his family that Cabral met with the reception due to one who had secured such important benefits to his country. Immense, however, as had been the successes of Cabral in some respects, it will have been seen that he had not been so fortunate as he had wished in establishing a factory at Calicut, although he had left

[3] Portions of mummy that had been prepared with bitumen were in those days used as a drug. It is now used as a pigment.

[4] The Aniba is an aromatic wood from Guyana, with which Vespucci may have made acquaintance in the West, and perhaps without sufficient precision have mentioned it among these eastern products.

some agents behind at Cochin. Nevertheless he had paved the way for effecting the object he had in view, which was not long in being carried into execution.

Before Cabral's return King Manoel had sent out a noble Galician named Juan de Nova with four vessels. He set sail from Belem on the 5th of March, 1501. In his voyage out he discovered the island of Ascension, but which he called the island of Conception. It appears first to have received its name of Ascension from Alfonso d' Albuquerque, who saw it again in May, 1503, and mentioned it in his journal, probably by mistake, under the latter name, which it has ever since retained. On the 7th of July, De Nova anchored at the watering-place of San Bras, beyond the Cape of Good Hope. Here Pedro de Ataide, who had been separated from Cabral in the great storm already described, had left in a shoe, so as to be sheltered from the winds, a letter announcing his having passed that way, and with what object, and urging all captains bound for India to go by way of Mombaza, where they would find other letters in charge of one Antonio Fernandes. By this means De Nova, who of course possessed no further information of those parts than what had been gathered from Vasco da Gama, became aware of the existence of two friendly and safe ports in India where he could take in a cargo, namely, Cochin and Cananor. At Quiloa he fell in with Antonio Fernandes, who delivered him Cabral's letter. He then proceeded to Cananor, where he was well received by the rajah, who pressed him to freight his ship with spices from that port. From this De Nova courteously excused himself, stating that he had orders from the king to take a cargo first from the place where his agents had been left. He however desired that while he went to Cochin, a certain quantity of ginger, cinnamon, and other drugs, should be got in readiness, which quantity he would deduct from the cargo he would take in at Cochin. On the way he encountered the fleet of the King of Calicut, and with his artillery sunk five large vessels and nine proas. At Cochin he was received with great warmth on account of the victory he had gained over the Rajah of Calicut, and the King of Cochin readily met the wishes of De Nova. The latter added six or seven men to the number of agents already settled there, returned to Cananor, completed the freighting of his ships with a rich cargo, and set sail for Portugal. On his homeward voyage another piece of good fortune awaited him in the discovery of the island of St. Helena, which seemed to be providentially placed by the Almighty as a watering-station for vessels returning from India. De Nova reached Portugal on the 11th of September, 1502, and was received by the king with distinguished honour for the valuable services which he had rendered to the country.

Meanwhile, in 1503, Antonio de Saldanha, on his way to India, had given his name to the Agoada de Saldanha, near the Cape of Good Hope, a fact to which we shall presently have occasion to refer; and in this year the two Albuquerques, Francisco and Affonso, sailed for India. The former restored to the King of Cochin his territory, from which he had been driven by the King of Calicut, and founded the first Portuguese fort in India at Cochin, leaving the famous Duarte Pacheco Pereira defender of the kingdom. Affonso de Albuquerque, after touching on the coast of the Terra de Santa Cruz discovered by Cabral, reached Coulam, now Quilon, in Travancore, as yet unknown to the Portuguese, made terms of friendship with its king, and established a factory there.

In 1504, Diogo Fernandes Pereira wintered at Socotra, which had not previously been reached by the Portuguese.

In 1505, King Manoel sent out a great expedition of two-and-twenty ships and fifteen thousand men, which sailed from Lisbon on March 25th, 1505, under Dom Francisco de Almeida, the first viceroy of the Indies, with instructions to build fortresses at Sofala and Quiloa, and to free the Portuguese commerce in India from the difficulties with which it was oppressed. Juan de Nova sailed in this expedition. As a proof of his success Almeida sent back, in the beginning of the following year, eight ships loaded with spices to Portugal, under the command of Fernam Soares. On their way they discovered, on the 1st of February, 1506, the east coast of the island of Madagascar. In his outward passage Almeida conquered Quiloa, and dethroned the king, who refused to pay the stipulated tribute, and who had showed himself an enemy to the Portuguese. He set a new king on the throne, and himself crowned him with great solemnity. He also founded a fort there, which he named Santiago. On his arrival in India he founded the forts of Anchediva and Cananor. He solemnly crowned the King of Cochin, to whom King Manoel sent a rich crown of gold. Almeida also received ambassadors from the King of Narsinga and other princes, with whom he had entered on terms of alliance and friendship.

In 1505, Francisco de Almeida's son, Lourenço, discovered Ceylon, already known by overland accounts. He entered the Porto de Galle, and made its king an annual tributary to Portugal of four hundred bahars (about 300 pounds each) of cinnamon.

In this year also Pedro de Anhaya made the King of Sofala tributary to Portugal, and laid the foundations of a fort there on the 21st of September.

The high command which had been given to Almeida had been intended by the king for Tristam da Cunha, who was prevented from accepting it by a malady in the eyes, but, that obstacle being now removed, he was sent out on the 6th of April, 1506, with the command of sixteen vessels and thirteen hundred men to strengthen the dominion of Portugal in Africa and India. Affonso d'Albuquerque went out under his orders. It was in this voyage that the three islands bearing the name of Tristam da Cunha were discovered. In consequence of information brought to the king by Diogo Fernandes Pereira, the discoverer of the island of Socotra, to the effect that the Moors had a fortress therein, and held the Christians in subjection, Tristam da Cunha and Albuquerque were commissioned to take the fortress, which they succeeded in doing.

In this year João Gomez d'Abreu discovered the west coast of Madagascar on the 10th of August, St. Laurence's Day, from which circumstance the island received the name of San Lourenço.

In 1506 Affonso de Albuquerque returned to India to succeed Francisco de Almeida so soon as the term of his governorship should expire, and on his way explored the strait of Bab-el-Mandeb. In this year the first elephant was sent to Portugal from India by Francisco de Almeida. In 1507 Lourenço de Almeida discovered the Maldives. In this year Duarte de Mello founded the fort of Mozambique. Affonso de Albuquerque explored the coasts of Arabia and Persia, made the King of Ormuz tributary to Portugal, and on the 24th of October laid the foundations of the fort there, which he named Nossa Senhora da Vittoria.

In 1508 Albuquerque landed envoys charged with letters from himself to the King of Abyssinia, at a point three leagues from Cape Guardafui, who succeeded in reaching the court of Abyssinia, which was then governed by Helena, the grandmother of King David, who was in his minority. The result of this embassy was that an Armenian named Matthew was, some years after, sent as envoy from Abyssinia to the King of Portugal, and met with a gratifying reception from the king in the month of February, 1514.

In 1508 Diogo Lopes de Sequeira was commissioned by the king to examine the coasts of Madagascar and to discover Malacca. On the 11th of September, 1509, he anchored at Malacca, the great emporium of the east, to which were brought cloves from the Moluccas, nutmegs from Banda, sandal-wood from Timor, camphor from Borneo, gold from Sumatra and Loo Choo, and gums, spices, and other precious commodities from China, Japan, Siam, Pegu, &c. There he established a factory. Fernam de Magalhaens was in this expedition.

In the year 1510 the illustrious Francisco d' Almeida, the first Viceroy of India, on his way home to Portugal, was slain on the 1st of March in an encounter with the natives in the Agoada de Saldanha, near the Cape of Good Hope, which had been, as already stated, discovered by Antonio de Saldanha in 1503.

On the 25th of November, 1510, Affonso de Albuquerque conquered Goa, where he built a fort, and organized a municipal government, adopting measures of wise administration which paved the way for this city becoming the capital of the eastern empire of Portugal. In 1511 he conquered the city of Malacca, the king of which had treacherously plotted the death of Sequeira, with whom he had made terms of friendly intercourse. He then sent out expeditions to Siam, Birmah, and the East India Islands, and in this year and 1512, Antonio de Abreu discovered the island of Amboyna, and Francisco Serrão went to Ternate in the Moluccas. In 1512 or 1513 the Mascarenhas islands are supposed to have been discovered by Pedro de Mascarenhas, who appears to have sailed for India in 1511, and to have remained a considerable time during 1512 at Mozambique, but nothing certain is known of this discovery. In 1517 Fernam Peres de Andrade sailed to China, and entered into commercial relations with the governor of Canton. He also sent to Nankin as ambassador Thomé Pires, who, however, was cast into prison and died after a captivity of many years, in consequence of his commission to the emperor not being worded in conformity with the rules of Chinese etiquette, that sovereign being addressed by the governor of the Indies in the same style as he was accustomed to address the Indian rajahs who were tributary to Portugal. Andrade returned to India in 1519.

CHAPTER XVI.

RESULTS SOUTHWARD.

1513—*circa* 1530.

THE discovery of the New World was a fertile source of misconstruction and misnomer. Columbus to his dying day believed that Cuba was a part of Asia. Three years after his death the vast continent which his genius and perseverance had disclosed received a name which was other than his, and when at length the great ocean which bathed the western shores of that continent was revealed, the very points of the compass were dislodged from their natural position in the process of providing it a name. A glance at the map of the world is enough to show that the Atlantic and Pacific Oceans in their general extent lie east and west of America, yet from the simple accident that the Pacific lay south of that part of America (the Isthmus of Darien) from which it was first discovered, it received the inappropriate name of the South Sea. This designation was applied to it even in its most northern part, and, by way of antithesis, the Atlantic has occasionally been called the North Sea, even in its most southern part.

From 1505 to 1507 the court of Spain was earnestly engaged in the project of finding a direct route to the Spice Islands by the west, and on the 29th of June, 1508, Vicente Yañez Pinzon and Juan Diaz de Solis, reputed to be the ablest navigator and pilot of his day, sailed from San Lucar and explored the coasts of South America from Cape St. Augustine to the fortieth degree of south latitude, and yet missed the mouth of the La Plata. It was not till 1513, on the 25th of September, that Vasco Nuñez de Balboa, who had in 1510 been placed in command of a small colony at Santa Maria on the Gulf of Darien, perceived the Pacific from the ridge of the Sierra de Quarequa. Kneeling on the scarped summit from which he gazed on this vast and unknown ocean, he raised his hands to heaven in wonder and gratitude at the immensity of the revelation that had been made to him. But he had to encounter the resistance of the natives before he reached the shore. These he managed without much difficulty to subdue. Meanwhile he despatched Francisco Pizarro, Juan de Escaray, and Alonzo Martin de San Benito in search of the shortest pathway to the sea. Alonzo Martin on reaching the shore threw himself into a canoe which happened to be lying alongside, and was the first European who can be said to have navigated the Pacific. On the evening of the 29th of September, Balboa, with twenty-six of his companions, reached the strand, and walking into the water knee-deep, with his sword in one hand and the flag of Spain in the other, took formal possession of the newly-found ocean on behalf of his sovereign the King of Spain, and vowed to defend it against all his enemies. In token of possession he erected piles of stones on the shore. When the King of Spain heard of this discovery, he sent out Pedro Arias d'Avila as governor of Darien. Avila sailed from San Lucar with fifteen vessels and fifteen hundred men, and by his tyranny and exactions after his arrival spread desolation over the whole country from the Gulf of Darien to the Lake of Nicaragua. A dissension arose between him and Balboa, and in 1517 the latter, charged with calumny against the Government, was put in chains, tried, condemned, and beheaded.

In October, 1515, Juan Diaz de Solis was sent out with the express purpose of discovering a passage to the Moluccas by the west, and in January, 1516, he entered the Rio de la Plata, to which was originally given the name of Rio de Solis. The name of La Plata, which means "silver," was not given it till 1527, when Diego Garcia found some plates of that metal, probably from the mines of Potosi, in the hands of the Guarani Indians. The expedition was fatal to De Solis. Having anchored in the mouth of the river, he attempted a descent in the country, and he and eight of his men were massacred by the natives, and their bodies were cut in pieces, roasted, and devoured in sight of the ships. This was probably in August, 1516. The survivors had no heart to proceed farther, but returned to Europe, and thus King Ferdinand died without seeing the accomplishment of the great object of his anxiety.

It was not till 1517 that Magalhaens laid before Charles V., at Valladolid, his proposals for effecting the great discovery, but here we have to deal with a character and an achievement of colossal proportions, which demand especial description in a work devoted to the "Results" of the life of Prince Henry the Navigator.

Fernam de Magalhaens, better known by the Spanish form of his name, Magellan, was of noble Portuguese parentage, but we know little for certain of his early youth, except that he was brought up in the household of Queen Leonora, the wife of Dom João II. The instruction in mathematics and geography which he would there receive would be of an advanced kind, as at that time these sciences, which had received large development in Portugal under the auspices of Prince Henry, were taught by the two eminent Jews, named Josef and Rodrigo, of whom mention has been already made. He afterwards entered the service of Dom Manoel. In March, 1515, when little more than twenty years old, he joined the expedition of Francisco d' Almeida, first viceroy of the Indies, to Quiloa, in which were João de Nova, the constant rival of Albuquerque, already known to the reader as the discoverer of St. Helena, Diogo Correa, and Magalhaens' own bosom friend João Serrão. We have also seen that he was at the discovery of Malacca by Diogo Lopez de Sequeira in 1509. His sojourn in India and his campaigns in the extreme East, enabled him to gather information on which he afterwards based his memorable enterprise. One of his cousins, Francisco Serrão, who in 1511 first went to Ternate, married a woman of that island, and settled there, having contrived to secure the good-will of the Malay sovereign. He thence communicated to Magalhaens the great commercial advantages which might be secured by foreigners from intercourse with his adopted country.

Duarte Barbosa, also, the future brother-in-law of Magalhaens, contributed by his explorations, the account of which he completed in 1516, to that information which influenced the subsequent movements of Magalhaens. After his return from the East, Magalhaens served in Africa, and during a razzia at Azamor, was wounded in the knee, from which wound he remained lame all the rest of his life. In the distribution of some cattle then captured some disagreement arose, which led to complaints against him at court, and to much dissatisfaction. Conceiving himself unjustly treated by the king in the matter of these complaints and the mode of their reception, Magalhaens resolved to renounce his nationality, and to leave Portugal. His experience in navigation, and his acquaintance with the geography of the Moluccas, made him an acceptable visitor to Charles V., who was then but just returned from Flanders. Magalhaens arrived in Seville on the 20th of October, 1517, accompanied by two other malcontents, Rui Falciro, a learned cosmographer, and Christovam de Haro, a wealthy merchant, who already possessed immense commercial relations with India. The Papal Bull of Alexander VI., which had determined that a line drawn from pole to pole a hundred leagues west of the Azores should be the boundary between the claims of Spain and Portugal, was practically indecisive on account of the difficulty of measuring longitudes. Nor were matters improved by the Convention of 1494, in which the line of demarcation was removed to three hundred and seventy leagues west of the Azores, for though Portugal thereby gained in South America, Spain became also a considerable gainer in the East, the sea way to which had been first opened up by Portugal. The Moluccas formed, moreover, the very garden of those spices, the commerce of which was so eagerly coveted. Magalhaens gave it as his opinion that the Moluccas fell within the Spanish boundary, and undertook to take a fleet thither by the south of the American continent. The position of Magalhaens at Seville was strengthened by his marriage, in January, 1518, with the daughter of his relative, Diogo Barbosa, with whom he had taken up his quarters, and who had sailed to the Indies in 1501 under the order of Juan de Nova. He was now Commander of the Order of Santiago, and lieutenant to the alcaide of the Castle of Seville. Magalhaens had further the good fortune to secure the friendship and aid of Juan de Ovando, the principal factor of the Contratacion or chamber of commerce. To the latter was mainly owing the arrangement with the Emperor for that great expedition which was afterwards to hold so distinguished a position in the history of nautical discovery.

In August, 1519, Charles V. gave Magalhaens five ships, with the rank of Captain General, and it is remarkable that every one of the vessels was accompanied by a Portuguese pilot. The "Trinidad," of one hundred and twenty tons,[1] on board of which Magalhaens hoisted his flag, had Stevam Gomez for pilot; the "San Antonio," also of one hundred and twenty tons, commanded by Juan de Cartagena, had indeed a Spaniard, Andres de San Martin, for pilot, but he was accompanied by the Portuguese pilot, João Rodrigues de la Mafra; the "Concepcion," of ninety tons, commanded by Gaspar de Quesada, had for pilot the Portuguese, João Lopez de Caraballo; the "Vittoria," of eighty-five tons, under the command of Luis de Mendoza, was piloted by the Portuguese, Vasco Gallego; and the "Santiago," of seventy-five tons, was commanded by João Serrão, a Portuguese pilot, on whose skill and knowledge of the East, especially of the Moluccas, of which they were in search, Magalhaens placed great reliance.

The fleet, which consisted of two hundred and sixty-five persons, set sail from San Lucar de Barrameda on the 21st of September, 1519, and reached what is now called Rio de Janeiro on the 13th of December. Magal-

---

[1] To produce a correct impression on our minds of the size of these vessels, one-fifth may be added to the recorded tonnage to make the equivalent of the measurement of the present day; e. g. the "Trinidad," recorded as of 120 tons, may be estimated at 144 tons.

haens named it Porto de Santa Lucia. Thence they came to the Rio de la Plata, where at first they supposed they had found a channel to the Pacific; but giving up this hope, they proceeded south, and on the 31st of March, 1520, entered Port St. Julian, where Magalhaens stayed five months. The voyage, if destined to be a great one in the world's history, was a most unhappy one. It is not improbable that national jealousy had much to do with the insubordination exhibited by some of the Spanish captains on the one side, and the extreme severity resorted to by Magalhaens by way of repression. The revolt was initiated off the coast of Africa by Juan de Cartagena, captain of the "San Antonio." Discontent had arisen from Magalhaens having deviated from the course previously settled in a consultation with the principal officers, and by which deviation, unfortunately, much time was lost. Juan de Cartagena took upon himself to remonstrate with Magalhaens, who simply replied that it was his duty to follow his commander, and not call him to account. On a later occasion, this was followed by conduct so mutinous that Cartagena was not only deprived of his command, but made a prisoner, and the command of his vessel—the "San Antonio"—was given to a kinsman of Magalhaens, Alvaro de Mezquita. This led to worse. On the morrow of their arrival at Port St. Julian, which was Easter Day, the whole fleet was summoned to attend mass on shore; but Luis de Mendoza and Gaspar de Quesada, the captains of the "Vittoria" and "Concepcion," absented themselves. This looked strongly like disaffection, and so it proved. Magalhaens having decided to winter at Port San Julian, and finding fish abundant, judged it expedient to retrench the allowance of provisions. This, with the cold and barrenness of the country, caused great murmuring, and the crews desired that their commander would either issue the usual allowance, or return, for they had already gone farther than any other, and it was impossible to say what dangers lay before them. To this Magalhaens replied that what he had undertaken he intended to perform: that the king had ordered the voyage, and that it was his duty to go on till he found a termination to the land, or a strait. He reminded them that the place where they were to winter abounded in wood and water and fish and fowl, and he engaged that they should have no lack of bread and wine. He further held out to them the confident hope that they should discover a world as yet unknown. But they contended that all the spices of the Moluccas were not worth so long a voyage, in which they had to cross the line and coast the whole of Brazil, spending seven or eight months in passing through so many climates, and to reach a point so much easier of attainment in the opposite direction. But besides these reasonings, no doubt, the being commanded by a Portuguese was hateful to them, and they mistrusted his loyalty to their country. The result was, that one night Gaspar de Quesada boarded and took possession of the "San Antonio," made Alvaro de Mezquita, the captain, and Mafra, the pilot, prisoners, and released Juan de Cartagena.

Magalhaens now saw plainly that summary measures were more prudent than leniency. He first secured the "Vittoria" by sending thirty men on board her under Gonzalo Gomez de Espinosa, who by the commander's orders poniarded Mendoza. At midnight it happened that the ebb-tide caused the "San Antonio" to drag her anchors, and to float down the river towards Magalhaens' ship, who supposing her to be come with the intention of fighting, fired into her a ball, which made its way into the cabin, and passed between the legs of Mafra, the pilot, who was confined there. The ship was presently boarded, and Quesada, with the rest of the mutineers, was captured. The "Concepcion" after this surrendered at discretion. After a long inquiry, Quesada was condemned to be strangled, and a servant of his, who would otherwise have been hanged, was reprieved on condition of his being the executioner. Juan de Cartagena was sentenced to be put on shore with a French priest who had shared in the mutiny. The rest by a wise policy were pardoned, and the regulations respecting the provisions were modified.

When May set in, João Serrão was sent southward to examine the coast, and at twenty leagues' distance discovered on the 3rd of May a river, which in honour of the day he named Santa Cruz, but he had only passed three leagues beyond it, when his ship, the "Santiago," was driven violently ashore by a gust of wind from the east, and became a total wreck. The crew, who happily were all saved, contrived in a few days, during which they had to live on herbs and shell-fish, to make a small boat of some planks which were driven on shore, and by this means two men crossed the Santa Cruz and managed to reach Port San Julian, though in a most exhausted state. Assistance and provisions were immediately sent overland, but the weather was so severe that they had to thaw ice for drink. The crew were rescued and distributed among the other ships, Serrão being appointed to the command of the "Concepcion," and Duarte Barbosa to the "Vittoria."

It was not till they had lain two months in Port St. Julian that any sign of a native appeared. At length a man of gigantic size was seen on the beach, singing and dancing and sprinkling dust upon his head. As this was supposed to imply friendliness, a sailor was sent on shore to imitate his movements, which he did so well that the giant accompanied him on board. He first pointed to the sky, by way of asking whether they had come down from that region. When he saw his reflection in a looking-glass, he started back with such sudden surprise that he overturned four Spaniards who were behind him. Other natives soon came, the smallest of whom was taller and stouter than the largest Spaniard. They had bows and arrows, and coats made of skins. A kettle full of pottage with biscuit was served to them, enough for twenty Spaniards, but six of these men ate it all up. They then went on shore.

Two of them the next day brought some of the meat of the animals whose skins they wore, and were much pleased with the present of a red jacket to each in return. One of them came often afterwards, and having been taught the Lord's Prayer, was baptized and received the name of Juan Gigante (John Giant). Observing that the mice were thrown overboard, he begged to have them to eat, and took on shore all that they could give him, but after six days they saw no more of him. In all they saw only eighteen of the natives. They wore shoes made of the skins of the guanaco, which gave their feet the appearance of paws, for which reason Magalhaens gave them the name of Patagones, *pata*, in Spanish, meaning a paw. After a lapse of twenty days, four of them reappeared, and a most treacherous plan was resorted to in order to capture them, the object being to carry away the two youngest and to exchange the other two for their wives, with the view of importing this gigantic race into

Europe. After the two youngest had had their hands filled with presents of different kinds, bright iron rings were offered them, but as, much as they wished for them, they could not take them in their hands, it was proposed to put them on their legs, and thus unsuspectingly they were chained. As soon as they perceived the ungenerous trick, they struggled furiously, imploring Setebos, their demon, to come to their help. Nine Spaniards seized the other two and with difficulty bound them, but one broke loose at the time and the other afterwards escaped. The next day seven of the Spaniards had an encounter with nine of the natives, in which one of the former was shot; to avenge whose death, Magalhaens sent out twenty men to take or slay all they might meet, but happily, though they were eight days absent, they encountered none. The natives were wanderers, and carried with them their huts, which were made of light framework covered with skins. The men were about seven feet six inches high, and remarkably swift of foot; the women not so tall, but stouter.

After taking possession of the country for the King of Spain, by erecting a cross on a hill which they named Monte Christo, the ships set sail on the 24th August, leaving Juan de Cartagena and Sanchez de Reino on shore, with a supply of bread and wine.

Finding in the river of Santa Cruz a great abundance of fish, with wood and water, the fleet put in there till the 18th of October, when they proceeded southward, and on the 21st reached a cape, from which the coast turned directly *due west*. In honour of the day, which was the feast of St. Ursula, they named the cape Cabo de las Virgenes (Cape of the Virgins). Magalhaens then sent on two small ships to explore the inlet, but not to be absent more than five days. At the end of that time they returned with the report that while one of them had only found some bays containing many shoals, the other had sailed three days westward without finding an end to the strait, and that the tide was stronger when it flowed westward than when it ran to the east. This news was so encouraging that the whole fleet entered the channel. The "San Antonio" was sent on to explore, and after sailing fifty leagues brought back the same promising account as the others. There now remained only provisions enough for three months, and Magalhaens wisely called a council of the officers, at which the majority agreed with him in the desirableness of proceeding, but Stevam Gomez was for returning to Spain, lest they might be caught in calms and perish of starvation. Magalhaens, however, declared that "even if they were to be reduced to eating the leather on the ship's yards, he would fulfil his promise to the emperor, and, by the help of God, he hoped to succeed." He accordingly set sail, forbidding any on pain of death to say a word about returning to Spain, or about shortness of provisions.

In consequence of many fires being seen on the southern shore of the strait, Magalhaens named that country Tierra del Fuego (the Land of Fire).

As they proceeded westward another arm of the sea towards the south-east made its appearance and invited examination, and the "San Antonio" was sent to explore it, with orders to return in three days. As six days passed without her reappearance, the "Vittoria" went in search of her, and subsequently the whole fleet: but as no sign appeared of her, it was concluded that she had sailed for Spain, as afterwards proved to be the case.

The fleet now resumed its course westward, and on the 27th of November, 1520, thirty-seven days after the discovery of the eastern entrance, emerged from the strait into an open sea. The cape which terminated the strait at the westward on Tierra del Fuego was named Cabo Deseado (the Desired Cape), and that inflexible man, whom neither danger could deter nor death intimidate, is said to have wept tears of gratitude as he beheld this realization of his hopes. His illustrious name, as was only just, was subsequently given to the strait which had thus been traversed, although at first it was named after the "Vittoria," which had first sighted the eastern entrance.

Now that the great discovery was effected, it was desirable to make for the warm latitudes, and Magalhaens with the three remaining ships, the "Trinidad," the "Vittoria," and the "Concepcion," steered north-west. On their way they discovered on the 24th of January, 1521, an uninhabited island in 16° 15' S., which they named San Pablo (Saint Paul), probably from the remaining Patagonian, who, dying on the passage, had been baptized in that name. His fellow-captive had been carried off in the "San Antonio," on board of which he also perished as he neared the warm latitudes. Two days the ships remained off San Pablo in the hope of recruiting their diminished stores with fish, but without success. At two hundred leagues' distance they discovered on the 4th of February, another equally profitless, which from the number of sharks near it, they named Tiburones. In their disappointment they named the two islands, though so wide apart, Las Desventuradas (the Unfortunate Islands), for their distress was becoming so great that they even ate sawdust and the leather on the rigging. To save the fresh water, they mixed one-third of salt water with the fresh to boil their rice, which brought on the scurvy, and twenty of the men died of that disease.

They crossed the line on the 13th of February, and on the 6th of March, they had the happiness of reaching some beautiful islands, the natives of which came out to meet them in canoes bringing cocoa-nuts, yams, and rice. They were a sturdy race, with olive complexions and long hair. They dyed their teeth red and black, and were naked with the exception of an apron of bark.

Magalhaens would gladly have stayed here, but the pilfering habits of the people made it impossible. After some contentions on this account, at length they stole a skiff, which act Magalhaens punished by landing ninety men, and firing their houses. Several natives were killed, and all the provisions that could be found were carried off. The skiff was soon set adrift and recaptured, but the event made Magalhaens decide on leaving these islands, which from the propensity of their inhabitants received the name of the Ladrones (the Thieves).

From the Ladrones, Magalhaens steered W. and by W.S.W., and on the 16th of March reached a group of islands to which he gave the name of Archipielago de San Lazaro, a name which was afterwards replaced by that of the Philippines. On the 18th nine natives came out to him in a canoe from the island of Zuluan. He received them cordially, and they gave him fruits and palm wine. They afterwards brought provisions in exchange for trinkets, and the ships remained there nine days. These people were tattooed and went nearly naked, but some of the chiefs wore earrings and bracelets of gold, and a light covering of cotton, embroidered with silk, on the head. Their weapons also were sometimes ornamented with gold. On the 28th of March, Magalhaens anchored off Mazagua, with the chief of which island he entered into very friendly relations. On the 31st of March, being Easter day, mass was celebrated on shore with great solemnity. The rajah, who was named Colambu, and his brother were present, and when the Spaniards knelt in adoration, they followed their example. On inquiry Magalhaens found that they worshipped a supreme being, whom they named Abba.

On the 5th of April Magalhaens sailed, under the guidance of Colambu himself, to the large island of Zebu, the king of which was Colambu's relation. They reached the town of Zebu on the east side of the island on the 7th. Their arrival at first occasioned great alarm, which was allayed by Colambu, who represented the new-comers as a peaceable people who wished to barter goods with the islanders. At length all difficulties were removed and presents were interchanged. Here Magalhaens obtained supplies of provisions in great abundance.

Being anxious to introduce the Christian religion, for which the people seemed favourably inclined, with the king's consent he erected a stone chapel on the shore, and it having been duly consecrated, and also ornamented with tapestry and palm branches, he landed on Sunday, the 14th April, with many of his people to hear mass. The procession was headed by the royal ensigns and two men in complete armour. The king and a large number of natives came to observe the service, and behaved with the greatest decorum. By means of the interpreter, a native of Sumatra, who had accompanied the expedition, the priest endeavoured to instruct them in the Christian faith, and soon the king and the chief of Mazagua requested to be baptized. The former had given him the name of Carlos, from the emperor. Colambu was named Juan, and in a short time the queen, the princesses, and the residents of the town followed their example. Unfortunately, while explaining the duties required by Christianity, the foremost of which was the destruction of their idols, Magalhaens held out an inducement to conversion which savoured much more of worldliness than of the religion he was advocating. He assured the King of Zebu that one of the benefits of Christianity would be the power of easily subduing his enemies. Now the island contained several little independent sovereignties which were often at war with each other, and a temptation like this was a great provocation to his zeal. Whether, resting on so insecure a foundation, it was likely to be permanent, we shall presently see. To show the King of Zebu the value of Spanish protection, Magalhaens called a meeting of the other chiefs, four of whom attended. These he required on pain of death to pledge themselves to obey the new Christian king. They yielded, but one of them afterwards slighting the command, was attacked in the night by Magalhaens with forty men, who ransacked and burnt one of his villages and set up a cross on the spot.

Near Zebu was a small island named Matan, to the chief of which, who was named Cilapulapo, he sent a similar requirement that he would submit to the Christian King of Zebu, on pain of having his town, named also Matan, similarly destroyed. The gallant chief replied that he wished to be on good terms with the Spaniards, and to prove his words sent them a present of provisions, but absolutely refused to obey strangers of whom he knew nothing, or to submit to those whom he had long been accustomed to command. Against the advice of the King of Zebu as well as of João Serrão, Magalhaens determined to punish the chief of Matan for his contumacy. At midnight, on the 26th of April, Magalhaens sailed for Matan with three boats and sixty men, accompanied by the King of Zebu and a thousand natives. It wanted two hours of daylight when they arrived, but it was low water, and while waiting for the morning, Magalhaens sent a messenger to the chief, proposing that if he would then make submission, all would be forgotten. The only answer was a defiance. The King of Zebu would have led the attack with his thousand men, but his offer was declined, and he himself ordered to remain quiet with his men in their canoes and see how the Spaniards would fight. Eleven men were left to guard the boats, and forty-nine, including Magalhaens, landed. They first set fire to some houses, when a strong body of Indians appeared in one direction, and as soon as the Spaniards had prepared to attack them, another body of Indians made their appearance from another quarter. Magalhaens was thus obliged to divide his little band into two. The battle was kept up with projectiles during the greater part of the day, the Indians using stones, lances, and arrows, and the Spaniards their muskets and cross-bows. After a time it was perceived that the fire of the Spanish musketry was not so deadly as had been apprehended, and the islanders had further noticed that the legs of their enemies could be assailed with greater effect than their heads and bodies, which were covered with armour. Moreover, Magalhaens had detached a small party to set fire to some houses, more than twenty of which were burnt, but two of the party were killed by

the Indians. The latter became now bolder, and
approached nearer with a view to taking the life of
Magalhaens himself. His ammunition now began to
fail, and he ordered a retreat, but immediately after
received a wound from an arrow in the leg. It was
some distance to the boats, and the Spaniards lost all
order in their retreat, but Magalhaens himself bravely
confronted the Indians, looking back from time to time
to see if the men had reached the boats. He had just
slain an Indian by hurling back at him his own lance,
when in attempting to draw his sword, he found that a
wound in the right arm prevented him from doing so
more than halfway. The islanders seeing this, attacked
him boldly. A severe wound in the right leg caused
him to fall forward on his face, and he was speedily
despatched. In obedience to the unfortunate order
which he had received, the King of Zebu and his people
had remained in their canoes, looking quietly on, but seeing the failing condition of the Spaniards at the close, came
to their relief and saved many of them. Eight Spaniards
died with Magalhaens, and twenty-two were wounded.

Thus fell this great navigator, second only to Columbus in the history of nautical exploration. Midway in
the execution of a feat such as the world had never
witnessed, the very hardihood which already had
rendered that achievement possible, had now, by degenerating into presumption, deprived him of the glory of
its fulfilment.

The Spaniards who escaped elected Duarte Barbosa
and the pilot João Serrão, as joint commanders-in-chief.
We have now to witness the hollowness of that rapid
conversion to Christianity professed by the King of Zebu,
which very naturally betrayed itself so soon as the false

hope on which he had depended was proved to be unfounded. The defeat of Magalhaens was the most conclusive proof that Christianity did not insure victory in battle. The friendly co-operation of allies was now replaced by the basest treachery. On Wednesday, May the 1st, this Christian king invited the commanders and officers to an entertainment on shore, in order that he might deliver to them the presents intended for the emperor, which were now ready. But he plotted their death, a threat from the King of Matan rendering it necessary for him to prove himself their enemy. Against the advice of Serrão, who had his misgivings, Barbosa accepted the invitation, and by means of an unmerited taunt, induced Serrão to accompany him. Twenty-six Spaniards went on shore, and in the midst of the feast were attacked by a body of armed men, who had been concealed. All of them were murdered with the exception of the interpreter and Serrão, who had been a favourite amongst them and was spared. The Spaniards on board hearing the cry of the victims, whose bodies were presently dragged to the shore and cast into the sea, weighed anchor and fired upon the town. The Indians now brought forward Serrão, naked and in chains, who implored his countrymen to desist from firing and to ransom him; but Caraballo, the principal officer then in command, knowing that Serrão's detention left him without a superior, threw aside every feeling of humanity and made sail, basely abandoning Serrão to the mercy of the natives, who, doubtless, put him to death.

About one hundred and fifteen only now survived of the armada, too small a number to manage the three remaining ships. They sailed for the island of Bohol, S.E. of Zebu, where they burned the "Concepcion," which was the oldest of their three vessels. Caraballo was elected commander-in-chief, and Goncalo Gomez de Espinosa was appointed to the command of the "Vittoria."

From Bohol they sailed S.S.W., and after touching on the west coast of Mindanao, passed by Cagayan to the island of Palawan, and thence to Borneo.

It is amusing to observe how completely explorers coming into new countries, the natural phenomena of which they witness for the first time, have been deceived by nature herself, when she has beneficently contrived a deception for the sake of preserving the creatures of her own hand. In Palawan, a long strip of an island, which stretches away north-west and south-east from the northernmost point of Borneo, they came upon specimens of the remarkable orthopterous insect, the *phyllium*, or walking leaf, whose wings are like leaves, its head like a broken-off stalk, and its eggs like seeds. The following is Pigafetta's account of them in this voyage:—

"In this island are found certain trees, the leaves of which when they fall, are animated and walk. They are like the leaves of the mulberry-tree, but not so long; they have the leaf-stalk short and pointed, and near the leaf-stalk they have on each side two feet. If they are touched they escape, but if crushed, they do not give out blood. I kept one for nine days in a box. When I opened it the leaf went round the box. I believe they live upon air."

On the 8th of July, 1521, they anchored at about three leagues distance from the city of Borneo, and the next morning were visited by the king's secretary, inquiring their business and whence they came. They sent a present to the king, whose name was Siripada, and received from him an invitation for two of the Spaniards to visit the city. Espinosa, Captain of the "Vittoria," accordingly landed with six men, and was conveyed on an elephant to the king, who when he had satisfied his curiosity, dismissed him with a present of Chinese damask. This city was inhabited by Mahometans, but there was another larger one inhabited by the earlier natives, who worshipped the sun and moon. Both cities were built on piles over the water. As the people continued friendly, and the Spaniards had occasion to caulk the ships, five men were sent to the city of Borneo to procure wax to serve instead of pitch for that purpose, but as three days elapsed without their returning, and some large junks were seen to enter the port and anchor near them, while a host of smaller craft put off from the shore, the Spaniards tripped their anchors, attacked and captured two of the junks, and with their artillery dispersed the smaller vessels. Two days after, the 31st of July, they captured another junk, containing one hundred men, and among them, one of the King of Borneo's generals, said to be the son of the King of Luzon. This man was sent on shore with several others to the king, to tell him that if the five Spaniards were not restored, every vessel coming into the port should be destroyed. Two of them only were returned, but the Spaniards being anxious to proceed on their voyage, set sail a few days after without the other three; an inexplicable proceeding, as they had so large a number of natives to give in exchange. It afterwards appeared that Caraballo had privately released the son of the King of Luzon for a sum of money, a circumstance which caused his removal from the command by general consent when the ships were ready to sail. Espinosa was made commander-in-chief, and Juan Sebastian del Cano, a

Biscayan, was appointed to the command of the "Vittoria."

Off the coast of Mindanao, they captured a vessel of the country containing some of the chiefs of Mindanao, by whose instructions they altered their course to southeast with the view of finding the Moluccas. In the passage their Mindanao prisoners leaped overboard in the night-time, and made their escape. It was on Wednesday, November 6th, 1521, that four islands were descried, which, as they learned from one of the pilots, who being wounded could not escape, were the long-sought-for Molucca Islands, the object for the discovery of which by a western route this most wearisome voyage was undertaken.

On Friday, the 8th, they anchored at Tidor, and the next day the king, whose name was Almanzor, richly dressed in embroidered linen and silks, came on board the "Capitana," where he met with a cordial welcome, and on taking leave embraced the captain, expressing himself much gratified with his reception. As at first the demand for spices was not promptly responded to, the Spaniards thought of seeking a cargo at one of the other islands, but when the king heard this, he made a solemn promise to them on the Korán, to provide them with all the spices they desired if they would engage not to seek them elsewhere. To this Espinosa consented, and to show his consideration for the king, at his request liberated his prisoners and killed all the hogs on board, the dislike of the Mohammedans to these animals being intense. By way of compensation, the king made the Spaniards an ample present of goats and poultry.

On the 13th of November, a Portuguese named Pedro Affonso de Lorosa, who had come to the Moluccas with the first discoverers, came from Ternate and informed the Spaniards that the news of their voyage had reached the Moluccas, nearly twelve months before. Francisco Serrão, the discoverer, had died at Ternate eight months previously. Lorosa begged permission to return with his wife to Europe in the Spanish ships, which was granted.

On the 25th, Almanzor having procured a large quantity of cloves from the neighbouring islands, invited the Spaniards to a banquet on shore, saying that it was customary to entertain merchants on the occasion of their first taking in a cargo. But the Spaniards having a wholesome recollection of the fatal feast at Zebu, prudently declined the invitation with thanks.

Having laid in their stock of spices and provisions, they prepared to sail on Wednesday, December 18th, and the kings of the islands came to pay their farewell visit, but while the "Trinidad" was weighing, it was found that she had sprung a leak. As several days were spent in vain endeavours to remedy the mischief, or to find out where the water entered, it was resolved that the "Vittoria" should sail forthwith to Europe by the Cape of Good Hope, and that the "Trinidad," after repairing, should sail eastward for Panama. The "Vittoria" had in her forty-seven Europeans, and thirteen Indians. The "Trinidad" fifty-three Europeans. The King of Tidor sent two pilots to steer the "Vittoria" clear of the neighbouring islands, and she proceeded on her homeward voyage.

On the 10th of January they reached Mallua or Ombay, where they remained fifteen days to repair, and on the 26th they came to the island of Timor, where they took in white sandal-wood, cinnamon, and wax. Here a mutiny broke out, in which several lives were lost. Some of the mutineers were executed, and others left the ship.

On February 11th they sailed from Timor, and in order to avoid Portuguese ships in rounding the Cape, sailed as far south as 42° S., but with all their caution, when they passed the Cape on the 6th of May, they approached it within five leagues. Their sufferings must have been great, for the ship was leaky and provisions scarce, and at all hazards, when they reached the Cape Verde Islands, they were compelled to put in at Santiago, for their provisions were now exhausted. This was on the 9th of July.

To prevent the Portuguese from suspecting whence they came, they said that they had come from America, and thus they procured some rice from the shore. It was here they discovered that in sailing round the world they had lost a day in reckoning their time, for whereas at Santiago it was Thursday, the 10th of July, the "Vittoria's" account made it Wednesday, the 9th.

Through the imprudence of one of the sailors who offered spices in payment for what he wanted to purchase, the remnant of this extraordinary expedition narrowly escaped even at this late period from a ruinous disaster. The boat was stopped, and the Portuguese made preparations to attack the ship, but fortunately the movement was perceived in time, and Del Cano weighed anchor and left the island.

On Saturday, the 6th of September, 1522, the "Vittoria" arrived at San Lucar, with eighteen survivors only of the noble fleet which had sailed from the same port on the 20th of September, 1519. Thus three years, all but fourteen days, had been expended in this most eventful and wonderful voyage—a miracle of resolute perseverance under inconceivable hardships. It was appropriate that the only ship which had effected this great achievement should have borne the name of "Vittoria," for a victory had been gained such as the world had never witnessed. On his arrival, Del Cano, the fortunate recipient of the honours which had been toiled for and deserved by the talents and indomitable resolution of his great commander, Magalhaens, was summoned by the emperor to Valladolid, and received with great distinction. A life pension of five hundred ducats was conferred on him, with a patent of nobility. The coat of arms granted him by the emperor bore branches of the clove, cinnamon, and nutmeg trees, with a globe for a crest, and the motto, "*Primus circumdedisti me.*"

Thus far we have had great things to record as links in one continuous chain of magnificent discoveries. Eastward and westward the bold hand of man had torn away the veil from the bosom of ocean, and at length he has encircled her waist with his grasp. One little century has transpired since the budding manhood of Prince Henry had seen him bent upon the investigation of the unknown paths of the Atlantic, and now the world has been encompassed by men whose daring was fostered by the example of his perseverance. A century shall not have transpired since his first feeble but persistent efforts had succeeded in rounding the then formidable Cape Bojador, before another gem shall be added to the crown of that glorious little nation, to whose courageous efforts his genius and constancy had given the first impulse.

The great discoveries of Francisco Pizarro and Diego de Almagro on the western coast of South America soon followed.

It was not long after the completion of the ever memorable voyage which has been just related, before Australia, that vast insular continent, with whose discovery we are accustomed generally to connect the name of our illustrious Cook, or at furthest that of Dampier, was explored both on its eastern and western sides. True, the knowledge of this fact lay dormant till the close of the last century, hidden in the testimony of some valuable old French manuscript maps, whose worth and importance, nay, even whose existence, appears to have been unrecognized till after the gallant Cook had completed his unrivalled series of explorations.[2] Long previously, no doubt, the great fact had been faintly indicated on engraved maps, but in a fashion far less definite than on these yet older manuscript maps, which, drawn before copper plates were used for cartography, tell forth unequivocally the story of the important discovery. The earliest *engraved* indication of Australia occurs on a mappe-monde, in the third volume of the Polyglot Bible of Arias Montanus, dated 1571, and is the more striking that it stands unconnected with any

[2] It is greatly to be regretted that Alexander Dalrymple, at that time Hydrographer to the Admiralty and East India Company, to whom England is largely indebted for its commercial prosperity, and who panted for the glory of discovering a great southern continent, should have allowed his jealousy of Captain Cook's appointment to the "Endeavour" to lead him into an injurious insinuation that the great Captain's discoveries on the coast of New Holland were the result of his acquaintance with one of these pre-existent maps. This he bases on the resemblance of the names of bays and coasts on the map to those given by Captain Cook to parts of New Holland which he had himself discovered. The unworthy insinuation met with a sensible and generous refutation from the pen of a Frenchman, M. Frederic Metz, in a paper printed at p. 261, Vol. 47, of *La Revue, ou Décade Philosophique, Littéraire et Politique*, Nov., 1805.

other land whatever, and bears no kind of description. It is simply a curved line indicating the north part of an unexplored land exactly in the position of the north of Australia, distinctly implying an imperfect discovery. In the other *engraved* maps of the sixteenth century, we find the Terra Australis occupying the whole of the southern part of the globe, that portion which lay in the real longitude of Australia being brought up to its right position, far more to the north than elsewhere; thus recognizing the genuine discovery of the north part of that continent. The vast remainder was but a fancied continuation of the Tierra del Fuego, the southern point of which not having been yet discovered, was supposed to form a portion of a great southern land which from remote ages had been imagined to be in existence, and as Magalhaens had been the discoverer of this Tierra del Fuego in passing through the strait which bears his name, this supposed great southern continent received from its reputed discoverer the name of Terra Magellanica. In some of these early engraved maps, New Guinea and the Terra Australis are united, but no greater proof can be adduced of the fact, that Australia was then known to be discovered, although as yet no *authenticated* discovery by any given ship or navigator had been recorded, than the fact that on other maps of this period is found the legend, " Nova Guinea, quæ an sit insula aut pars continentis adhuc ignotum est." " New Guinea, which whether it be an island or part of the continent is as yet unknown." These facts respecting the early *engraved* maps are interesting, because while utterly distinct from the earlier and more valuable manuscript documents, even they precede the period of what, for want of a better word, I must call the earliest authenticated discovery of Australia, *i.e.*, first made *by a known ship or navigator*. This was effected on the 18th of November, 1605, by the Dutch yacht, the "Duyfhen," which had been despatched from Bantam to explore the island of New Guinea, and which sailed along what was thought to be the west side of that country to $19\frac{3}{4}°$ of south latitude.[3]

But all this, though far from irrelevant to our subject, is a digression from the more important consideration of the story told by the invaluable manuscript maps of the beginning of the sixteenth century. It occurs in similar form on seven maps, five of them in England and two in France, on which, immediately below Java and separated from that island only by a narrow strait, is drawn a large country stretching southward to the verge of the several maps. The first of these maps to which a fixed date is attached, are two in one atlas, which was made in 1542 by a Frenchman named Jean Rotz, who came to England and dedicated his work to Henry VIII. Another, probably older but without a date, is anonymous, but as it bears the arms of the Dauphin, it appears to have been executed in the time of Francis I. for his son the Dauphin, afterwards Henry II. Both this map and the atlas by Rotz are in the British

---

[3] In the year 1861 I lighted on a manuscript mappe-monde in the British Museum, which to all reasonable appearance, enabled me to carry back the first *authenticated* discovery to the year 1601, and to transfer the honour thereof from the Dutch to the Portuguese. This, however, proved, subsequently, to be an abominable imposture. For the sake of those whose tastes are sufficiently antiquarian to take an interest in the matter, I have given the whole story in an Appendix, but purposely omit it from the current text, because it is necessarily explanatory instead of being purely narrative; and, moreover, it does not fall within the century of discoveries of which this book professes to treat.

Museum. On the Dauphin map this great country is called "Jave la Grande;" on Rotz's map "The Londe of Java," and is distinguished from the smaller island of Java itself by the latter being called "The lytil Java."

There are three points, then, which demand our consideration. 1st. What the large country is which is thus delineated to the south of Java. 2nd. What was the approximate period of the discovery. 3rd. Who were the discoverers.

As the other maps all tell the same story, it will be needless here to make any further reference to them.[1]

1st. Happily, Rotz's map is an exception to the rest in one important respect. Whereas the other maps connect this great country with a vast continent occupying the whole south part of the globe, including and, as it were, springing from the Tierra del Fuego, from whose discoverer it is called Magellanica, Rotz's map exhibits the degrees of latitude in which both the western and eastern coasts were supposed to cease. On the western side the coast-line ceases altogether at 35°, the real south-western point of Australia. On the eastern coast, evidently the remotest for investigation, there is greater inaccuracy, the line terminating in the sixtieth degree, a parallel far exceeding in its southing even the southernmost point of Tasmania, which is in 43° 35′, but there is strong reason for supposing that the eastern side of Tasmania was included in this line. At the same time, while there is no other country but Australia lying between the same parallels and of the same extent, between the east coast of Africa and the west coast of America, Australia does in reality lie between the same

[1] For a more detailed account of these maps see my "Early Voyages to Terra Australis," printed for the Hakluyt Society, 1859.

meridians as the great mass of the country here laid down.

There are also many points of correctness in contour. As regards the west coast, a single glance of the eye is sufficient to detect the general resemblance. On the eastern side, as might be expected, the discrepancies are much greater, but nothing can be more remarkable than the great number of islands and reefs laid down along the north-east coast as coinciding with the Great Barrier Reefs, and with the Cumberland and Northumberland Islands, and a host of others, which skirt this part of the shores of Australia.

2ndly. Such an amount of comparative accuracy extending over so vast a field of exploration, fairly throws back the original discovery to a period very much earlier than 1542, the date of Rotz's map, so that we may legitimately include some portion at least of the immense continental island within our century of discoveries.

3rdly. Who were the discoverers? In reply we can only say, that some of the names of places are beyond all question Portuguese, while others bear the appearance of being Provençal. In the presence of such facts we must content ourselves with the certainty that Australia was discovered at that early period, and live in the hope that some documents may one day be found which may throw a light on the actual discoverers. It should be mentioned that New Zealand is also shown by these early maps to have been then discovered.

We have now seen how, within the small compass of a hundred years, from the date of the rounding of Cape Bojador, more than one-half of the world was opened up to man's knowledge, and brought within his reach by an unbroken chain of discovery which originated in the genius and the efforts of one whose name is all but unknown.

The Coasts of Africa visited; the Cape of Good Hope rounded; the New World disclosed; the sea-way to India, the Moluccas, and China, laid open; the globe circumnavigated, and Australia and New Zealand discovered: such were the stupendous results of a great thought and of indomitable perseverance in spite of twelve years of costly failure and disheartening ridicule. Had that failure and that ridicule produced on Prince Henry the effect which they ordinarily produce on other men, it is impossible to say what delays would have occurred before these mighty events would have been realized; for it must be borne in mind that the ardour not only of his own sailors, but of surrounding nations, owed its impulse to this pertinacity of purpose in him. True it is, that the great majority of these vast results were effected after his death; and it was not granted to him to affix his quaint signature to charters and grants of territory in those Eastern and Western Empires which at length were won by means of the explorations he had

I[FFANTE] D[OM] A[NRIQUE].

fostered. True, he lived not to see the proof, in his own case unparalleled, that the courageous pursuit of a grand idea may produce consequences even greater than that idea had comprehended. No doubt that from Sagres no beam of light brought to his mental vision the prospect of an America to brighten the horizon of the Sea of Darkness; yet enough has, I trust, been said in the preceding pages to establish the correctness of the statement with which I set out, that "if, from the pinnacle of our present knowledge, we mark on the world of waters those bright tracks which have led to the discovery of mighty continents, we shall find them all lead us back to that same inhospitable point of Sagres, and to the motive which gave to it a royal inhabitant."

APPENDIX.

In the year 1861, I laid before the Society of Antiquaries, and thereby made known to the world for the first time, the apparently important fact that the great continental island of Australia had been discovered in the year 1601 by a Portuguese navigator, named Manoel Godinho de Eredia. Up to that time the earliest *authenticated* discovery of any part of the great southern land, was that made a little to the west and south of Cape York, by the commander of the Dutch yacht the "Duyfhen" or "Dove," about the month of March, 1606. Thus the supposed fact which I announced in 1861, gave a date to the first authenticated discovery of Australia earlier by five years than that which had been previously accepted in history, and transferred the honour of that discovery from Holland to Portugal. The document on which this assumption was based, was a MS. mappe-monde in the British Museum, in which on the north-west corner of a country which could be shown beyond all question to be Australia, stood a legend in Portuguese to the following effect: "Nuça Antara was discovered in the year 1601 by Manoel Godinho de Eredia, by command of the viceroy Ayres de Saldanha." This mappe-monde had the great disadvantage of being only a copy, possibly made even in the present century, from one, the geography of which proved it to be some two centuries older. Still the mere fact of its being a copy laid it open to a variety of possible objections, which fortunately I was able to forestall by arguments that I believed to be unanswerable, but which need not be repeated here. I need now merely say that I had the good fortune at the time to find an apparently happy confirmation of what was stated in the map, in a little printed work which described the discoverer as a learned cosmographer and skilful captain, who had received a special commission from the viceroy at Goa to make explorations for gold-mines, and at the same time to verify the descriptions of the southern islands. The viceroy thus mentioned was the immediate predecessor of Ayres de Saldanha, under whose viceroyalty the map declares the discovery to have been made.

The map, as I afterwards discovered from a letter addressed to Navarrete by the Vicomte de Santarem in 1835, was a copy by a foreign hand from one in a MS. Atlas made in the seventeenth century by one Teixeira. The name "Nuça Antara" is shown in Sir Stamford Raffles' "Java" to apply also to the island of Madura, north east of Java, but as that island was distinctly laid down in this very mappe-monde, it seemed clear that no mistake was involved on that account; and that the country delineated was really Australia was proved by a second legend in Portuguese below the first to this effect, "Land discovered by the Dutch, which they called Endracht or Concord." Eendraghtsland, as we all know, was the name given to a large tract on the west coast of Australia, discovered by the Dutch ship, the "Eendraght," in 1616. The reader, then, will see that in 1861, I had before me in a map (the original of which was made two centuries and a quarter ago), a distinct and unequivocal declaration of the actual discovery of a country which the map itself showed to be Australia, by a man whom contemporary history described as a distinguished cosmographer, and at a time which corresponded with the periods of office of the two viceroys mentioned respectively in the printed document quoted, and in the map. The viceroyalty of Francisco de Gama, from whom Eredia first received his commission to make similar explorations, extended from 1597 to 1600, and the asserted discovery was made in 1601, under the viceroyalty of Ayres de Saldanha, the immediate successor of Da Gama. I am not ashamed that I accepted the declaration as sound. It was so accepted by all who had the above evidence before them, and became recognized as an historical fact. Being so recognized, it carried back, as I have said, the first discovery of Australia by *any known ship or navigator* from 1606 to 1601, and transferred the honour of such discovery from the Dutch to the Portuguese. One thing, of course, remained to be desired; viz. that the original report of the discovery might some day be found. That day at length arrived. In the year 1871, M. Reulens, the librarian of the Royal Burgundian Library at Brussels, discovered among the MSS. there, the original report of Eredia to Philip III. of all his doings in the South Seas, and his excellency the Chevalier d'Antas was good enough to have a transcript made for me of all that portion which related to my subject. I no sooner looked into this more ample statement than I detected the work of an imposter, and as in the preparation of my work on " Early Voyages to Terra Australis," my memory had become charged with all the details of the subject, I was able to trace not only the documents which, as he was not a discoverer in reality, supplied him with the materials for being a discoverer on paper, but also blunders in those documents of which I was cognizant, but he had not been, and which, as he had been himself deceived, clearly betrayed the utter falsity of his statements. Believing, for reasons which I shall presently explain, that there were wealthy countries in the south which had never been explored, Eredia procured for himself the appointment of official " Discoverer" in those regions, an ambiguous and misleading title which implies by anticipation the credit due only to success. The delusion which the ambiguity of that title rendered possible became a reality, for we have seen that on the map which came before me in 1861, the declaration was distinct and absolute " Nuça Antara was discovered in the year 1601 by Manoel Godinho de Eredia," whereas the pretended discoveries described in the report are not professed to have been made by Eredia in *propriâ personâ*.

Before giving the translation of the words of Eredia's report, I will merely premise that the reputed country in the south, about which he treats, has received from him the name of " India Meridional," a designation which I will retain in preference to Southern India, for the sake of avoiding confusion with the country to which the latter name more properly belongs. I shall presently explain how this country received its existence on maps, became a subject of ambitious thought to Manoel Godinho de Eredia, and finally became identified with the genuine Australia, of which he really had no knowledge whatever.

"The India Meridional [or Southern India]," says Eredia, "is that continent which extends from the Promontory of Beach, the province of gold, in 16 degrees of south latitude, to the tropic of Capricorn and Antarctic circle, with many large provinces, such as Maletur, Locach, and others as yet unknown in that sea, in which lies the island called Java Minor, so celebrated by the ancients and so unknown by the moderns, with other adjacent islands, such as Petan, Necuran, Agania; and nearly all these produce a great quantity of gold, cloves, mace, nutmegs, sandal-wood, and spices not known or seen in Europe, as is testified by Ptolemy and Vartomannus in their writings, and by Marco Polo from eye-witness, for he lived a long time in Java Minor!" [here follows a learned dissertation on Marco Polo and Java Minor which need not be quoted until he approaches the part which concerns our subject]. "The annals of Java Major," he says, "make mention of the India Meridional and of its commerce and of the ancient navigation from Java Major to Java Minor, where was the greatest emporium in the world for gold and spices. This commerce was subsequently stopped by wars for the space of 331 years until the year 1600, when by chance a boat from Luça Antara, in the India Meridional, driven by weather and currents, arrived in the harbour of Balambuan in Java Major, where the king of the province, who was present at the time with some Portuguese, gave them a good reception and entertainment. These strangers of Luça Antara, although in form and features like the Javanese of Bantam, differed from them in language, and showed themselves to be Javanese of another race. This novelty caused so much pleasure to the Javanese, and satraps of Balambuan, and especially to Chiaymasiuro, King of Damuth, that the latter, being a prince, resolved for curiosity's sake to venture on the discovery of Luça Antara. Embarking with some companions in a calaluz or rowing-boat provided with necessaries, he left the port of Balambuan for the South, and after twelve days' voyage arrived at the said harbour of Luça Antara, a peninsula or island of 600 leagues in circumference, where he was well and hospitably received by the Xabandar of the country; and while Chiaymasiuro was enjoying the freshness of the country, he took note of its wealth, for he observed in it much gold, cloves, mace, nutmegs, sandal-wood, both white and coloured, with other spices and aromatics of which he took samples. With the south monsoon he returned safely to the harbour of Balambuan, where he was received by the king in presence of the Portuguese and particularly of Pedro de Carvalhães, overseer at Malacca, who will bear witness to his arrival and to his voyage from Luça Antara to Balambuan in the year 1601. According to the roteiro or log of Chiaymasinro's voyage, Luça Antara must be the general name of that peninsula, in which are the harbours of the kingdoms of Beach and Maletur, because between the sixteen degrees of latitude of Beach and the nine degrees of Balambuan is a space of eight degrees, which amount to the 140 Spanish leagues of Chiaymasiuro's twelve days' voyage from Balambuan to Luça Antara. This shows that Luça Antara cannot be the Java Minor of Marco Polo, because it is in a higher latitude of the tropic of Capricorn; viz. in 23° 30'. And for this enterprise was Manoel Godinho de Eredia at the same time despatched in the said year of 1601 and provided with the habit of the Order of Christ and the title of Adelantado of the India Meridional, to pass to the southward in order to carry out the southern discoveries and to take possession of these lands for the crown of Portugal. But this did not take place, because, being in Malacca ready to make the voyage of the India Meridional, there supervened the wars of that fortress with the Malays and Dutch, which prevented the discoveries, as the people were wanted for the defence of Malacca, the Governor of which was Andrea Furtado de Mendoça."

This is Eredia's report, and it is followed by a statement to the same effect written by Chiaymasiuro, King of Damuth, to the King of Pam, but embodying the following additional facts. The king of the country presented Chiaymasiuro with handfuls of gold coin, such as that of Venice. The natives wore their hair long, down to the shoulders and had the head bound with a fillet of wrought gold. They wore kreeses adorned with precious stones and with curved blades like the kreeses of Bali. Their common pastime was cockfighting. This letter of Chiaymasiuro's is followed by a like statement, agreeing in all particulars with the two preceding, indited by the Portuguese, Pedro de Carvalhães, who declares that he received it from the lips of Chiaymasiuro and his companions whom he met in Surabaya. This document contains one statement in addition to the foregoing; viz. that Luça Antara contained many populous cities and towns. At the close of the document Carvalhães swears on the holy Gospels to the truth of his statement and signs it with his name. Accompanying the extract which I received from Brussels were two maps, also by Eredia, the one of Luça Antara and its surroundings, the other a map of the world, in which Luça Antara is placed on the N.W. of that part of the great southern land, which, if it represented a truth, *could* only tally with what we know to be Australia. Now it does not require much knowledge of geography to see that the Luça Antara of Eredia, thus described, would in no way agree with what we know of Australia. Here, therefore, I might stop; but when I reflect how many thousands have been led by my means erroneously to connect the name of Eredia with the first authenticated discovery of Australia, I think it likely that some may look to me for the completion of the story.

Not being Australia, then, what was Luça or Nuça Antara? Finding that in Sunda " Nusa " is the ordinary, and in Java the

X

ceremonial, word for "island," while to the eastward and northward not Nusa, but Pulo and other equivalents are used for that word, and remembering that "Luça Antara" was an alternative name for the island of Madura, which lies close to the east coast of Java itself, I reverted to the description of Luça Antara given by the native prince Chiaymasiuro and by P. Carvalhães and found that it tallied with Madura to a nicety. The men of Luça Antara who were driven by stress of weather into the port of Balambuan are described as in figure, face, and complexion like the Javanese of Bantam, but differing somewhat in their language, insomuch as they showed themselves to be Javanese of another species or race. Crawford, in his History of the Indian Archipelago, t. 2, p. 69, says that the languages of the two islands are scarcely more like than any other two languages of the western portion of the Archipelago. The long hair down to the shoulders, the fillet of cloth of gold round the head, the kreese adorned with precious stones and with the blade curved, the cock-fighting, the gold and spices and sandal-wood, all bear their abundant testimony to the fitness of the application of the description to the island of Madura. The island itself was described as six hundred leagues in circuit and containing well-peopled cities and towns, which is all in accordance with the real description of Madura, nor can we find any other island presenting such elements of identity. Here, then, we come to the first stage of the great falsehood. The Javanese prince reports himself to have made a voyage of twelve days to the *south* from Balambuan to reach an island whose name and description in every particular belong to an island lying *north* of Balambuan. The distance from Balambuan to the coast assumed to be reached by the southward course, viz. Australia, would be about six hundred miles; that by the northern course to Madura would be barely ninety, and the time occupied in accomplishing the voyage with oars, viz. twelve days, would apply much more reasonably to the former distance than the latter. The question, then, naturally arises, how came Eredia, having elected the island of Madura, under its little known Malay name of Luça Antara, as the source from which to draw the materials for circumstantial description in his report to Philip III. to apply that description to a locality which corresponds, as our map shows, with a country which, had he been speaking truth, *could* be no other than Australia? A fact of which he was utterly ignorant, but which had come to my knowledge in the elaboration of my " Early Voyages to Terra Australis" for the Hakluyt Society in 1859, laid bare to me the whole machinery of this impostor's process of deception, and showed how, in attempting to deceive the king, he himself was deceived by the blunders of others who had gone before him. The facts are as follows :—In the seventh chapter of the third book of Marco Polo's travels we read these words :—

" When you leave Java and sail for 700 miles on a course between south and south-west you arrive at two islands, a greater and a less. The one is called Sondur and the other Condur. As there is nothing about them worth mentioning, let us go on five hundred miles beyond Sondur and then we find another country which is called Locach. In this country the brazil which we make use of grows in great plenty, and they also have gold in incredible quantity. They have elephants likewise and much game. In this kingdom, too, are gathered all the porcelain shells which are used for small change in all those regions."

Now, although all the manuscripts and texts of Marco Polo read as above " when you leave Java," Marsden has shown that the point of departure should really be Champa, a name in old times applied by Western Asiatics to a kingdom which embraced the whole coast between Tongking and Cambodia, including all that is now called Cochin China. Colonel Yule has shown that the country meant by Locach was Lo-kok, or the kingdom of Lo, which, previous to the middle of the fourteenth century, formed the lower part of what is now Siam. Sondur and Condur are the Pulo Condore Islands. The introduction of the word Java into the text instead of Champa was a digression, the retention of which inevitably led geographers to place Locach in the Southern Ocean. So much for blunder number one, of which Eredia knew nothing; we now come to blunder number two, of which he was equally unconscious. In the Basle edition of Marco Polo in 1532, the printer unluckily altered the L into a B, and the first c into an e, so that the word Locach became Boeach. This was afterwards shortened into Beach, and the blunder was repeated in books and on maps with so much confidence that we find it

even occurring on a semi-globe which adorns the monument of
the learned Sir Henry Savile in Merton College Chapel, Oxford;
and strangely enough, it is the only geographical name thereon
inscribed. As, however, some editions of Marco Polo retained the
word Locach and others Beach, both names came to be copied
on to maps, and the point of departure being Java, the map-
makers, following the course indicated in Marco Polo, laid these
countries down as forming part of the great southern land which
was supposed to occupy the entire south part of the globe. This
was the India Meridionalis of Eredia's dreams and ambition. It
will have been observed that Luça Antara was said to be also
reached by Chiaymasiuro after a voyage of twelve days *south*
from Java, and accordingly it is domiciled by Eredia on this same
southern land with Locach and Beach, a thought evidently
suggested by Marco Polo's text. But it will also have been
noticed that in this Locach, mis-spelt Beach, there was gold in
considerable quantity. And the result was, that Beach was
specially described on many of the maps of that time as "provin-
cia aurifera," and Eredia at the commencement of his report
speaks of it as "the province of gold." Let us now trace the
effect which this produces on Eredia's geography. In the first
place he lays down *both* Locach and Beach, showing in common
with the other geographers his ignorance of the misprint. To
these he adds Luça Antara with an elaborate and complex outline,
even with the rocks and shoals minutely laid down, which I fear
he never derived from the surveying skill of his friend Chiaymasiuro, but, in the same manner as the Portuguese named the Cape
Verde islands from the promontory off which they lay; so also off
the coast of Beach, Eredia lays down an island to which he gives
the name of Luça Veach. In Spain and Portugal the B and V
are interchangeable. "The island," says Eredia, "is called Luça
Veach, because among the natives of Ende, Sabbo, and Java
'Luça' signifies 'an island' and 'Veach' 'of gold.'" The
printer's devil in Basle, in 1532, little dreamed that he was
inventing a Javanese word, nor does Crawford, the great Malay
authority, corroborate that he did so. So far is it otherwise that
in a list of all the words representing "gold" throughout the

Archipelago, not one in the slightest degree approaches to either Beach or Veach. Nevertheless the next chapter in Eredia's report consists of a certification from our friend Pedro de Carvalhães, captain of the fortress of Ende, in which he swears on the holy Gospels that it is all true, and affixes his signature thereto under date of "Malacca, 4th of October, 1601," the same date as his other certificate.

In one of the chapters of Eredia's report, entitled "Of Discovery by Chance," he tells us that a vessel from Malacca was carried to the south by the Bali currents between Java and Bima, and discovered the islands of Luça Tambini, peopled only by women, like Amazons, who with bows and arrows prevented any one from landing. "These women" he says, "must have their husbands from another separate island." Every one has heard of the fable of the Male and Female Islands. It has existed from time immemorial, and was repeated by Marco Polo, but I doubt if the noble Venetian would have sworn on the holy Gospels, as of his own knowledge in the character of a local and official authority, that a vessel from Malacca went there. This, however, Pedro de Carvalhães did in his last mentioned certification, and I am glad that he tells us that after having discovered the island of women, Pulo Tambini, they then came in sight of Luça Veach. The one statement deserved to be made in the same breath with the other. I need not weary the reader with any further details from the utterances of these vile accomplices. Suffice it that there are plenty more falsehoods in them, built up on the basis of the low country maps, the conjectural or imaginary portions of which are dressed up by Eredia as solid realities, confirmed by all the circumstance of detail. That Eredia received a commission from the Viceroy Ayres de Saldanha to make discoveries of supposed islands in the south is pretty certain. The Alvará, or patent, signed 5th of April, 1601, accompanies the report. It constitutes him Governor-in-chief of any such islands falling within the limits of the crown of Portugal, promises him the Order of Christ, and engages that in the event of his death being ascertained, provision should be made for the honourable marriage of his daughter, to whom the extreme recompense and honours would be accorded as the services of her father might merit. He was to receive also the twentieth part of the profit of his discoveries, or what his majesty was in the habit of giving to discoverers of mines in his own kingdoms. It is very clear that he occupied a responsible position, and that much might be expected from him. Carvalhães in both his certificates uses the words " The discoverer, Manoel Godinho de Eredia, asked me for this information for the good of his voyage and for the accomplishment of the service of the king." It was evidently requisite that he should be a discoverer on paper, since fate had not made him a discoverer at sea. In the map of the world which accompanies his report, and which is itself a reduction from a map by Ortelius, he writes on the southern land, " India Meridional descoberta anno 1601." The map-maker who followed him, and from whose handiwork was made the copy which I brought forward in 1861, had a constructive mind. On a country which bore a legend which proved it to be Australia, he with unflinching positiveness grouped into one distinct declaration the reputed discovery, the date, the name of Eredia, and the name of the viceroy. " Nuça Antara was discovered in 1601 by Manoel Godinho de Eredia, by order of the Viceroy Ayres de Saldanha." I repeat that I am not ashamed that with the amount of evidence that then lay before me I believed him; but I am very happy in the thought, that, so soon as the field of evidence was enlarged, it was I, who alone had been responsible for its promulgation, that had the good fortune at once to detect the imposture.

THE END.

INDEX.

Abraham of Beja, (Rabbi), sent by João II., with Joseph of Lamego, to meet Covilham, 213.

Abreu (Antonio de) discovers Amboyna, &c., 1511-12, 268.

Abreu (João Gomez d') discovers the west coast of Madagascar, 1506; names it San Lourenço, 266.

Abyssinia, Journey of Covilham to, 214.

—— Tristam da Cunha (1507) his expedition, 266.

Affonso V. his surname of "the African," 178.

—— determines to attack Alcaçar Seguer, and sails on the expedition, 30th Sept., 1458, 178.

—— lands at Sagres, where he is received by Prince Henry, 178.

—— Alcaçar surrendered, 180.

—— his grief for the death of Prince Henry, 181.

—— commissions Fra Mauro to construct a mappemonde, 188.

—— in 1469 makes an arrangement with Fernam Gomez, that the latter shall cause to be explored 100 leagues of coast annually, 198.

—— confers honour upon Gomez, 200.

—— his death, 200.

Affonso, eldest son of the King of Congo, set aside by his father in favour of the younger brother; recovers his rights; his zeal for Christianity, 208.

Affonso (Alvaro) goes with Zarco's expedition, 58.

—— explores the coast of Madeira, 59.

Affonso (Diogo) goes with Gonsalves to the Rio d'Ouro, 1445, 96.

Affonso (Fernando d') goes out to Cape Verde with Vallarte, 118.

—— returns to Portugal after Vallarte falls into the hands of the natives, 119.

Affonso (Stevam) with Lançarote in his first expedition, 95.

—— with Lançarote's second expedition, 102.

—— his encounter with the African at the mouth of the Senegal, 105-106.

Ahude Maymom exchanges with Gonsalves negroes and gold for articles of trifling value, 98.

—— his kind treatment of Fernandes, 99.

Alarves or Azanegues, 98.

Albergaria (Vasco Martinez de), his bravery at Ceuta, 32.

Albert Nyanza, described by Pigafetta, from Duarte Lopes, 1591, 208.

Albuquerque, Francisco and Affonso de, sail for India, 1503, 264.

—— (Francisco de) restores to the King of Cochin his territory, and founds there the first Portuguese fort in India, 264.

—— (Alfonso de) reaches Coulam, now Quiloa, makes terms with the king, and establishes a factory there, 264.

—— in 1506 returns to India to succeed Almeida, 266.

—— explores the strait of Bab-el-Mandeb, 266.

—— in 1507 explores the coast of Arabia and Persia, 267.

—— in 1508 sends a mission to Abyssinia, 267.

Alcaçar Seguer, besieged by Affonso V., 178.

Alcaçar Seguer, the surrender; Duarte de Menezes made governor, 179.
—— besieged by the King of Fez; gallant defence; the Moors repulsed, 179.
—— Dom Duarte constructs the mole, 180.
Alcaforado (Francisco) his original narrative of Machin's discovery, and its disappearance from de Mello's library, 57.
—— was present in Zarco's expedition, 58.
Algoa Bay, pillar set up in an island there by Dias, 219.
Aljubarrota, battle of, 14—17.
Almada (João Vaz de) at the siege of Ceuta, 35.
Almeida (Francisco de), first Viceroy of the Indies; his expedition in 1505; discovers the east coast of Madagascar; founds a fort at Quiloa, settles the affairs in India, and founds the forts of Anchediva and Cananor, 265.
—— sends the first elephant to Portugal, 266.
—— is slain, 1510, near the Cape of Good Hope, 267.
Almeida (Lorenço de) discovers Ceylon, 1505, 265.
—— in 1507 discovers the Maldives, 266.
Alvares (Rodrigo) with Lançarote on his first expedition, 95.
Amboyna (Island) discovered by Antonio de Abreu, 268.
America, first suggestion of name, 236.
—— adoption of suggestion, 387, 240.
Andrade (Fernam Peres de), 1517, sailed to China, and entered into commercial relations with the Governor of Canton, 268.
—— returns to India, 1519, 268.
Angra dos Cavallos, 72.
Angra de Gonsalo de Cintra, 95.
Angra dos Ruivos, 70.
Angra dos Vaqueiros (Flesh Bay), 218.
Angra das Voltas, 218.
Anhaya (Pedro de), 1505, makes the King of Sofala tributary to Portugal, 266.
Annobon, discovered 1st January, 1471, by Martin Fernandez of Lisbon, and Álvaro Esteves of Lagos, 199.

Antonio de Lisboa (Father) sent out by João II. with Pedro de Montarryo, to seek the country of Prester John by land, 212.
Arabs, early knowledge of Africa, 47.
Arguin (Island of), discovered by Nuño Tristam, 1443, 93.
—— situation, 94.
—— (Fort of), foundations laid by the Prince, 1448, 94.
—— erected under João II., 201.
Arrayolos (Count de) at the siege of Tangier, 76.
—— returns to Portugal after the defeat, 83.
Astrolabe used by Da Gama, 245.
Atayde (Pedro de) leaves letters with directions to captains bound for India at San Bras and Mombaza, of which Juan de Nova avails himself, 263.
Australia, early discoveries of, 294—298, 301—310.
Aveiro (João Affonso d'), his mission to King of Benin, 211.
Avila (Pedro Arias de) sent out by the King of Spain as Governor of Darien; his quarrel with Balboa, 270.
Azambuja (Diogo de) commands the fleet sent out with materials for building the fort of S. Jorge da Mina, 201.
—— concludes a treaty with Bezegniche, and has an interview with Caramansa, 201; obtains his consent to the erection of a church and fort, 202.
Azanegues (the), Antam Gonsalves' voyage, 1441, 89.
—— Tristam's voyage, 1443; finds the island of Arguin, 93.
—— Lançarote expedition, 1444, 94.
—— Fernandez' account of his sojourn among them, 98.
—— their food, customs, and character, 142.
Azores, The, 130.
—— name first given to the islands of Santa Maria and San Miguel from hawks, or rather kites, being found there in 1444, 132.
—— claims of the Flemings, as made by Josué van den Berge, in 1445; disproved, 133.

Azurara, quoted, upon the number of caravels sent up to 1446, and the distance they had gone, 116.
—— his testimony to the Prince's compassion for the slaves, 120, 121.
—— his description of Prince Henry, 183.

Balboa (Vasco Nuñez de) discovers the Pacific, 1510; the quarrel between him and Avila; his trial and execution, 1517, 271.
Baldaya (Affonso Gonsalves) goes out with Gil Eannes, 1435, and reaches the Rio d'Ouro, 69.
—— sends two young men to reconnoitre, 70.
—— returns to Portugal without effecting the capture of any of the natives, 1436, 72.
Balthazar goes out with Gonsalves, 92.
Barbosa (Duarte), information given by him to Magalhaens, 272.
—— made joint-commander with João Serrao after the death of Magalhaens; murdered by the people of Zebu, 287.
Barcellos (Count de), illegitimate brother of the Prince, 21.
—— is with the Princes at the siege of Ceuta, 32.
—— his share of the spoils of Ceuta, 37.
Barros (João de), quoted as to the limited knowledge of the Portuguese at sea before the Prince's time, 44.
Batalha, Queen Philippa buried there, 27.
—— King João's burial, 65.
—— Dom Fernando's, 85.
—— Prince Henry's, 181.
Batti Mansa, negro king, makes a treaty with Cadamosto, 164.
—— receives Diogo Gomez with favour, 173.
Behaim (Martin Von) accompanies Diogo Cam, 1484, 205.
Bemoi, Prince of the Jaloffs, his war with his brothers; alliance with the Portuguese; is defeated, and takes refuge in Portugal, 215.
—— his reception, baptism, and knighting; returns to his country, and is basely slain by Pedro Vas da Cunha, 216.
Benin, between Congo and Fort S. Jorge da Mina; unsuccessful mission; unwholesome climate, 211.
Bernaldes (João) with Lançarote, in his first expedition, 95.
Beseghichi, or Bezeguiche, Diogo Gomez, after taking him on board his caravel, sets him free, and bespeaks his kindness to the Christians, 176.
Bethencourt, Jean de, his expedition to the Canaries, 123.
Bianco (Andrea) engaged on the mappemonde of Fra Mauro, 188.
Bisboror, nephew of Budomel, entertains Cadamosto, 147.
—— his serpent-charming, 152.
Boor, King of the land where Vallarte went on shore, near Cape Verde, 118.
Boyador (Cape), the doubling accomplished by Gil Eannes, 69.
Braganza, royal house of, sprung from the marriage of King João's illegitimate son Affonso, Count of Barcellos, and the daughter of the Constable Nuño Alvares Pereira, 21.
Bruco, a chieftain of Gomera who assisted the Portuguese against Palma, 124.
Bruges (Jaques de), Prince Henry's grant of the captaincy of Terceira to, 133.
Budomel, the country south of the Jaloffs, 146.
—— the people wonderful swimmers, 147.
—— the government, religion, and customs, 147—156.
Budomel, Lord of the country of that name, 146.
—— his hospitable reception of Cadamosto, 147.
—— his domestic life, 148.
—— his court, 149.
—— his religion, 150.

Cabo dos Corrientes, 190.
Cabo dos Mastos, 199.
Cabo Mesurado, 197.
Cabo del Monte, 197.
Cabo do Resgate, 98.
Cabo Roxo, 168—196.

Cabo de Santa Anna (North), 100.
Cabo de Santa Anna (South), 197.
Cabral (Ferdinand Alvarez), his gallantry at the siege of Tangier, 78.
Cabral (Gonzalo Velho), 1431, sent out by Prince Henry in search of the Azores, 131.
—— receives the command of San Miguel, 132.
Cabral (Pedro Alvarez), his expedition to Calicut with Bartholomeu Dias and Coelho, 1500, 257.
—— change of purpose; reaches the coast of Brazil, 259.
—— encounters a dreadful storm off the Cape, in which Bartholomeu Dias is lost, 260.
—— he proceeds to Calicut, and establishes a factory, 260.
—— the wealth brought back, 261.
Caçuta, one of the King of Congo's subjects who went to Portugal with Diogo Cam, and was baptized; he went back with the expedition sent to christianize his people, 1490, 205.
Cadomosto's first voyage; sets out from Venice, 1454, 138.
—— his interview with Prince Henry, which results in his undertaking his voyage of discovery, 139.
—— Porto Santo and Madeira, 139.
—— Canary Islands, 141.
—— describes the curious traffic between the blacks of Melli and another tribe of negroes, exchanging salt for gold, 141.
—— reaches the Senegal, 143.
—— describes the country of the Jaloffs and the customs of the people, 143—146.
—— is hospitably received by Budomel, 146.
—— describes the government, religion, customs, &c., 146—156.
—— takes leave of Budomel; joins Uso di Mare; passes Cape Verde, 156.
—— he passes the country of the Barbacins and the Serreri; discovers the mouth of a river, which he calls the Barbacins (the Joal?), and arrives at another river (the Joombas), 157.
—— arrives at the mouth of the Gambia, 158.

Cadomosto has an encounter with the natives, 159.
—— returns to Portugal, 161.
—— sets out on his second voyage with Uso di Mare, 162.
—— discovers four islands, 162.
—— names two of them Boavista and Santiago, 163.
—— enters the river Gambra, 163.
—— buries one of the sailors on an island, which is named after him, Saint André; has a peaceful interview with some of the natives, 163.
—— makes a treaty with Batti Mansa, 164.
—— describes elephant-hunting, 166.
—— takes back parts of a young elephant as curiosities to present to the Prince, 167.
—— obliged to leave the country of Batti Mansa on account of the sickness of the men, 167.
—— passes Cape St. Mary, Casa Mansa river, Cabo Roxo, Rio de Santa Anna (the Cacheo), S. Domingo river (Rio de Jatte), and reaches the Rio Grande (the river Jeba), 168.
—— returns to Portugal, 169.
Calicut, De Gama's arrival there, 250.
Cam (Diogo), 1484, passes Cape St. Catherine and reaches the mouth of a large river, which he calls Rio do Padrao, afterwards named the Congo, and sets up a pillar on the south side, 204.
—— brings some of the negroes to Portugal to learn the language, 204.
—— accompanied by Martin Behaim, 205.
—— revisits Congo, and proceeding southwards plants two pillars, one St. Augustine, the other at Manga das Areas, now Cape Cross, at the beginning of the country of the Hottentots, 205.
—— on his way back to Portugal is received with affection by the King of Congo, 205.
Camara dos Lobos, the terminus of Zarco's exploration of the coast of Madeira, 61.
Camelo (Alvaro Gonsalves de) sent to gain information about Ceuta, 23

Index. 315

Canary Islands, or Fortunate Isles of the ancients, 122.
—— enterprise of Jean de Bethencourt, 123.
—— the descent of João de Castilha and others upon, 124.
—— Azurara's account of the, 126.
Cano (Juan Sebastian del) appointed commander of the *Vittoria*, 289.
—— his arrival at San Lusar, 1522; honours bestowed on him, 293.
Cape Bojador, *see* Bojador.
Cape Branco, Ibn Said relates the chance arrival of some Arabs, 47.
Cape Diab, 189.
Cape of Good Hope. See *Good Hope*.
Cape Ledo, 196.
Cape Lopez, 200.
Cape Non, stated as the limit of exploration by Ibn Khaldoun, 46.
Cape Sagres of Guinea, 195.
Cape St. Catherine, discovered by Sequeira, 200.
Cape Verde Islands, discovery of, 163.
Cape Verga, 195.
Canamansa, his interview with Diogo de Azambuja, 202.
Cartagena (Juan de) with Magalhaens' expedition, 274.
—— his mutiny, 275.
Casa Mansa (river), 168.
Castilha (João de) joins Lançarote's expedition, in a caravel belonging to Alvaro Gonsalves de Atayde, 102.
—— joins with the *Picanço*, and the caravel from Tavila, in a descent on the Islands of Palma, 124.
—— after having gained the help of the people of Gomera in the expedition, on his return he treacherously seizes about twenty of the Gomerans, but is not allowed by the prince to retain them, 125.
Castro (Dom Pedro de) arrives with reinforcements at Tangier, 78.
Ceuta, siege of, 29—41.
—— the Princes land there on their way to Tangier, 75.
—— the treaty for its surrender to the Moors, 81.
—— the Cortes refuse to give it up, 83.

Ceuta (Bishop of), his intrepidity at the siege of Tangier, 80.
Ceylon, 1505, discovered by Lourenço de Almeida, 265.
China, 1517, Fernam Peres de Andrade sailed there, and entered into commercial relations with the Governor of Canton, 268.
Cintra (Diogo Gomez de), his testimony to the prince's compassion for the captives, 121.
Cintra (Gonsalo de) goes out in 1445, and, disobeying his orders, is slain on the island of Naar, 95.
Cintra (Pedro de) sent out by Affonso V.; goes to the mouth of the Rio Grande and to the Beseque; finds and names Cape Verga and Cape Sagres, of Guinea, 195.
—— his discoveries, 196—198.
Cochia or Kukia, 171.
Coelho (Nicolas) sails in Da Gama's expedition in the *Berrio*, 211.
—— goes out with Cabral's expedition, 1500, 258.
—— sent to examine the coast of Brazil, 259.
Columbus (Christopher), his sojourn in Portugal from 1470—1484, 222.
—— his marriage with the daughter of Perestrello, Governor of Porto Santo, 222.
—— he lives at Porto Santo with his wife's mother, who gives him the papers, &c., of Perestrello, 222.
—— incidents which confirm him in the idea of land to the West, 223, 224.
—— studies geographical authors, and among them the Cardinal Pierre d'Ailly's "Imago Mundi," 224.
—— Marco Polo and Sir John Mandeville, 225.
—— while at Lisbon writes to Toscanelli, and receives from him a chart which confirms his idea of reaching Asia by the West, 225.
—— he submits to the King of Portugal his proposition, but is opposed by the Council, 226.
—— leaves Lisbon, 1484, in disgust at the dishonest scheme of some of the councillors, 227.
—— having overcome all obstacles, he

sets sail 3rd of August, 1492, and comes in sight of land on the 12th of October, 227.

Columbus (Christopher), the islands he discovered; his return, 229.

—— his reception in Spain, and triumphal entry into Barcelona, 229.

—— numerous editions of the description of his voyage, 357; narrative poem by Giuliano Dati, 230.

—— his second voyage and the results, 230, 231.

—— his third voyage, 231—233.

—— his arrival in Spain, 233.

—— his fourth and last voyage, 234, 235.

—— his loyalty and magnanimity while suffering from ingratitude and misfortune, 235, 236.

—— his death in 1506, 236.

—— monuments to his memory, 366.

Columbus (Ferdinand), his assertion that in Portugal the admiral first conceived the thought of finding lands westward, 222.

Commerce of the interior of Africa, 93.

Congo (King of), his affectionate reception of Diogo Cam, and great desire to become Christian; sends an embassy to Portugal to beg that priests might be sent out, 205.

—— his state reception of Ruy de Sousa, 206.

—— his baptism; his dissatisfaction at the restriction to one wife; his death, 207.

Correa (Diego) with the expedition of Almeida, 1505, 272.

Cortereal (Vasco Eannes de), the first to pass through the Almina Gate at the siege of Ceuta, 31.

Costa (Soeiro da) with Lançarote's expedition, 102.

—— his discovery of the river at first named after him, but now called Great Bassam, or Assinie River, 198.

Covilham (Pedro de), 1487, sent out by João II. with Affonso de Payva to find the country of Prester John by land; parts with Payva at Aden; goes to the Malabar coast; passes over to Sofala, 212—214.

Covilham (Pedro de), his letter to King João proves him to be the *theoretical* discoverer of the Cape of Good Hope, 214.

Cunha (Pedro Vaz de), in a fit of anger basely kills Bemoi, prince of the Jaloffs, 216.

Cunha (Tristam da), 1506, Affonso d'Albuquerque goes with him; discovers the three islands that bear his name; they take the fortress of Socotra, 266.

Da Gama (Paolo) sails in his brother's expedition in the *San Raphael*, 244.

Da Gama (Vasco) made commander of the fleet of the Indus; sails 8th July, 1497, 244; the fleet anchors in the bay of St. Helena, where they become acquainted with the Bosjesmans, 245.

—— passes the Cape of Good Hope, 245.

—— passes the extreme point of Dias's discovery, and reaches Natal, 246; Rio do Cobre; goes on to a river, which he names Rio dos Boos Signaes, where he erects a pillar, which he calls padrao of San Rafael; 10th of March, anchors off Mozambique, 247; reaches Mombaza, 248; reaches Melinda, 248.

—— 20th of May anchors off Calicut, 250.

—— erects a pillar which he calls Santa Maria, 253.

—— reaches Anchediva, 254.

—— reaches Magadoxo, 256.

—— raises a pillar on one of the Ilhas de Sam Jorge, 257.

Dalmeida (Diego Lopez) sent by Baldaya to reconnoitre at the Rio d'Ouro, 71.

Dati (Giuliano), his narrative of the discovery by Columbus in ottava rima, 230.

De Nova (Juan), sent out by King Manoel, 1501, discovers the island of Ascension, 263; proceeds to Cananor; encounters the fleet of the King of Calicut, 264; discovers St. Helena on the way home, and on his arrival is received with distinguished honour by the king, 264.

De Nova (Juan), sails in Almeida's expedition, 265.

Dias (Bartholomew), 1486, with his brother, Pedro Dias, and João Infante, goes out in search of the country of Prester John, 217.

—— erects a pillar at Angra dos Ilheos, now Dias Point, 217.

—— passes Cape Voltas, and is driven south, 218.

—— finding no land when he steers eastward, sails north, and finds Angra dos Vaqueiros (Flesh Bay), 218.

—— reaches Algoa Bay; sets up a pillar on a small island there; the first land beyond the Cape trodden by Europeans, 219.

—— finds a river, which he names Rio do Infante, from João Infante, 219.

—— is obliged by his crew to return, 220.

—— names the Cape, Cabo Tormentoso (Stormy Cape), 220.

—— on his return to Portugal, the king named it Cape of Good Hope, 220.

—— was to have accompanied the expedition of Da Gama, but is subsequently ordered to sail for San Jorge el Mina, 244.

—— goes out with Cabral's expedition, 1500, 258.

—— perishes in a storm off the Cape of Good Hope, 260.

Dias (Diniz), obtains permission to make explorations in the service of Prince Henry; sails past the Senegal to the land of the Jaloffs, the first real blacks, 96.

—— reaches Cape Verde, to which he gives its name, 97.

—— from Lisbon, joins Lançarote's expedition, 102.

Dias (João) with Lançarote in his first expedition, 102.

Dias (Lourenço), with Lançarote's expedition, is the first to reach the island of Arguin, 217.

Dias Vicente, sailing captain of Cadamosto's caravel, 139.

Dragon's-blood, 139.

Duarte (Dom), 26.

—— present at the queen's death, 30.

Duarte (Dom) lands with Prince Henry at Ceuta, 31.

—— knighted by the king, 36.

—— takes great interest in meteorology, 49.

—— testifies his satisfaction with Prince Henry's efforts by the charters of the 26th of September, 1433, and of the 26th of October, 1434, giving him the islands of Madeira, Porto Santo, and the Desertas, 68.

—— his personal qualities, 73.

—— new title given to his heir, 73.

—— gives a reluctant consent to the attack on Tangier, 74.

—— applies to the Pope, but makes preparations before receiving an answer, and sends out the expedition, 75.

—— his grief at the disastrous result and the fate of his brother Fernando, 83.

—— attempts his brother's rescue, but in vain, 83.

—— his grief for his brother's sufferings undermines his health, 85.

—— his death, 87.

—— his character, 87.

—— Leal Conselheiro, 87.

Edward III. of England, the prince's great-grandfather, 5.

Elephant-hunting, described by Cadamosto, 166.

English esquires, at the battle of Aljubarrota, 14.

English ships, which joined in the expedition against Ceuta, 40.

Equator first crossed, 1471, 200.

Equatorial Nile Lakes, first mentioned by Pigafetta from Duarte Lopes, 208.

Escobar (Pedro de), commander selected by Fernam Gomez for the expedition beyond Sierra Leona, 198.

—— discovers La Mina, and goes 37 leagues beyond Cape Lopo Gonsalves, 199.

Esteves (Alvaro), of Lagos, pilot in Fernam Gomez' expedition; reputed the best navigator in Portugal, 199.

—— discovers Principe, Annabon, and S. Thomé, 199, 200.

Evora (Bishop, of), at the siege of Tangier, 76.

Faleiro (Rui), accompanies Magalhaens to Seville, 273.
Fayal, first donatary, Jobst Van Heurter, 135.
Fernandes (Alvaro), joins Lançarote's expedition, 102.
—— is the first to go to the Madeleine Islands, 108.
—— reaches a cape, which he names Cabo dos Mastos, 109.
—— in 1446 passes beyond Cape Verde; is wounded with a poisoned arrow, but recovers by the use of an antidote, 112, 113.
—— reaches 110 leagues south of Cape Verde, 113.
—— meets with Ahude Maimom at the Cabo do Resgate, 114.
—— is rewarded by the regent and Prince Henry for having gone further south than any of his predecessors, 114.
Fernandes (Joeo) goes with Gonsalves to the Rio d'Ouro, and remains seven months in the interior, 96.
—— found on the shore by Gonsalves, 98.
—— gives the prince an account of his sojourn with the Moors, 98—100.
—— goes with Diogo Gil to Messa, 117.
Fernandez (Martin), of Lisbon, pilot in Fernam Gomez' expedition, 199.
—— discovers Principe, Annabon, and S. Thomé, 199, 200.
Fernando (King), eldest surviving son of Pedro the Severe and his successor, 6.
—— his guilty and unhappy marriage, and unfortunate reign, 6, 7.
Fernando (Dom), the Constant Prince, his earnest desire to make the attack on Tangier, 74.
—— lands at Ceuta with Prince Henry, 75.
—— takes part in the attack, 76.
—— is given as hostage, with twelve other nobles, for the performance of the treaty, 81.
—— is conducted to Arzilla by Zalá ben Zalá, and treated with insult by the Moors, 83.
Fernando (Dom) is transferred to the King of Fez, and treated with the greatest cruelty, 84.
—— his death, 84.
—— his body exposed by the Moors, his heart brought to Portugal by his faithful servants, and buried at Batalha, 85.
—— his body recovered from the Moors, and buried at Batalha, twenty-two years after, 85.
Fernando (Dom), Duke of Beja, nephew of Prince Henry, is appointed to convey his body to Batalha, 182.
Fernando Po. See *Pó, Fernam do.*
Ferreira (Gonzalo Ayres), goes with Zarco's expedition, 58.
—— the first Portuguese who had children born in Madeira, 58.
—— sent to explore the interior of Madeira, 60.
Formosa (Ilha). See *Pó, Fernam do.*
Forosangoli, Prince of Gambra, 164.
Foscari (Doge), quotation from his letter, 190.
Fra Mauro, commissioned to construct a mappemonde for Affonso V., 188—190.
Frangazick, negro chief, nephew of Farisangul, 170.
Freitas, (Alvaro da), with Lançarote's expedition, 102.
—— declares his intention of going southward with Lançarote and Pires, 104.
Funchal, derivation of the name, 57.

Gadifer de la Salle, with Bethencourt in his expedition, 123.
Gambia (River), described by Cadamosto, 163—167.
Gil Eannes, his expedition, 1433, 68.
—— succeeds in doubling Cape Boyador, 1434, 69.
—— goes again with Baldaya, 1435, and reaches the Rio d'Ouro, 70.
—— with Lançarote in his first expedition, 95.
—— with Lançarote's second expedition, 102.
Giocondi (Giuliano), sent by Dom

Manuel, King of Portugal, to win over Vespucci to his service, 236.

Giocondi (Fra Giovanni), translated Vespucci's letter to Lorenzo di Pier Francisco de' Medici, from Italian into Latin, 236.

—— built the bridge of Notre Dame at Paris, 236.

Gomez (Diogo), his explorations, 170—177.

Gomez (Fernam), his contract with Affonso V. to explore 100 leagues of coast annually; sends out João de Santarem and Padro de Escobar; they discover the coast afterwards called La Mina, 198—200.

Gomez (Stevam), Magalhaens' pilot, 274.

Gonsalves (Antam), expedition, 1441, 89.

—— goes out in 1445 with Diogo Affonso and Gomes Pires to the Rio d'Ouro, 95.

—— finds Fernandez, 98.

—— goes to the Rio d'Ouro in 1447, 117.

Gonsalves (Jorge), 1447, goes to the Rio d'Ouro, 117.

Good Hope discovered by Bartholomew Dias, and named by him Cabo Tormentoso, 1486; received its present name from King João II., 220.

—— re-discovery by Da Gama, 245.

Guinea coast, as now understood, began to be known by that name after the construction of the Fort la Mina in 1481, 97.

Guitanye, governor of the country where Vallarte landed, 119.

Gummi Mansa, a negro chief, showed Cadamosto a young elephant that he had killed, 166.

—— and gave him parts of it to take back to Portugal as curiosities, 167.

Haagen (Willem van der), or Da Silveira, founds the city of Topo, in Sam Jorge; removes to Fayal, 133.

Henry IV. of England, the prince's uncle, 5.

Henry (Prince), his parentage, 5.

—— desires to receive the honour of knighthood with his two elder brothers, 22.

Henry (Prince) prepares for the expedition against Ceuta, 25.

—— is present at the death of his mother, and receives her dying charge, 26.

—— starts with the expedition to Ceuta, 28.

—— his courage and presence of mind, 28.

—— lands at Ceuta, 30.

—— his gallantry during the siege, 32—34.

—— knighted by the king, 36.

—— created Duke of Viseu and Lord of Covilham, 40.

—— goes to the help of the Governor of Ceuta against the King of Granada, 41.

—— his adopted motto, 43.

—— his renown in Europe, 43.

—— his first exploring expeditions, 44.

—— gathers information from the Moors in Africa, 46.

—— his desire to further the cause of Christianity, 46.

—— takes up his abode at Sagres, 48.

—— supposition that he established the chair of mathematics in Lisbon, 50.

—— discovery of Porto Santo and Madeira by Zarco and Vaz, 1418—1420, 51.

—— is exhorted by the king on his death-bed to persevere in his efforts, 67.

—— receives by charter from King Duarte the islands of Madeira, Porto Santo, and the Desertas, 68.

—— sends out the expedition of Gil Eannes, 1433, 68.

—— who succeeds in doubling Cape Boyador, 1434, 69.

—— the expedition of Gil Eannes and Baldaya, 69.

—— they reach the Rio d'Ouro, 70.

—— joins Dom Fernando in urging King Duarte to fit out an expedition to attack Tangier, 74.

—— lands at Ceuta with his brother and the forces, 75.

—— the siege, 76—81.

Henry (Prince) is obliged to conclude a treaty, and to leave Dom Fernando as hostage, 81.
—— leaves Tangier, 81.
—— retires to Ceuta, and falls ill with grief, 83.
—— hopes to release his brother, but is driven by tempest to the Algarves, 83.
—— retires to Sagres, till the death of Dom Duarte, 88.
—— causes of a break of three or four years in the explorations, 88.
—— sends out Gonsalvez and Tristam, 89.
—— sends to the Pope to pray for a concession to Portugal of the lands to be discovered from Cape Boyador to the Indies, 91.
—— receives a charter from the regent, granting him a fifth of the produce, &c., 91.
—— is summoned to Coimbra by the regent, to invest with knighthood his eldest son Pedro, 101.
—— sends out Cabral in search of the Azores, 131.
—— gives Cabral the command of San Miguel, 132.
—— bestows on the Order of Christ the tithes of San Miguel and one-half of the sugar revenues, 132.
—— his grant of the captaincy of Terceira to Jacques de Bruges, 133.
—— fits out a new caravel for Cadamosto, 139.
—— gives his approbation to Cadamosto's second voyage, 162.
—— equips a caravel and appoints Diogo Gomez captain, 170.
—— sends the Abbot of Soto de Cassa to christianize Nomimansa and his people, 177.
—— receives King Affonso at Sagres, 178.
—— is present at the siege of Alcaçar, 179.
—— his donation of the ecclesiastical revenues of Porto Santo and Madeira to the Order of Christ, 180.
—— the Order of the Garter conferred on him in 1442-3, 183.
—— his illness and death, 181.
—— his tomb, 182.

Henry (Prince), description of him by Azurara, 183.
—— the sums he expended on explorations, 190.
—— called "Protector of the Studies of Portugal," and "the Navigator," 191.
—— statue erected by Dom Manuel at Belem, monument at Sagres, 191, 245.
Heurter (Jobst van), father-in-law of Martin Behaim, first captain donatary of Fayal, 134.
Homem (Hector), sent by Baldaya to reconnoitre at the Rio d'Ouro, 71.

Ilha dos Bancos, 197.
Ilha Formosa. See Pó, Fernam do.
Imago Mundi of Pierre d'Ailly, studied by Columbus, 224.
Infante (João) goes out with Bartholomeu Dias, 212.

Jaloffs, the people on the south of the Senegal, 143—145.
João I., King of Portugal, father of Prince Henry, 5.
—— is the youngest and illegitimate son of Pedro the Severe, 6.
—— at the age of seven made Grand Master of the Order of Aviz, 6.
—— after the accession of his brother Fernando, his life is endangered by Queen Leonora, 7.
—— is made regent after the death of his brother, 9.
—— succeeds in defending Lisbon from the King of Castile, 10, 11.
—— is proclaimed king, 12.
—— wins the battle of Aljubarrota, 14—17.
—— his marriage with the Princess Philippa, daughter of the Duke of Lancaster, 19.
—— receives the Order of the Garter, 20.
—— his children, 20, 21.
—— entertains the idea of taking Ceuta, 22.
—— sends envoys to gather information, 23.
—— makes preparations for the siege of Ceuta, 25.
—— is present at the queen's death, 26.
—— sails on the Feast of St. James, 28.

João I., King of Portugal, confers knighthood on his sons, 36.
—— takes possession of Ceuta, 36.
—— makes the Count de Viana governor, and returns to Portugal, 38.
—— sends help to the Governor against the King of Granada, 41.
—— his declining health and death, 64.
—— his burial at Batalha, 65.
—— his character, 65.
—— the buildings he founded in Portugal, 66.
—— the Gospels, the life of Christ, and other spiritual books translated by his order, 66.
—— the affection of his people, 67.
—— on his death-bed exhorts Prince Henry to persevere in his explorations, 67.
João II., succeeds Affonso V.; orders the completion of the fort of Arguin, 200.
—— sends an expedition under Diogo de Azambuja to build the fort of Sam Jorge da Mina, 201.
—— designs the stone pillars to be erected by discoverers, 203.
—— his reception of the negroes brought by Diogo Cam, 204.
—— takes the title of Lord of Guinea, 205.
—— he and his queen stand sponsors for Caçuta, 205.
—— is told by the negro ambassador from Benin of a powerful monarch in the interior, 211.
—— concludes that this must be Prester John, and determines to seek this kingdom by land and by sea, 212.
—— gives the name to the Cape of Good Hope, 220.
—— his illness from poisoned water, 242.
—— he sinks under his anxieties; his death; his designation of "the Perfect Prince," 243.
João (the Iffante Dom), goes with Prince Henry to the relief of Ceuta, 41.
—— joins Prince Henry at Ceuta, and resolves to attempt the rescue of Dom Fernando, after the siege of Tangier, 83.

John of Gaunt, Prince Henry's grandfather, 5.
—— arrives at Corunna to enforce his claim to the crown of Castile, 18.
—— marriage of his daughter Philippa with the King João I., 19.
Joseph of Lemago, sent by João II. to meet Covilham, 213.

Ladrones (The) discovered by Magalhaens, 282.
Lagos, the inhabitants appeal to the prince for permission to fit out a fleet to revenge the death of Gonsalo da Cintra, 101.
La Mina (coast) discovered 1470 by João de Santarem and Pedro de Escobar, sent out by Fernam Gomez, 199.
—— for the fort, see *Mina*.
Lançarote, receives permission from the prince to make the voyage to Africa, 94.
—— sails in 1444 with 6 caravels and returns with about 200 captives from the bay of Arguin, 95.
—— entrusted with the command of the 14 caravels from Lagos, 102.
—— they sail on the 10th of August, 1445, 102.
—— after the successful encounter with the natives, he assembles the commanders of the fleet, and announces that the object of the expedition is accomplished, and they are free to follow their own course, 103.
—— returns to Portugal, 107.
"Leal Conselheiro," of Dom Duarte XIII., 87.
Lopes (Duarte), his mission from the King of Congo to Pope Sixtus V. and Philip II. related to Felipe Pigafetta, 208.
Lourenco (João) goes out with Zarco's expedition, 58.
Lud (Walter), Secretary to René II., Duke of Lorraine, and canon of the cathedral of St. Dié, establishes a college under the Duke's auspices, and sets up a printing-press, 238.

Machico, derivation of the name, 57.

Y

Machin (Robert), his romantic story, 55.
—— discovery of his tomb by Ruy Paes, 59.
—— a chapel founded on the spot by Zarco, 61.
Madagascar discovered by Almeida, 1505, 265.
—— west coast discovered by João Gomez d'Abreu, 1506, 266.
—— Sequeira commissioned to examine the coast, 267.
Madeira, discovery of, 54—63.
—— Cadamosto's description, 139—141.
Magalhaens (Ferham de), or Magellan, his parentage and education, 271.
—— enters the service of Dom Manoel, 272.
—— his marriage, 273.
—— gains the friendship of Juan de Ovando, 274.
—— Charles V. gives him the command of 5 ships, 274.
—— names of ships and commanders, 274.
—— sets sail, 1519, and reaches Rio de Janeiro in December, 274.
—— revolt headed by Juan de Cartagena, 275.
—— Patagonia, 278.
—— Tierra del Fuego, 280.
—— they pass the Straits, 281.
—— the Ladrones, 282.
—— the Philippines, 282.
—— his quarrel with the chief of Matan, 285.
—— his death, 286.
Mahometanism professed by the Jaloffs, 144.
—— by the people of Budomel, 150.
Malacca, in 1508, Sequeira commissioned to discover; establishes a factory there, 267.
Maldives discovered in 1507 by Lourenço de Almeida, 266.
Mandeville (Sir John), influence of his travels on the mind of Columbus, 225.
Manga das Areas (Cape Cross), pillar set up there by Diogo Cam, 205.
Mani Sono, uncle of the King of Congo, he and his son the first of the people baptized, 206.

Manoel (Dom) has a statue of Prince Henry placed at Belem, 245.
—— succeeds John II., and resumes the maritime explorations, 243.
—— makes Vasco da Gama commander of the fleet of the Indies, 243.
—— subsequently built the splendid Temple of Belem, 244.
—— receives the news of Cabral's discovery, 259.
—— establishes a colony in Brazil, 260.
—— sends out Juan de Nova to India, 263.
—— receives him on his return with great honour, 264.
—— sends out a great expedition under Almeida, 265.
—— sends a crown of gold to the King of Cochin, 265.
—— receives an embassy from Abyssinia, and sends one in return, 267.
—— sends out Sequeira to explore Madagascar and discover Malacca, 267.
Map in Laurentian library at Florence, 1351, 54, 130.
—— of Fra Mauro, 1459, 188.
—— by Pigafetta after Duarte Lopes, showing Lakes Victoria and Albert Nyanza, and Lake Tanganyika in 1591, 208.
—— of Africa, to illustrate Portuguese discoveries, *end of volume*.
Marocco (King of), comes to the aid of the Moors at Tangier, 78.
Martin (Alonzo), the first European who navigated the Pacific, 270.
Martinez (Fernando), correspondence with Toscanelli, 225.
Mascarenhas (Pedro de), supposed to have discovered the Mascarenhas Islands, 1512 or 1513, 268.
Matthew, an Armenian, sent as envoy from Abyssinia to the King of Portugal, 267.
Melli, in the empire of the negroes, 141.
—— the traffic of the people with another tribe of negroes; exchanging salt for gold, 141.

Mello (Duarte de), 1507, founded the fort of Mozambique, 266.
Mello (Francisco Manoel de) gives the story of Machin, from the MS. of Alcaforado, 57.
Mello (Martin Alfonso de) declines the dangerous honour of being Governor of Ceuta, 38.
Mendez (Scioro), commander of the fort at Arguin, 194.
Mendoza (Affonso Furtado de) sent as envoy to Sicily, but really to gain information about Ceuta, 23.
Meneses (Dom Pedro de), Count di Viana, first Commander of Ceuta, 38.
—— keeps the Moors in check for three years, 40.
—— receives aid from Portugal under the command of Prince Henry and Dom João, 41.
Meneses (Duarte de) made Governor of Alcaçar; his gallant defence against the King of Fez, 179, 180.
Menendus, Mondo, or Mongo, a wealthy Englishman, who brought four ships to the siege of Ceuta, 28.
Mina, surname given to Fernam Gomez in honour of the discovery, 200.
Mina (Fort of S. Jorge da), built by João II., 1482, 201.
Molućcas (The). Francisco Serrao went to Ternate, 1511, 268.
Morales (Juan de), as fellow captive, hears from Machin's people of the discovery of Madeira; imparts this knowledge to Zarco, and goes with him to the rediscovery, 56—58.

Natal, named by Da Gama, 246.
Neale, (Dr. J. Mason), his description of Batalha, 182.
Negro fair, 154.
Negus (The), Prince of Abyssinia, detains Covilham in his dominions and treats him with honour, 211.
Nile of the Negroes (the Senegal), 104.
Nile, Equatorial lakes first mentioned by Pigafetta, from Duarte Lopes, 208.
Nile, sources of, referred to by Pigafetta, from Duarte Lopes, 1591, 210.

Nomimansa, King of the Barbacins, makes peace with Diogo Gomez, 174.
Nomimansa wishes to be baptized, 175.
—— the prince sends the Abbot of Soto de Cassa to instruct him and his people in the faith, 177.
Nova (Juan de), expedition, 263.

Ouro (Rio d'), whence it received its name, 93.
Ovando (Juan de), his friendship for Magalhaens, 274.

Pacheco (Gonsalo), his expedition, 100.
Paes (Ruy), goes out with Zarco's expedition, 58.
—— finds the tomb of Machin, 59.
Pallenço, with Lançarote's expedition, 102.
Panso Aquitimo, younger son of the King of Congo, rejects the faith, 207.
Patagonia, discovered by Magalhaens, 278.
Payva (Affonso de), sent out with Covilham by João II., but after parting with him at Aden, dies on the journey, 212.
Pedro (Dom), second brother of the prince, present at the queen's death, 26.
—— knighted by the king, 36.
—— receives the titles of Duke of Coimbra, &c., 39.
—— his travels, 50.
—— receives from the Venetians a copy of Marco Polo's travels, and a map, 51.
—— visits England, and is made Knight of the Garter, 52.
—— shares Prince Henry's studies, 52.
—— sends out Gomes Pires, in 1415, with Andam Gonsalves, to the Rio d'Ouro, 96.
—— summons Prince Henry to Coimbra to invest with knighthood his eldest son Pedro, 101.
—— rewards Alvaro Fernandes for going further south than any of his predecessors, 114.
Pereira (Diogo Fernandes). 1504, win-

tered at Socotra, then first reached by Portuguese, 265.

Pereira (Nuño Alvarez), called the Holy Constable, his important help to the Grand Master after the siege of Lisbon, 10.
—— at the battle of Aljubarrota, 14.
—— his victory at Valverde, 18.
—— retires to the convent of Carmo, 64.

Perestrello (Bartholomeu), accompanies Zarco and Vaz in their expedition to Porto Santo, 63.
—— receives the governorship of the island, 63.
—— father-in-law of Columbus, 222.

Philesius. See *Ringmann*.

Philippa, Queen, Prince Henry's mother, 5.
—— arrives at Corunna with her father, the Duke of Lancaster, 18.
—— her marriage with King João, 19.
—— receives an embassy from the Queen of Granada; her reply, 24.
—— her illness, 25.
—— solemn leave-taking, and charge to her sons, 26.
—— her death, 26.
—— her character, 26.
—— her funeral, 27.

Philippines (The) discovered by Magalhaens, 282.

Picanço (The), or the Wren, a caravel in Lançarote's expedition, 104.
—— joins the caravel from Tavila and João de Castilha in an expedition to the Island of Palma, 124.
—— the caravel of Diogo Gomez, 170.

Pico, captaincy granted to Jobst van Heurter, 135.

Pigafetta (Felipe), publishes description of the equatorial Nile lakes in Duarte Lopes' Congo, 208.

Pires (Gomes), goes with Gonsalves to the Rio d'Ouro, 96.
—— with Lançarote's expedition, 102.
—— declares his intention to go on to the land of the negroes, 103.
—— attempts to conciliate the people at the Madeleine Islands, 107.
—— becomes separated from the other caravels, and returns to Portugal, 107.

Pires (Gomes), goes to the Rio d'Ouro, 1446, 115.

Pires (Thomé) sent by Andrade as ambassador to Nankin, and dies in captivity there, 268.

Piste, a chieftain of Gomera, who assisted the Portuguese against Palma, 124.
—— and afterwards came to live in Portugal under the protection of the prince, 125.

Pó, Fernam do, discovered 1471, or 1486, 199.

Porto Santo, the discovery, 54.
—— Zarco's expedition in 1420 arrives there, 54.
—— its colonization, 54.
—— Perestrello made Governor, 63.

Quesada (Gaspar de) with Magelhaen's expedition, 274.
—— mutinies, 275.
—— his execution, 277.

Regras (João das), his able advocacy of the claims of the Grand Master to the throne, 12.

René II. (Duke of Lorraine), the printing-press at St. Dié under his patronage, 238.
—— his secretary, Walter Lud, 238.

Ringmann (Mathias), or Philesius, studies at Paris at the same time that Fra Giocondi was there, 237.
—— returns to his native Alsace, and is subjected to a brutal assault from rival students, 237.
—— is the originator of the name of America, 238.
—— in 1505 he edits an edition of Giocondi's translation of Vespucci's letter, 238.
—— becomes professor of Latin at the college of St. Dié, and corrector of the press in the printing-office, 238.

Rio Grande, so called by Cadamosto, supposed to be the river Jeba, 169.

Rio do Infante, Great Fish River, 219.

Rio d'Ouro, found by Gil Eannes and Baldaya, 70.

Rio de la Plata, 1516, discovered by Juan Dias de Solis, 271.

Rio Roxo, 196.
Rio de Santa Anna (the Cacheo), 168.
Rio do Seyxo, in Madeira, 59.
Rio Verde, 196.

S. Augustine at Cape Negro, pillar set up by Diogo Cam, 205.
S. Bras, named by Bartholomeo Dias, 219.
S. Dié, a printing-press established there by a cluster of learned priests, under the auspices of René II., Duke of Lorraine, 238.
S. Domingo River (Rio de Jatte), 168.
S. Gabriel, pillar erected by Da Gama at Calicut, 253.
S. Gabriel (The), Da Gama's ship, 214.
S. Jorge, colonization attempted by Willem van der Haagen, *alias* Da Silveira, 134.
S. Jorge, pillar set up by Diogo Cam at R. Zaire, 204.
—— for the fort, see *Mina*.
S. Maria discovered in 1432 by Gonsalo Velho Cabral, 131.
S. Maria, pillar erected by Da Gama on an island of the group that now bears the name, 253.
S. Maria das Neves (river), 197.
S. Miguel, rediscovered, 1444, by Gonsalo Velho Cabral, 131.
S. Rafael, pillar erected by Da Gama at the Rio dos Boos Signaes, 253.
S. Thomé discovered on the 21st Dec., 1470, 199.
S. Vicente (river), 196.
Sá de Bandeira (his Excellency the Marquis de), at his instance a monument was erected to Prince Henry at Sagres, 191.
—— plan of Sagres given by him, 192.
Sagres, the chosen residence of the prince, 1.
Saldanha (Antonio de), 1503, gave his name to the Agoada da Saldanha, near the Cape of Good Hope, 264.
Santa Cruz, in Algoa Bay, pillar set up on the island of the same name by Bartholomeu Dias, 219.
Santiago, pillar set up by Bartholomeu Dias, at Serra Parda (Dias or Pedestal point), 217.
Senegal (river), passed by Diniz Dias, 96.

Senegal (river), Cadamosto's description of the, 143.
Sequeira, discovers Cape St. Catherine, 2° south of the equator, 200.
Sequeira (Diogo Lopez de), 1508, discovers the islands of Santa Clara; sails for Malacca; establishes a factory there; Magalhaens in this expedition, 267.
Serpent-charming, 152.
Serrao (Francisco), went to Ternate in the Moluccas, 1611-1612, 268.
—— marries and settles at Ternate; communicates to Magalhaens the great advantages to be gained by intercourse therewith, 272.
Serrao (João) with Magalhaens' expedition, 274.
—— joint commander with Barbosa after the death of Magalhaens; his unhappy fate, 287.
Sierra Leona, 196.
Socotra, discovered by Diogo Fernandez Pereira, 1504, 265.
Sodrè (Vasco Gil), first colonizer of Terceira, 133.
Solis (Juan Dias de), with Pinzon, explored the coasts of South America, 1508, 269; in 1516 enters the Rio de la Plata, which originally bore his name, 271.
—— massacred by the natives, 271.
Souza (Gonzalo de), takes out the expedition to Congo, but dies at Cape Verde, and is succeeded by his nephew, 206.
Souza Holstein (Marquis de) casts made by his order from the statues of Dom João and Queen Philippa, 65.
Straits of Magellan, first named Vittoria, 281.
Swimming extraordinary, 147.

Tanganyika (Lake), apparently referred to by Pigafetta from Duarte Lopes, 1591, 208.
Tangier, Dom Duarte is persuaded by Prince Henry and Dom Fernando to fit out an expedition for the conquest, 74.
Tangier, the siege, 76—81.
Tegazza, 141.
Terceira, first named Ilha de Jesu

Christo, discovered between 1444 and 1450, 132.
Terceira, captaincy given by Prince Henry to Jacques de Bruges, 1450, 133.
Terra da Boa Gente, 246.
Theriack, antidote to poison, 113.
Tierra del Fuego, 280.
Tinoco (Aires), with one sailor and three boys manages to steer the caravel of Nuño Tristam back to Lisbon, after the death of Tristam and the rest of the crew, 112.
Toison d'Or, Order of, established in honour of the marriage of the Princess Isabella to the Duke of Burgundy, 20.
Toscanelli sends a chart to Columbus, which confirms him in the idea of reaching Asia by the West, 225.
Trevigiano (Stefano) brings to Portugal the mappemonde of Fra Mauro, 188.
Trinidad (The), Magalhaens' ship, 274.
Tristam (Nuño), joins Antam Gonsalveo; succeeds in making a capture; knights Gonsalves; pursues his voyage till he reaches Cape Branco, to which he gives that name, 89, 90.
—— returns to Portugal, 90.
—— goes out in 1443; finds an island which he calls Gete (Isle of Arguim), 93.
—— makes a capture, and obtains important information; finds the Ilha das Garças; returns, 94.
—— makes another voyage, 1446; and according to Azurara, "was the first who saw the country of the blacks," 110.
—— 1446, reaches the Rio Grande; in an encounter with the natives he is slain, with almost all his crew, by poisoned arrows, 111.

Uniamuezi, first mentioned by Pigafetta from Duarte Lopes, 209.
Uso di Mare with Cadomosto, 156—162.

Vallarte, a Danish nobleman begs permission of Prince Henry to go to Cape Verde, 1448, 118.
Vallarte, falls into an ambush of the natives; his uncertain fate, 119.
Valverde, battle of, 18.
Vaz (Tristam), his rediscovery of Porto Santo and Madeira, 54.
—— the northern half of Madeira is given to him, 61.
—— joins Lançarote's expedition (from Madeira), 102.
Vespucci (Amerigo), description of his third voyage, translated by Fra Giovanni Giveondi, 236.
Victoria Nyanza, described by Pigafetta from Duarte Lopes, 1591, 208.
Vittoria (The) sails in Magalhaens' expedition, commander Luis de Mendoza, 274.
—— strait named after her, 281.
—— Espinoza captain, 289.
—— Juan Sebastian del Cano commander, 289.
—— arrival at San Lucar, 292.

Waldseemüller, (Martin), Hylacomylus, joins the circle of learned men at St. Dié, 238.
Walking leaves in Palawan, 288.

Zalá ben Zalá, Governor of Ceuta, 30.
—— fears the result of the siege, 31.
—— determines on flight, 35.
—— at the siege of Tangier, 75.
—— his son hostage on the side of the Moors for the conditions of the treaty at the end of the siege, 83.
—— transfers Dom Fernando to the King of Fez, 84.
Zarco (João Gonsalvez), his rediscovery of Porto Santo and Madeira, 54.
—— captures the vessel in which Juan de Morales was returning, and learns from him the discovery by Machin, 56.
—— takes possession of and explores the island, 59.
—— receives the title of Count of Camara dos Lobos, 61.
—— receives the government of the southern half of the island; erects a church at Funchal; sets fire to the forests, 61.
Zeno (Marco), Venetian knight with whom Cadamosto sailed, 138.

LONDON:
GILBERT AND RIVINGTON, PRINTERS,
ST. JOHN'S SQUARE.

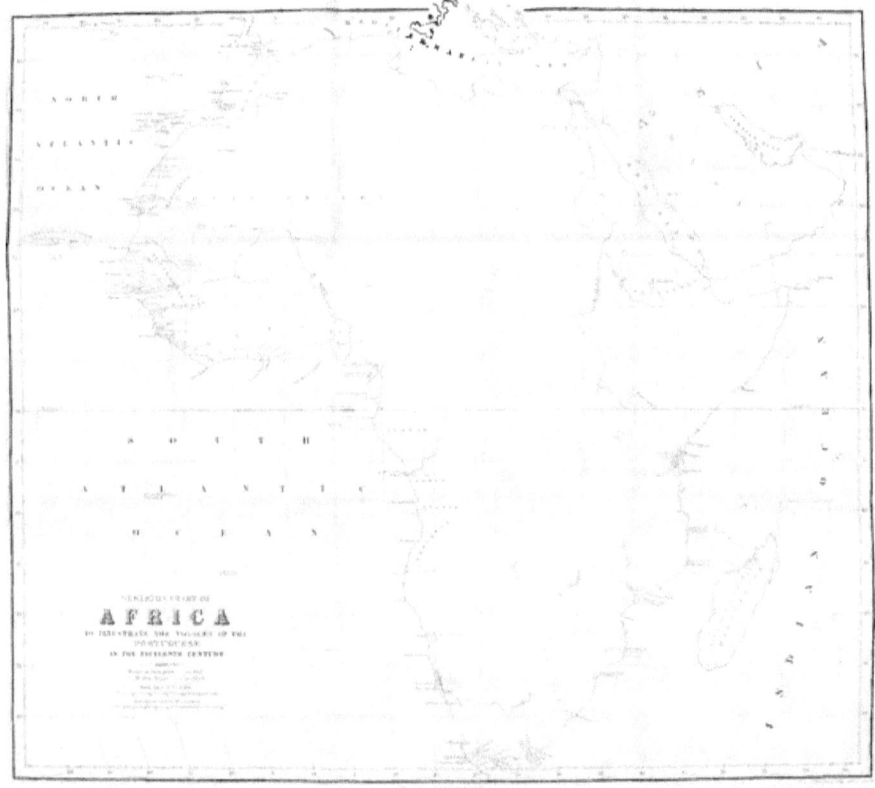

www.ingramcontent.com/pod-product-compliance
Lightning Source LLC
Chambersburg PA
CBHW020235240426
43672CB00006B/532